FREEBSD® DEVICE DRIVERS

FREEBSD® DEVICE DRIVERS

A Guide for the Intrepid

by Joseph Kong

no starch press

San Francisco

ISBN-10: 1-59327-204-9
ISBN-13: 978-1-59327-204-3

Publisher: William Pollock
Production Editor: Alison Law
Cover and Interior Design: Octopod Studios
Developmental Editor: William Pollock
Technical Reviewer: John Baldwin
Copyeditor: Damon Larson
Compositor: Susan Glinert Stevens
Proofreader: Ward Webber
Indexer: BIM Indexing & Proofreading Services

For information on book distributors or translations, please contact No Starch Press, Inc. directly:

No Starch Press, Inc.
38 Ringold Street, San Francisco, CA 94103
phone: 415.863.9900; fax: 415.863.9950; info@nostarch.com; www.nostarch.com

Library of Congress Cataloging-in-Publication Data
A catalog record of this book is available from the Library of Congress.

This book is dedicated to the FreeBSD community.

BRIEF CONTENTS

CONTENTS IN DETAIL

3
DEVICE COMMUNICATION AND CONTROL   27

4
THREAD SYNCHRONIZATION   53

5
DELAYING EXECUTION

6
CASE STUDY: VIRTUAL NULL MODEM

7
NEWBUS AND RESOURCE ALLOCATION

8
INTERRUPT HANDLING 125

9
CASE STUDY: PARALLEL PORT PRINTER DRIVER 141

10
MANAGING AND USING RESOURCES   165

11
CASE STUDY: INTELLIGENT PLATFORM
MANAGEMENT INTERFACE DRIVER   183

12
DIRECT MEMORY ACCESS   193

17
NETWORK DRIVERS, PART 2:
PACKET RECEPTION AND TRANSMISSION 299

ABOUT THE AUTHOR

The author of *Designing BSD Rootkits* (No Starch Press), Joseph Kong works on information security, operating system theory, reverse code engineering, and vulnerability assessment. Kong is a former system administrator for the city of Toronto.

ABOUT THE TECHNICAL REVIEWER

John Baldwin has been working on various portions of the FreeBSD operating system for 12 years. His main areas of interest include SMP, PCI, ACPI, and support for *x86*. He has served as a member of both the FreeBSD core team and the release engineering team.

FOREWORD

While most portions of an operating system are maintained and developed by individuals who specialize in a given operating system, device drivers are unique: They're maintained by a much broader spectrum of developers. Some device driver authors have extensive experience with a particular operating system, while others have detailed knowledge of specific hardware components and are tasked with maintaining device drivers for those components across multiple systems. Too, device drivers are often somewhat self-contained, so that a developer can maintain a device driver while viewing other parts of the system as a black box.

Of course, that black box still has an interface, and each operating system provides its own set of interfaces to device drivers. Device drivers on all systems need to perform many common tasks, such as discovering devices, allocating resources for connected devices, and managing asynchronous events. However, each operating system has its own ways of dealing with these tasks, and each differs in the interfaces it provides for higher-level tasks. The key to writing a device driver that is both robust and efficient lies in understanding the specific details of the interfaces that the particular operating system provides.

FreeBSD Device Drivers is an excellent guide to the most commonly used FreeBSD device driver interfaces. You'll find coverage of lower-level interfaces, including attaching to eligible devices and managing device resources, as well as higher-level interfaces, such as interfacing with the network and storage stacks. In addition, the book's coverage of several of the APIs available in the kernel environment, such as allocating memory, timers, and synchronization primitives, will be useful to anyone working with the FreeBSD kernel. This book is a welcome resource for FreeBSD device driver authors.

John Baldwin
Kernel Developer, FreeBSD
New York
March 20, 2012

ACKNOWLEDGMENTS

No book is an island. You would not be holding this book in your hands without the help and support of a host of people to whom I am most grateful.

Foremost, thanks to Bill Pollock and the gang at No Starch Press for giving me the opportunity to write this book and for helping me along the way. Special thanks to Alison Law, Riley Hoffman, and Tyler Ortman for pulling things together. Alison, you deserve to be mentioned at least twice, if not more. Thanks for entering corrections multiple times and for keeping me on schedule (sort of). Thanks, too, to copyeditors Damon Larson and Megan Dunchak and to Jessica Miller for writing the back cover copy.

I couldn't have done this without John Baldwin's excellent technical review. He patiently answered all of my (inane) questions and helped to improve my code. To my brother, Justin Kong, thank you for reviewing this book multiple times. You definitely deserve the "Iron Man" award. Thanks to Aharon Robbins for his review and to my friend Elizabeth C. Mitchell for drawing my diagrams (and for baking me brownies). And thanks to George Neville-Neil and Michael W. Lucas for your advice.

Thanks, Dad, for lending me your expertise on hardware and for lending me actual hardware, which made it possible for me to write this book. Thanks, Mom, for your love and support. I know you pray for me every day. Thanks also go to my friends for their support.

And last but not least, thanks to the open source software and FreeBSD communities for your willingness to share. Without you, I'd be a lousy programmer, and I'd have nothing to write about.

INTRODUCTION

Welcome to *FreeBSD Device Drivers*! The goal of this book is to help you improve your understanding of device drivers under FreeBSD. By the time you finish this book, you should be able to build, configure, and manage your own FreeBSD device drivers.

This book covers FreeBSD version 8, the version recommended for production use as of this writing. Nonetheless, most of what you'll learn will apply to earlier versions and should apply to later ones as well.

Who Is This Book For?

I wrote this book as a programmer, for programmers. As such, you'll find a heavy focus on programming, not theory, and you'll examine real device drivers (namely, ones that control hardware). Imagine trying to write a book without ever having read one. Inconceivable! The same thing goes for device drivers.

Prerequisites

To get the most out of this book, you should be familiar with the C programming language. You should also know something about operating system design; for example, the difference between a process and a thread.

If you lack the necessary background, I recommend reading the following three books prior to this one, or just keeping them around as references:

- *The C Programming Language*, by Brian W. Kernighan and Dennis M. Ritchie (Prentice Hall PTR, 1988)
- *Expert C Programming*, by Peter van der Linden (Prentice Hall, 1994)
- *The Design and Implementation of the FreeBSD Operating System*, by Marshall Kirk McKusick and George V. Neville-Neil (Addison-Wesley Professional, 2005)

Contents at a Glance

FreeBSD Device Drivers contains the following chapters.

Chapter 1: Building and Running Modules
Provides an overview and introduction to basic device driver programming concepts and terminology.

Chapter 2: Allocating Memory
Describes FreeBSD's kernel memory management routines.

Chapter 3: Device Communication and Control
Teaches you how to communicate with and control your device drivers from user space.

Chapter 4: Thread Synchronization
Discusses the problems and solutions associated with multithreaded programming and concurrent execution.

Chapter 5: Delaying Execution
Describes delaying code execution and asynchronous code execution, and explains why these tasks are needed.

Chapter 6: Case Study: Virtual Null Modem
Contains the first of several occasions where I walk you through a real-world device driver.

Chapter 7: Newbus and Resource Allocation
Covers the infrastructure used by FreeBSD to manage the hardware devices on the system. From here on, I deal exclusively with real hardware.

Chapter 8: Interrupt Handling
Discusses interrupt handling in FreeBSD.

Chapter 9: Case Study: Parallel Port Printer Driver
Walks through lpt(4), the parallel port printer driver, in its entirety.

Chapter 10: Managing and Using Resources
Covers port-mapped I/O and memory-mapped I/O.

Chapter 11: Case Study: Intelligent Platform Management Interface Driver
Reviews the parts of `ipmi(4)`, the Intelligent Platform Management Interface driver, which uses port-mapped I/O and memory-mapped I/O.

Chapter 12: Direct Memory Access
Explains how to use Direct Memory Access (DMA) in FreeBSD.

Chapter 13: Storage Drivers
Teaches you how to manage storage devices, such as disk drives, flash memory, and so on.

Chapter 14: Common Access Method
Provides an overview and introduction to Common Access Method (CAM), which you'll use to manage host bus adapters.

Chapter 15: USB Drivers
Teaches you how to manage USB devices. It also walks through `ulpt(4)`, the USB printer driver, in its entirety.

Chapter 16: Network Drivers, Part 1: Data Structures
Describes the data structures used by network drivers. It also goes over Message Signaled Interrupts (MSI).

Chapter 17: Network Drivers, Part 2: Packet Reception and Transmission
Examines the packet reception and transmission components of `em(4)`, the Intel PCI Gigabit Ethernet adapter driver.

Welcome Aboard!

I hope you find this book useful and entertaining. As always, I welcome feedback with comments or bug fixes to *joe@thestackframe.org*.

Okay, enough with the introductory stuff. Let's begin.

1

BUILDING AND RUNNING MODULES

This chapter provides an introduction to FreeBSD device drivers. We'll start by describing the four different types of UNIX device drivers and how they are represented in FreeBSD. We'll then describe the basics of building and running loadable kernel modules, and we'll finish this chapter with an introduction to character drivers.

NOTE   *If you don't understand some of the terms used above, don't worry; we'll define them all in this chapter.*

Types of Device Drivers

In FreeBSD, a *device* is any hardware-related item that belongs to the system; this includes disk drives, printers, video cards, and so on. A *device driver* is a computer program that controls or "drives" a device (or sometimes numerous devices). In UNIX and pre-4.0 FreeBSD, there are four different types of device drivers:

- Character drivers, which control character devices
- Block drivers, which control block devices
- Network drivers, which control network devices
- Pseudo-device drivers, which control pseudo-devices

Character devices provide either a character-stream-oriented I/O interface or, alternatively, an unstructured (raw) interface (McKusick and Neville-Neil, 2005).

Block devices transfer randomly accessible data in fixed-size blocks (Corbet et al., 2005). In FreeBSD 4.0 and later, block drivers are gone (for more information on this, see "Block Drivers Are Gone" on page 15).

Network devices transmit and receive data packets that are driven by the network subsystem (Corbet et al., 2005).

Finally, a *pseudo-device* is a computer program that emulates the behavior of a device using only software (that is, without any underlying hardware).

Loadable Kernel Modules

A device driver can be either statically compiled into the system or dynamically loaded using a loadable kernel module (KLD).

NOTE *Most operating systems call a loadable kernel module an* LKM—*FreeBSD just had to be different.*

A *KLD* is a kernel subsystem that can be loaded, unloaded, started, and stopped after bootup. In other words, a KLD can add functionality to the kernel and later remove said functionality while the system is running. Needless to say, our "functionality" will be device drivers.

In general, two components are common to all KLDs:

- A module event handler
- A `DECLARE_MODULE` macro call

Module Event Handler

A *module event handler* is the function that handles the initialization and shutdown of a KLD. This function is executed when a KLD is loaded into the kernel or unloaded from the kernel, or when the system is shut down. Its function prototype is defined in the `<sys/module.h>` header as follows:

```
typedef int (*modeventhand_t)(module_t, int /* ❶modeventtype_t */, void *);
```

Here, ❶ modeventtype_t is defined in the `<sys/module.h>` header like so:

```
typedef enum modeventtype {
        ❶MOD_LOAD,       /* Set when module is loaded. */
```

```
❷MOD_UNLOAD,      /* Set when module is unloaded. */
❸MOD_SHUTDOWN,    /* Set on shutdown. */
❹MOD_QUIESCE      /* Set when module is about to be unloaded. */
} modeventtype_t;
```

As you can see, modeventtype_t labels whether the KLD is being ❶ loaded into the kernel or ❷ unloaded from the kernel, or whether the system is about to ❸ shut down. (For now, ignore the value at ❹; we'll discuss it in Chapter 4.)

Generally, you'd use the modeventtype_t argument in a switch statement to set up different code blocks for each situation. Some example code should help clarify what I mean:

```
static int
modevent(module_t mod __unused, int ❶event, void *arg __unused)
{
        int error = 0;

        switch (❷event) {
❸case MOD_LOAD:
                uprintf("Hello, world!\n");
                break;
❹case MOD_UNLOAD:
                uprintf("Good-bye, cruel world!\n");
                break;
❺default:
                error = EOPNOTSUPP;
                break;
        }

        return (error);
}
```

Notice how the ❶ second argument is the ❷ expression for the switch statement. Thus, this module event handler prints "Hello, world!" when the KLD is ❸ loaded into the kernel, prints "Good-bye, cruel world!" when the KLD is ❹ unloaded from the kernel, and returns EOPNOTSUPP (which stands for *error: operation not supported*) prior to ❺ system shutdown.

DECLARE_MODULE Macro

The DECLARE_MODULE macro registers a KLD and its module event handler with the system. Here is its function prototype:

```
#include <sys/param.h>
#include <sys/kernel.h>
#include <sys/module.h>

DECLARE_MODULE(name, moduledata_t data, sub, order);
```

The arguments expected by this macro are as follows.

name

The name argument is the module name, which is used to identify the KLD.

data

The data argument expects a filled-out moduledata_t structure, which is defined in the <sys/module.h> header as follows:

```
typedef struct moduledata {
        const char      ❶*name;
        modeventhand_t  ❷evhand;
        void            ❸*priv;
} moduledata_t;
```

Here, ❶ name is the official module name, ❷ evhand is the KLD's module event handler, and ❸ priv is a pointer to private data (if any exists).

sub

The sub argument specifies the kernel subsystem that the KLD belongs in. Valid values for this argument are defined in the sysinit_sub_id enumeration, found in <sys/kernel.h>.

```
enum sysinit_sub_id {
        SI_SUB_DUMMY             = 0x0000000,    /* Not executed.      */
        SI_SUB_DONE              = 0x0000001,    /* Processed.         */
        SI_SUB_TUNABLES          = 0x0700000,    /* Tunable values.    */
        SI_SUB_COPYRIGHT         = 0x0800001,    /* First console use. */
        SI_SUB_SETTINGS          = 0x0880000,    /* Check settings.    */
        SI_SUB_MTX_POOL_STATIC   = 0x0900000,    /* Static mutex pool. */
        SI_SUB_LOCKMGR           = 0x0980000,    /* Lock manager.      */
        SI_SUB_VM                = 0x1000000,    /* Virtual memory.    */
...
     ❶SI_SUB_DRIVERS            = 0x3100000,    /* Device drivers.    */
...
};
```

For obvious reasons, we'll almost always set sub to ❶ SI_SUB_DRIVERS, which is the device driver subsystem.

order

The order argument specifies the KLD's order of initialization within the sub subsystem. Valid values for this argument are defined in the sysinit_elem_order enumeration, found in <sys/kernel.h>.

```
enum sysinit_elem_order {
        SI_ORDER_FIRST           = 0x0000000,    /* First.  */
        SI_ORDER_SECOND          = 0x0000001,    /* Second. */
        SI_ORDER_THIRD           = 0x0000002,    /* Third.  */
        SI_ORDER_FOURTH          = 0x0000003,    /* Fourth. */
```

```
❶SI_ORDER_MIDDLE        = 0x1000000,    /* Somewhere in the middle. */
   SI_ORDER_ANY         = 0xffffffff    /* Last.                    */
};
```

In general, we'll always set order to ❶ SI_ORDER_MIDDLE.

Hello, world!

You now know enough to write your first KLD. Listing 1-1 is the complete skeleton code for a KLD.

```
#include <sys/param.h>
#include <sys/module.h>
#include <sys/kernel.h>
#include <sys/systm.h>

static int
❶ hello_modevent(module_t mod __unused, int event, void *arg __unused)
{
        int error = 0;

        switch (event) {
        case MOD_LOAD:
                uprintf("Hello, world!\n");
                break;
        case MOD_UNLOAD:
                uprintf("Good-bye, cruel world!\n");
                break;
        default:
                error = EOPNOTSUPP;
                break;
        }

        return (error);
}

❷ static moduledata_t hello_mod = {
        "hello",
        hello_modevent,
        NULL
};

❸ DECLARE_MODULE(hello, ❹hello_mod, SI_SUB_DRIVERS, SI_ORDER_MIDDLE);
```

Listing 1-1: hello.c

This code contains a ❶ module event handler—it's identical to the one described in "Module Event Handler" on page 2—and a filled-out ❷ moduledata_t structure, which is passed as the ❹ second argument to the ❸ DECLARE_MODULE macro.

In short, this KLD is just a module event handler and a DECLARE_MODULE call. Simple, eh?

Compiling and Loading

To compile a KLD, you can use the `<bsd.kmod.mk>` Makefile. Here is the complete Makefile for Listing 1-1:

```
❶ KMOD=   hello
❷ SRCS=   hello.c

.include <bsd.kmod.mk>
```

Here, ❶ KMOD is the KLD's name and ❷ SRCS is the KLD's source files. Incidentally, I'll adapt this Makefile to compile every KLD.

Now, assuming Listing 1-1 and its Makefile are in the same directory, simply type make, and the compilation should proceed (very verbosely) and produce an executable named *hello.ko*, as shown here:

```
$ make
Warning: Object directory not changed from original /usr/home/ghost/hello
@ -> /usr/src/sys
machine -> /usr/src/sys/i386/include
cc -O2 -fno-strict-aliasing -pipe  -D_KERNEL -DKLD_MODULE -std=c99 -nostdinc
-I. -I@ -I@/contrib/altq -finline-limit=8000 --param inline-unit-growth=100 -
-param large-function-growth=1000 -fno-common  -mno-align-long-strings -mpref
erred-stack-boundary=2  -mno-mmx -mno-3dnow -mno-sse -mno-sse2 -mno-sse3 -ffr
eestanding -Wall -Wredundant-decls -Wnested-externs -Wstrict-prototypes  -Wmi
ssing-prototypes -Wpointer-arith -Winline -Wcast-qual  -Wundef -Wno-pointer-s
ign -fformat-extensions -c hello.c
ld  -d -warn-common -r -d -o hello.kld hello.o
:> export_syms
awk -f /sys/conf/kmod_syms.awk hello.kld  export_syms | xargs -J% objcopy % h
ello.kld
ld -Bshareable  -d -warn-common -o hello.ko hello.kld
objcopy --strip-debug hello.ko
$ ls -F
@@            export_syms  hello.kld    hello.o
Makefile      hello.c      hello.ko*    machine@
```

You can then load and unload *hello.ko* with kldload(8) and kldunload(8), respectively:

```
$ sudo kldload ./hello.ko
Hello, world!
$ sudo kldunload hello.ko
Good-bye, cruel world!
```

As an aside, with a Makefile that includes `<bsd.kmod.mk>`, you can use make load and make unload instead of kldload(8) and kldunload(8), as shown here:

```
$ sudo make load
/sbin/kldload -v /usr/home/ghost/hello/hello.ko
Hello, world!
```

```
Loaded /usr/home/ghost/hello/hello.ko, id=3
$ sudo make unload
/sbin/kldunload -v hello.ko
Unloading hello.ko, id=3
Good-bye, cruel world!
```

Congratulations! You've now successfully loaded code into a live kernel. Before moving on, one additional point is also worth mentioning. You can display the status of any file dynamically linked into the kernel using kldstat(8), like so:

```
$ kldstat
Id Refs Address    Size    Name
 1    4 0xc0400000 906518  kernel
 2    1 0xc0d07000 6a32c   acpi.ko
 3    1 0xc3301000 2000    hello.ko
```

As you can see, the output is pretty self-explanatory. Now, let's do something more interesting.

Character Drivers

Character drivers are basically KLDs that create character devices. As mentioned previously, character devices provide either a character-stream-oriented I/O interface or, alternatively, an unstructured (raw) interface. These (*character-device*) *interfaces* establish the conventions for accessing a device, which include the set of procedures that can be called to do I/O operations (McKusick and Neville-Neil, 2005). In short, character drivers produce character devices, which provide device access. For example, the lpt(4) driver creates the /dev/lpt0 character device, which is used to access the parallel port printer. In FreeBSD 4.0 and later, most devices have a character-device interface.

In general, three components are common to all character drivers:

- The d_foo functions
- A character device switch table
- A make_dev and destroy_dev function call

d_foo Functions

The d_foo functions, whose function prototypes are defined in the <sys/conf.h> header, are the I/O operations that a process can execute on a device. These I/O operations are mostly associated with the file I/O system calls and are accordingly named d_open, d_read, and so on. A character driver's d_foo function is called when "foo" is done on its device. For example, d_read is called when a process reads from a device.

Table 1-1 provides a brief description of each d_foo function.

Table 1-1: d_foo Functions

Function	Description
d_open	Called to open the device in preparation for I/O operations
d_close	Called to close the device
d_read	Called to read data from the device
d_write	Called to write data to the device
d_ioctl	Called to perform an operation other than a read or a write
d_poll	Called to check the device to see whether data is available for reading or space is available for writing
d_mmap	Called to map a device offset into a memory address
d_kqfilter	Called to register the device with a kernel event list
d_strategy	Called to start a read or write operation and then immediately return
d_dump	Called to write all physical memory to the device

NOTE   *If you don't understand some of these operations, don't worry; we'll describe them in detail later when we implement them.*

Character Device Switch Table

A character device switch table, struct cdevsw, specifies which d_foo functions a character driver implements. It is defined in the <sys/conf.h> header as follows:

```
struct cdevsw {
        int             d_version;
        u_int           d_flags;
        const char      *d_name;
        d_open_t        *d_open;
        d_fdopen_t      *d_fdopen;
        d_close_t       *d_close;
        d_read_t        *d_read;
        d_write_t       *d_write;
        d_ioctl_t       *d_ioctl;
        d_poll_t        *d_poll;
        d_mmap_t        *d_mmap;
        d_strategy_t    *d_strategy;
        dumper_t        *d_dump;
        d_kqfilter_t    *d_kqfilter;
        d_purge_t       *d_purge;
        d_spare2_t      *d_spare2;
        uid_t           d_uid;
        gid_t           d_gid;
        mode_t          d_mode;
        const char      *d_kind;
```

```
        /* These fields should not be messed with by drivers. */
        LIST_ENTRY(cdevsw)      d_list;
        LIST_HEAD(, cdev)       d_devs;
        int                     d_spare3;
        struct cdevsw           *d_gianttrick;
};
```

Here is an example character device switch table for a read/write device:

```
static struct cdevsw echo_cdevsw = {
        .d_version =    D_VERSION,
        .d_open =       echo_open,
        .d_close =      echo_close,
        .d_read =       echo_read,
        .d_write =      echo_write,
        .d_name =       "echo"
};
```

As you can see, not every d_foo function or attribute needs to be defined. If a d_foo function is undefined, the corresponding operation is unsupported (for example, a character device switch table for a read-only device would not define d_write).

Unsurprisingly, d_version (which denotes the version of FreeBSD this driver supports) and d_name (which is the driver's name) must be defined. Generally, d_version is set to D_VERSION, which is a macro substitution for whichever version of FreeBSD it's compiled on.

make_dev and destroy_dev Functions

The make_dev function takes a character device switch table and creates a character device node under */dev*. Here is its function prototype:

```
#include <sys/param.h>
#include <sys/conf.h>

struct ❶cdev *
make_dev(struct cdevsw *cdevsw, int minor, uid_t uid, gid_t gid,
    int perms, const char *fmt, ...);
```

Conversely, the destroy_dev function takes the ❶ cdev structure returned by make_dev and destroys the character device node. Here is its function prototype:

```
#include <sys/param.h>
#include <sys/conf.h>

void
destroy_dev(struct cdev *dev);
```

Mostly Harmless

Listing 1-2 is a complete character driver (based on code written by Murray Stokely and Søren Straarup) that manipulates a memory area as though it were a device. This pseudo (or memory) device lets you write and read a single character string to and from it.

NOTE *Take a quick look at this code and try to discern some of its structure. If you don't understand all of it, don't worry; an explanation follows.*

```
#include <sys/param.h>
#include <sys/module.h>
#include <sys/kernel.h>
#include <sys/systm.h>

#include <sys/conf.h>
#include <sys/uio.h>
#include <sys/malloc.h>

#define BUFFER_SIZE    256

/* Forward declarations. */
static d_open_t        echo_open;
static d_close_t       echo_close;
static d_read_t        echo_read;
static d_write_t       echo_write;

❶ static struct cdevsw echo_cdevsw = {
          .d_version =   D_VERSION,
          .d_open =      echo_open,
          .d_close =     echo_close,
          .d_read =      echo_read,
          .d_write =     echo_write,
          .d_name =      "echo"
};

typedef struct echo {
       ❷char buffer[BUFFER_SIZE];
       ❸int length;
} echo_t;

❹ static echo_t *echo_message;
❺ static struct cdev *echo_dev;

static int
❻ echo_open(struct cdev *dev, int oflags, int devtype, struct thread *td)
{
         uprintf("Opening echo device.\n");
         return (0);
}

static int
```

```
❼ echo_close(struct cdev *dev, int fflag, int devtype, struct thread *td)
{
        uprintf("Closing echo device.\n");
        return (0);
}

static int
echo_write(struct cdev *dev, struct uio *uio, int ioflag)
{
        int error = 0;

        error = copyin(uio->uio_iov->iov_base, echo_message->buffer,
            MIN(uio->uio_iov->iov_len, BUFFER_SIZE - 1));
        if (error != 0) {
                uprintf("Write failed.\n");
                return (error);
        }

        *(echo_message->buffer +
            MIN(uio->uio_iov->iov_len, BUFFER_SIZE - 1)) = 0;

        echo_message->length = MIN(uio->uio_iov->iov_len, BUFFER_SIZE - 1);

        return (error);
}

static int
echo_read(struct cdev *dev, struct uio *uio, int ioflag)
{
        int error = 0;
        int amount;

        amount = MIN(uio->uio_resid,
            (echo_message->length - uio->uio_offset > 0) ?
             echo_message->length - uio->uio_offset : 0);

        error = uiomove(echo_message->buffer + uio->uio_offset, amount, uio);
        if (error != 0)
                uprintf("Read failed.\n");

        return (error);
}

static int
echo_modevent(module_t mod __unused, int event, void *arg __unused)
{
        int error = 0;

        switch (event) {
        case MOD_LOAD:
                echo_message = malloc(sizeof(echo_t), M_TEMP, M_WAITOK);
                echo_dev = ❽make_dev(&echo_cdevsw, 0, UID_ROOT, GID_WHEEL,
                    0600, "echo");
```

```
                uprintf("Echo driver loaded.\n");
                break;
        case MOD_UNLOAD:
                destroy_dev(echo_dev);
                free(echo_message, M_TEMP);
                uprintf("Echo driver unloaded.\n");
                break;
        default:
                error = EOPNOTSUPP;
                break;
        }

        return (error);
}

DEV_MODULE(echo, echo_modevent, NULL);
```

Listing 1-2: echo.c

This driver starts by ❶ defining a character device switch table, which contains four d_foo functions named echo_foo, where foo equals to open, close, read, and write. Consequently, the ensuing character device will support only these four I/O operations.

Next, there are two variable declarations: an echo structure pointer named ❹ echo_message (which will contain a ❷ character string and its ❸ length) and a cdev structure pointer named ❺ echo_dev (which will maintain the cdev returned by the ❽ make_dev call).

Then, the d_foo functions ❻ echo_open and ❼ echo_close are defined—each just prints a debug message. Generally, the d_open function prepares a device for I/O, while d_close breaks apart those preparations.

NOTE *There is a difference between "preparing a device for I/O" and "preparing (or initializing) a device." For pseudo-devices like Listing 1-2, device initialization is done in the module event handler.*

The remaining bits—echo_write, echo_read, echo_modevent, and DEV_MODULE—require a more in-depth explanation and are therefore described in their own sections.

echo_write Function

The echo_write function acquires a character string from user space and stores it. Here is its function definition (again):

```
static int
echo_write(struct cdev *dev, ❶struct uio *uio, int ioflag)
{
        int error = 0;

        error = ❷copyin(❸uio->uio_iov->iov_base, ❹echo_message->buffer,
            MIN(❺uio->uio_iov->iov_len, ❻BUFFER_SIZE - 1));
```

```
        if (error != 0) {
                uprintf("Write failed.\n");
                return (error);
        }

❼*(echo_message->buffer +
        MIN(uio->uio_iov->iov_len, BUFFER_SIZE - 1)) = 0;

❽echo_message->length = MIN(uio->uio_iov->iov_len, BUFFER_SIZE - 1);

        return (error);
}
```

Here, ❶ struct uio describes a character string in motion—the variables ❸ iov_base and ❺ iov_len specify the character string's base address and length, respectively.

So, this function starts by ❷ copying a character string from ❸ user space to ❹ kernel space. At most, ❻ 'BUFFER_SIZE - 1' bytes of data are copied. Once this is done, the character string is ❼ null-terminated, and its length (minus the null terminator) is ❽ recorded.

NOTE *This isn't the proper way to copy data from user space to kernel space. I should've used uiomove instead of copyin. However, copyin is easier to understand, and at this point, I just want to cover the basic structure of a character driver.*

echo_read Function

The echo_read function returns the stored character string to user space. Here is its function definition (again):

```
static int
echo_read(struct cdev *dev, struct uio *uio, int ioflag)
{
        int error = 0;
        int amount;

        amount = ❶MIN(❷uio->uio_resid,
            ❸(echo_message->length - ❹uio->uio_offset > 0) ?
            echo_message->length - uio->uio_offset : 0);

        error = ❺uiomove(❻echo_message->buffer + uio->uio_offset, ❼amount,
            ❽uio);
        if (error != 0)
                uprintf("Read failed.\n");

        return (error);
}
```

Here, the variables ❷ uio_resid and ❹ uio_offset specify the amount of data remaining to be transferred and an offset into the character string, respectively.

So, this function first ❶ determines the number of characters to return—either the ❷ amount the user requests or ❸ all of it. Then echo_read ❺ transfers that ❼ number from ❻ kernel space to ❽ user space.

NOTE *For more on copying data between user and kernel space, see the copy(9) and uio(9) manual pages. I'd also recommend the OpenBSD uiomove(9) manual page.*

echo_modevent Function

The echo_modevent function is the module event handler for this character driver. Here is its function definition (again):

```
static int
echo_modevent(module_t mod __unused, int event, void *arg __unused)
{
        int error = 0;

        switch (event) {
        case MOD_LOAD:
                ❶echo_message = ❷malloc(sizeof(echo_t), M_TEMP, M_WAITOK);
                echo_dev = ❸make_dev(&echo_cdevsw, 0, UID_ROOT, GID_WHEEL,
                    0600, ❹"echo");
                uprintf("Echo driver loaded.\n");
                break;
        case MOD_UNLOAD:
                ❺destroy_dev(echo_dev);
                ❻free(echo_message, M_TEMP);
                uprintf("Echo driver unloaded.\n");
                break;
        default:
                error = EOPNOTSUPP;
                break;
        }

        return (error);
}
```

On module load, this function first calls ❷ malloc to allocate sizeof(echo_t) bytes of memory. Then it calls ❸ make_dev to create a character device node named ❹ echo under */dev*. Note that when make_dev returns, the character device is "live" and its d_foo functions can be executed. Consequently, if I had called make_dev ahead of malloc, echo_write or echo_read could be executed before ❶ echo_message points to valid memory, which would be disastrous. The point is: Unless your driver is completely ready, don't call make_dev.

On module unload, this function first calls ❺ destroy_dev to destroy the echo device node. Then it calls ❻ free to release the allocated memory.

DEV_MODULE Macro

The `DEV_MODULE` macro is defined in the `<sys/conf.h>` header as follows:

```
#define DEV_MODULE(name, evh, arg)                                      \
static moduledata_t name##_mod = {                                      \
    #name,                                                              \
    evh,                                                                \
    arg                                                                 \
};                                                                      \
❶ DECLARE_MODULE(name, name##_mod, SI_SUB_DRIVERS, SI_ORDER_MIDDLE)
```

As you can see, `DEV_MODULE` merely wraps ❶ `DECLARE_MODULE`. So Listing 1-2 could have called `DECLARE_MODULE`, but `DEV_MODULE` is cleaner (and it saves you some keystrokes).

Don't Panic

Now that we've walked through Listing 1-2, let's give it a try:

```
$ sudo kldload ./echo.ko
Echo driver loaded.
$ ls -l /dev/echo
crw-------  1 root  wheel   0, 95 Jun  4 23:23 /dev/echo
$ su
Password:
# echo "DON'T PANIC" > /dev/echo
Opening echo device.
Closing echo device.
# cat /dev/echo
Opening echo device.
DON'T PANIC
Closing echo device.
```

Unsurprisingly, it works. Before this chapter is concluded, a crucial topic bears mentioning.

Block Drivers Are Gone

As mentioned previously, block devices transfer randomly accessible data in fixed-size blocks; for example, disk drives. Naturally, *block drivers* provide access to block devices. Block drivers are characterized by the fact that all I/O is cached within the kernel's buffer cache, which makes block drivers unreliable, for two reasons. First, because caching can reorder a sequence of write operations, it deprives the writing process of the ability to identify the exact disk contents at any moment in time. This makes reliable crash recovery of on-disk data structures (for example, filesystems) impossible. Second, caching can delay write operations. So if an error occurs, the kernel cannot report to the process that did the write which particular operation failed. For these reasons, every serious application that accesses block devices specifies that a character-device interface always be used. Consequently, FreeBSD dropped support for block drivers during the modernization of the disk I/O infrastructure.

NOTE *Obviously, FreeBSD still supports block devices. For more on this, see Chapter 13.*

Conclusion

This chapter introduced you to the basics of FreeBSD device driver development. In the following chapters, we'll build upon the concepts described here to complete your driver toolkit. As an aside, because most FreeBSD device drivers are character drivers, don't think of them as a primary driver class—they're more like a tool used to create character device nodes.

2

ALLOCATING MEMORY

In the previous chapter we used malloc and free for the allocation and release of memory. The FreeBSD kernel, however, contains a richer set of memory allocation primitives. In this chapter we'll look at the stock kernel memory management routines. This includes describing malloc and free in more detail and introducing the malloc_type structure. We'll finish this chapter by describing the contiguous physical memory management routines.

Memory Management Routines

The FreeBSD kernel provides four functions for non-pageable memory allocation and release: malloc, free, realloc, and reallocf. These functions can handle requests of arbitrary size or alignment, and they are the preferred way to allocate kernel memory.

```
#include <sys/types.h>
#include <sys/malloc.h>

void *
malloc(unsigned long size, struct malloc_type *type, int flags);

void
free(void *addr, struct malloc_type *type);

void *
realloc(void *addr, unsigned long size, struct malloc_type *type,
    int flags);

void *
reallocf(void *addr, unsigned long size, struct malloc_type *type,
    int flags);
```

The malloc function allocates size bytes of memory in kernel space. If successful, a kernel virtual address is returned; otherwise, NULL is returned.

The free function releases the memory at addr—that was previously allocated by malloc—for reuse. Note that free doesn't clear this memory, which means that you should explicitly zero any memory whose contents you need to keep private. If addr is NULL, then free does nothing.

NOTE *If INVARIANTS is enabled, then free will stuff any released memory with 0xdeadc0de. Thus, if you get a page fault panic and the faulting address is around 0xdeadc0de, this can be a sign that you're using freed memory.[1]*

The realloc function changes the size of the memory at addr to size bytes. If successful, a kernel virtual address is returned; otherwise, NULL is returned, and the memory is left alone. Note that the returned address may differ from addr, because when the size changes, the memory may be relocated to acquire or provide additional room. Interestingly, this implies that you should not have any pointers into the memory at addr when calling realloc. If addr is NULL, then realloc behaves identically to malloc.

The reallocf function is identical to realloc except that on failure it releases the memory at addr.

The malloc, realloc, and reallocf functions provide a flags argument to further qualify their operational characteristics. Valid values for this argument are shown in Table 2-1.

---

1. INVARIANTS is a kernel debugging option. For more on INVARIANTS, see */sys/conf/NOTES*.

Table 2-1: malloc, realloc, and reallocf Symbolic Constants

Constant	Description
M_ZERO	Causes the allocated memory to be set to zero
M_NOWAIT	Causes malloc, realloc, and reallocf to return NULL if the allocation cannot be immediately fulfilled due to resource shortage; M_NOWAIT is required when running in an interrupt context
M_WAITOK	Indicates that it is okay to wait for resources; if the allocation cannot be immediately fulfilled, the current process is put to sleep to wait for resources to become available; when M_WAITOK is specified, malloc, realloc, and reallocf cannot return NULL

The flags argument must include either M_NOWAIT or M_WAITOK.

malloc_type Structures

The malloc, free, realloc, and reallocf functions include a type argument, which expects a pointer to a malloc_type structure; this structure describes the purpose of the allocated memory. The type argument has no impact on performance; it is used for memory profiling and for basic sanity checks.

NOTE *You can profile kernel dynamic memory usage, sorted by type, with the* vmstat -m *command.*

MALLOC_DEFINE Macro

The MALLOC_DEFINE macro defines a new malloc_type structure. Here is its function prototype:

```
#include <sys/param.h>
#include <sys/malloc.h>
#include <sys/kernel.h>

MALLOC_DEFINE(type, shortdesc, longdesc);
```

The type argument is the new malloc_type structure's name. In general, type should begin with M_ and be in uppercase letters; for example, M_FOO.

The shortdesc argument expects a short description of the new malloc_type structure. This argument is used in the output of vmstat -m. As a result, it shouldn't contain any spaces so that it's easier to parse vmstat -m's output in scripts.

The longdesc argument expects a long description of the new malloc_type structure.

MALLOC_DECLARE Macro

The MALLOC_DECLARE macro declares a new malloc_type structure with the extern keyword. Here is its function prototype:

```
#include <sys/types.h>
#include <sys/malloc.h>

MALLOC_DECLARE(type);
```

This macro is defined in the <sys/malloc.h> header as follows:

```
#define MALLOC_DECLARE(type) \
        extern struct malloc_type type[1]
```

As an aside, if you require a private malloc_type structure, you would prefix the MALLOC_DEFINE call with the static keyword. In fact, a non-static MALLOC_DEFINE call without a corresponding MALLOC_DECLARE call actually causes a warning under gcc 4.*x*.

Tying Everything Together

Listing 2-1 is a revision of Listing 1-2 that uses its own malloc_type structure instead of the kernel-defined M_TEMP.[2] Listing 2-1 should clarify any misunderstandings you may have about MALLOC_DEFINE and MALLOC_DECLARE.

NOTE   *To save space, the functions echo_open, echo_close, echo_write, and echo_read aren't listed here, as they haven't been changed.*

```
#include <sys/param.h>
#include <sys/module.h>
#include <sys/kernel.h>
#include <sys/systm.h>

#include <sys/conf.h>
#include <sys/uio.h>
#include <sys/malloc.h>

#define BUFFER_SIZE      256
```

❶ MALLOC_DECLARE(M_ECHO);
❷ MALLOC_DEFINE(M_ECHO, "echo_buffer", "buffer for echo driver");

```
    static d_open_t        echo_open;
    static d_close_t       echo_close;
    static d_read_t        echo_read;
    static d_write_t       echo_write;
```

---
2. M_TEMP is defined in */sys/kern/kern_malloc.c.*

```
static struct cdevsw echo_cdevsw = {
        .d_version =    D_VERSION,
        .d_open =       echo_open,
        .d_close =      echo_close,
        .d_read =       echo_read,
        .d_write =      echo_write,
        .d_name =       "echo"
};

typedef struct echo {
        char buffer[BUFFER_SIZE];
        int length;
} echo_t;

static echo_t *echo_message;
static struct cdev *echo_dev;

static int
echo_open(struct cdev *dev, int oflags, int devtype, struct thread *td)
{
...
}

static int
echo_close(struct cdev *dev, int fflag, int devtype, struct thread *td)
{
...
}

static int
echo_write(struct cdev *dev, struct uio *uio, int ioflag)
{
...
}

static int
echo_read(struct cdev *dev, struct uio *uio, int ioflag)
{
...
}

static int
echo_modevent(module_t mod __unused, int event, void *arg __unused)
{
        int error = 0;

        switch (event) {
        case MOD_LOAD:
                echo_message = malloc(sizeof(echo_t), ❸M_ECHO, M_WAITOK);
                echo_dev = make_dev(&echo_cdevsw, 0, UID_ROOT, GID_WHEEL,
                    0600, "echo");
                uprintf("Echo driver loaded.\n");
                break;
```

```
        case MOD_UNLOAD:
                destroy_dev(echo_dev);
                free(echo_message, ❹M_ECHO);
                uprintf("Echo driver unloaded.\n");
                break;
        default:
                error = EOPNOTSUPP;
                break;
        }

        return (error);
}

DEV_MODULE(echo, echo_modevent, NULL);
```

Listing 2-1: echo-2.0.c

This driver ❶ declares and ❷ defines a new malloc_type structure named M_ECHO. To use this malloc_type structure, malloc and free are ❸ ❹ adjusted accordingly.

NOTE *Because M_ECHO is used only locally, MALLOC_DECLARE is unnecessary—it's only included here for demonstration purposes.*

Now that Listing 2-1 uses a unique malloc_type structure, we can easily profile its dynamic memory usage, like so:

```
$ sudo kldload ./echo-2.0.ko
Echo driver loaded.
$ vmstat -m | head -n 1 && vmstat -m | grep "echo_buffer"
        Type InUse MemUse HighUse Requests  Size(s)
  echo_buffer    1     1K       -        1   512
```

Notice that Listing 2-1 requests 512 bytes, though sizeof(echo_t) is only 260 bytes. This is because malloc rounds up to the nearest power of two when allocating memory. Additionally, note that the second argument to MALLOC_DEFINE (echo_buffer in this example) is used in the output of vmstat (instead of the first argument).

Contiguous Physical Memory Management Routines

The FreeBSD kernel provides two functions for contiguous physical memory management: contigmalloc and contigfree. Ordinarily, you'll never use these functions. They're primarily for dealing with machine-dependent code and the occasional network driver.

```
#include <sys/types.h>
#include <sys/malloc.h>

void *
contigmalloc(unsigned long size, struct malloc_type *type, int flags,
    vm_paddr_t low, vm_paddr_t high, unsigned long alignment,
```

```
                         unsigned long boundary);

    void
    contigfree(void *addr, unsigned long size, struct malloc_type *type);
```

The contigmalloc function allocates size bytes of contiguous physical memory. If size is 0, contigmalloc will panic. If successful, the allocation will reside between physical addresses low and high, inclusive.

The alignment argument denotes the physical alignment, in bytes, of the allocated memory. This argument must be a power of two.

The boundary argument specifies the physical address boundaries that cannot be crossed by the allocated memory; that is, it cannot cross any multiple of boundary. This argument must be 0, which indicates no boundary restrictions, or a power of two.

The flags argument modifies contigmalloc's behavior. Valid values for this argument are shown in Table 2-2.

Table 2-2: contigmalloc Symbolic Constants

Constant	Description
M_ZERO	Causes the allocated physical memory to be zero filled
M_NOWAIT	Causes contigmalloc to return NULL if the allocation cannot be immediately fulfilled due to resource shortage
M_WAITOK	Indicates that it is okay to wait for resources; if the allocation cannot be immediately fulfilled, the current process is put to sleep to wait for resources to become available

The contigfree function releases the memory at addr—that was previously allocated by contigmalloc—for reuse. The size argument is the amount of memory to release. Generally, size should equal the amount allocated.

A Straightforward Example

Listing 2-2 modifies Listing 2-1 to use contigmalloc and contigfree instead of malloc and free. Listing 2-2 should clarify any misunderstandings you may have about contigmalloc and contigfree.

NOTE   *To save space, the functions echo_open, echo_close, echo_write, and echo_read aren't listed here, as they haven't been changed.*

```
#include <sys/param.h>
#include <sys/module.h>
#include <sys/kernel.h>
#include <sys/systm.h>

#include <sys/conf.h>
#include <sys/uio.h>
#include <sys/malloc.h>
```

```
#define BUFFER_SIZE     256

MALLOC_DEFINE(M_ECHO, "echo_buffer", "buffer for echo driver");

static d_open_t         echo_open;
static d_close_t        echo_close;
static d_read_t         echo_read;
static d_write_t        echo_write;

static struct cdevsw echo_cdevsw = {
        .d_version =    D_VERSION,
        .d_open =       echo_open,
        .d_close =      echo_close,
        .d_read =       echo_read,
        .d_write =      echo_write,
        .d_name =       "echo"
};

typedef struct echo {
        char buffer[BUFFER_SIZE];
        int length;
} echo_t;

static echo_t *echo_message;
static struct cdev *echo_dev;

static int
echo_open(struct cdev *dev, int oflags, int devtype, struct thread *td)
{
...
}

static int
echo_close(struct cdev *dev, int fflag, int devtype, struct thread *td)
{
...
}

static int
echo_write(struct cdev *dev, struct uio *uio, int ioflag)
{
...
}

static int
echo_read(struct cdev *dev, struct uio *uio, int ioflag)
{
...
}

static int
echo_modevent(module_t mod __unused, int event, void *arg __unused)
{
        int error = 0;
```

```
        switch (event) {
        case MOD_LOAD:
                echo_message = ❶contigmalloc(❷sizeof(echo_t), M_ECHO,
                    M_WAITOK | ❸M_ZERO, ❹0, ❺0xffffffff, ❻PAGE_SIZE,
                    ❼1024 * 1024);
                echo_dev = make_dev(&echo_cdevsw, 0, UID_ROOT, GID_WHEEL,
                    0600, "echo");
                uprintf("Echo driver loaded.\n");
                break;
        case MOD_UNLOAD:
                destroy_dev(echo_dev);
                contigfree(echo_message, sizeof(echo_t), M_ECHO);
                uprintf("Echo driver unloaded.\n");
                break;
        default:
                error = EOPNOTSUPP;
                break;
        }

        return (error);
}

DEV_MODULE(echo, echo_modevent, NULL);
```

Listing 2-2: echo_contig.c

Here, ❶ contigmalloc allocates ❷ sizeof(echo_t) bytes of ❸ zero-filled memory. This memory resides between physical address ❹ 0 and ❺ 0xffffffff, is aligned on a ❻ PAGE_SIZE boundary, and does not cross a ❼ 1MB address boundary.

The following output shows the results from vmstat -m after loading Listing 2-2:

```
$ sudo kldload ./echo_contig.ko
Echo driver loaded.
$ vmstat -m | head -n 1 && vmstat -m | grep "echo_buffer"
       Type InUse MemUse HighUse Requests  Size(s)
  echo_buffer    1     4K      -        1
```

Notice that Listing 2-2 uses 4KB of memory, though sizeof(echo_t) is only 260 bytes. This is because contigmalloc allocates memory in PAGE_SIZE blocks. Predictably, this example was run on an *i386* machine, which uses a page size of 4KB.

Conclusion

This chapter detailed FreeBSD's memory management routines and contiguous physical memory management routines. It also introduced the malloc_type structure.

Incidentally, most drivers should define their own malloc_type structure.

3

DEVICE COMMUNICATION
AND CONTROL

In Chapter 1 we constructed a driver that could read from and write to a device. In addition to reading and writing, most drivers need to perform other I/O operations, such as reporting error information, ejecting removable media, or activating self-destruct sequences. This chapter details how to make drivers do those things.

We'll start by describing the *ioctl interface*, also known as the *input/output control interface*. This interface is commonly used for device communication and control. Then we'll describe the *sysctl interface*, also known as the *system control interface*. This interface is used to dynamically change or examine the kernel's parameters, which includes device drivers.

ioctl

The ioctl interface is the catchall of I/O operations (Stevens, 1992). Any operation that cannot be expressed using d_read or d_write (that is, any operation that's *not* a data transfer) is supported by d_ioctl.[1] For example, the CD-ROM driver's d_ioctl function performs 29 distinct operations, such as ejecting the CD, starting audio playback, stopping audio playback, muting the audio, and so on.

The function prototype for d_ioctl is defined in the <sys/conf.h> header as follows:

```
typedef int d_ioctl_t(struct cdev *dev, u_long ❶cmd, caddr_t ❷data,
                      int fflag, struct thread *td);
```

Here, ❶ cmd is an ioctl command passed from user space. *ioctl commands* are driver-defined numeric constants that identify the different I/O operations that a d_ioctl function can perform. Generally, you'd use the cmd argument in a switch statement to set up a code block for each I/O operation. Any arguments required for an I/O operation are passed through ❷ data.

Here is an example d_ioctl function:

NOTE *Just concentrate on the structure of this code and ignore what it does.*

```
static int
echo_ioctl(struct cdev *dev, u_long ❶cmd, caddr_t ❷data, int fflag,
    struct thread *td)
{
        int error = 0;

        switch (❸cmd) {
        ❹case ECHO_CLEAR_BUFFER:
                memset(echo_message->buffer, '\0',
                    echo_message->buffer_size);
                echo_message->length = 0;
                uprintf("Buffer cleared.\n");
                break;
        ❺case ECHO_SET_BUFFER_SIZE:
                error = echo_set_buffer_size(*❻(int *)data);
                if (error == 0)
                        uprintf("Buffer resized.\n");
                break;
        ❼default:
                ❽error = ENOTTY;
                break;
        }

        return (error);
}
```

---

1. The d_ioctl function was first introduced in "d_foo Functions" on page 7.

Notice how the ❶ cmd argument is the ❸ expression for the switch statement. The constants ❹ ECHO_CLEAR_BUFFER and ❺ ECHO_SET_BUFFER_SIZE are (obviously) the ioctl commands. All ioctl commands are defined using one of four macros. I'll discuss these macros in the following section.

Additionally, notice how the ❷ data argument is ❻ cast—as an integer pointer—before it is dereferenced. This is because data is fundamentally a "pointer to void."

NOTE *Pointers to void can hold any pointer type, so they must be cast before they're dereferenced. In fact, you can't directly dereference a pointer to void.*

Finally, according to the POSIX standard, when an inappropriate ioctl command is received, the error code ENOTTY should be returned (Corbet et al., 2005). Hence, the ❼ default block sets ❽ error to ENOTTY.

NOTE *At one point in time, only TTY drivers had an ioctl function, which is why ENOTTY means "error: inappropriate ioctl for device" (Corbet et al., 2005).*

Now that you've examined the structure of a d_ioctl function, I'll explain how to define an ioctl command.

Defining ioctl Commands

To define an ioctl command, you'd call one of the following macros: _IO, _IOR, _IOW, or _IOWR. An explanation of each macro is provided in Table 3-1.

Table 3-1: ioctl Command Macros

Macro	Description
_IO	Creates an ioctl command for an I/O operation that transfers no data—in other words, the data argument in d_ioctl will be unused—for example, ejecting removable media
_IOR	Creates an ioctl command for a read operation; *read operations* transfer data from the device to user space; for example, retrieving error information
_IOW	Creates an ioctl command for a write operation; *write operations* transfer data to the device from user space; for example, setting a device parameter
_IOWR	Creates an ioctl command for an I/O operation with bidirectional data transfers

_IO, _IOR, _IOW, and _IOWR are defined in the <sys/ioccom.h> header as follows:

```
#define _IO(g,n)       _IOC(IOC_VOID,  (g), (n), 0)
#define _IOR(g,n,t)    _IOC(IOC_OUT,   (g), (n), sizeof(t))
#define _IOW(g,n,t)    _IOC(IOC_IN,    (g), (n), sizeof(t))
#define _IOWR(g,n,t)   _IOC(IOC_INOUT, (g), (n), sizeof(t))
```

The g argument, which stands for *group*, expects an 8-bit magic number. You can choose any number—just use it throughout your driver.

The n argument is the ordinal number. This number is used to differentiate your driver's ioctl commands from one another.

Finally, the t argument is the type of data transferred during the I/O operation. Obviously, the _IO macro does not have a t argument, because no data transfer occurs.

Generally, ioctl command definitions look like this:

```
#define FOO_DO_SOMETHING        _IO('F', 1)
#define FOO_GET_SOMETHING       _IOR('F', 2, int)
#define FOO_SET_SOMETHING       _IOW('F', 3, int)
#define FOO_SWITCH_SOMETHING    _IOWR('F', 10, ❶struct foo)
```

Here, 'F' is the magic number for these ioctl commands. Customarily, the first letter of your driver's name—in uppercase—is selected as the magic number.

Naturally, all of the ordinal numbers are unique. But they don't have to be consecutive. You can leave gaps.

Lastly, note that you can pass ❶ structures as the t argument. Using a structure is how you'll pass multiple arguments to an ioctl-based operation.

Implementing ioctl

Listing 3-1 is a revision of Listing 2-1 that adds in a d_ioctl function. As you'll see, this d_ioctl function handles two ioctl commands.

NOTE *Take a quick look at this code and try to discern some of its structure. If you don't understand all of it, don't worry; an explanation follows.*

```
#include <sys/param.h>
#include <sys/module.h>
#include <sys/kernel.h>
#include <sys/systm.h>

#include <sys/conf.h>
#include <sys/uio.h>
#include <sys/malloc.h>
#include <sys/ioccom.h>

MALLOC_DEFINE(M_ECHO, "echo_buffer", "buffer for echo driver");

❶ #define ECHO_CLEAR_BUFFER       _IO('E', 1)
❷ #define ECHO_SET_BUFFER_SIZE    _IOW('E', 2, ❸int)

static d_open_t        echo_open;
static d_close_t       echo_close;
static d_read_t        echo_read;
static d_write_t       echo_write;
static d_ioctl_t       echo_ioctl;

static struct cdevsw echo_cdevsw = {
```

```
        .d_version =    D_VERSION,
        .d_open =       echo_open,
        .d_close =      echo_close,
        .d_read =       echo_read,
        .d_write =      echo_write,
    ❹.d_ioctl =         echo_ioctl,
        .d_name =       "echo"
};

typedef struct echo {
    ❺int buffer_size;
        char *buffer;
        int length;
} echo_t;

static echo_t *echo_message;
static struct cdev *echo_dev;

static int
echo_open(struct cdev *dev, int oflags, int devtype, struct thread *td)
{
        uprintf("Opening echo device.\n");
        return (0);
}

static int
echo_close(struct cdev *dev, int fflag, int devtype, struct thread *td)
{
        uprintf("Closing echo device.\n");
        return (0);
}

static int
echo_write(struct cdev *dev, struct uio *uio, int ioflag)
{
        int error = 0;
        int amount;

        amount = MIN(uio->uio_resid,
            (❻echo_message->buffer_size - 1 - uio->uio_offset > 0) ?
            ❼echo_message->buffer_size - 1 - uio->uio_offset : 0);
        if (amount == 0)
                return (error);

        error = uiomove(echo_message->buffer, amount, uio);
        if (error != 0) {
                uprintf("Write failed.\n");
                return (error);
        }

        echo_message->buffer[amount] = '\0';
        echo_message->length = amount;

        return (error);
}
```

```
static int
echo_read(struct cdev *dev, struct uio *uio, int ioflag)
{
        int error = 0;
        int amount;

        amount = MIN(uio->uio_resid,
            (echo_message->length - uio->uio_offset > 0) ?
             echo_message->length - uio->uio_offset : 0);

        error = uiomove(echo_message->buffer + uio->uio_offset, amount, uio);
        if (error != 0)
                uprintf("Read failed.\n");

        return (error);
}

static int
echo_set_buffer_size(int size)
{
        int error = 0;

        if (echo_message->buffer_size == size)
                return (error);

        if (size >= 128 && size <= 512) {
                echo_message->buffer = realloc(echo_message->buffer, size,
                    M_ECHO, M_WAITOK);
                echo_message->buffer_size = size;

                if (echo_message->length >= size) {
                        echo_message->length = size - 1;
                        echo_message->buffer[size - 1] = '\0';
                }
        } else
                error = EINVAL;

        return (error);
}

static int
echo_ioctl(struct cdev *dev, u_long cmd, caddr_t data, int fflag,
    struct thread *td)
{
        int error = 0;

        switch (cmd) {
        case ECHO_CLEAR_BUFFER:
                memset(echo_message->buffer, '\0',
                    echo_message->buffer_size);
                echo_message->length = 0;
                uprintf("Buffer cleared.\n");
                break;
```

```
            case ECHO_SET_BUFFER_SIZE:
                    error = echo_set_buffer_size(*(int *)data);
                    if (error == 0)
                            uprintf("Buffer resized.\n");
                    break;
            default:
                    error = ENOTTY;
                    break;
            }

            return (error);
    }

    static int
    echo_modevent(module_t mod __unused, int event, void *arg __unused)
    {
            int error = 0;

            switch (event) {
            case MOD_LOAD:
                    echo_message = malloc(sizeof(echo_t), M_ECHO, M_WAITOK);
                    echo_message->buffer_size = 256;
                    echo_message->buffer = malloc(echo_message->buffer_size,
                        M_ECHO, M_WAITOK);
                    echo_dev = make_dev(&echo_cdevsw, 0, UID_ROOT, GID_WHEEL,
                        0600, "echo");
                    uprintf("Echo driver loaded.\n");
                    break;
            case MOD_UNLOAD:
                    destroy_dev(echo_dev);
                    free(echo_message->buffer, M_ECHO);
                    free(echo_message, M_ECHO);
                    uprintf("Echo driver unloaded.\n");
                    break;
            default:
                    error = EOPNOTSUPP;
                    break;
            }

            return (error);
    }

    DEV_MODULE(echo, echo_modevent, NULL);
```

Listing 3-1: echo-3.0.c

    This driver starts by defining two ioctl commands: ❶ ECHO_CLEAR_BUFFER (which clears the memory buffer) and ❷ ECHO_SET_BUFFER_SIZE (which takes an ❸ integer to resize the memory buffer).

NOTE   *Usually, ioctl commands are defined in a header file—they were defined in Listing 3-1 solely to simplify this discussion.*

Obviously, to accommodate adding in a d_ioctl function, the character device switch table was ❹ adapted. Moreover, struct echo was adjusted to include a variable (❺ buffer_size) to maintain the buffer size (because it can be changed now). Naturally, Listing 3-1 was ❻ ❼ altered to use this new variable.

NOTE *Interestingly, only echo_write had to be altered. The echo_open, echo_close, and echo_read functions remain the same.*

The echo_write, echo_set_buffer_size, echo_ioctl, and echo_modevent functions call for a more in-depth explanation and are therefore described in their own sections.

echo_write Function

As mentioned above, the echo_write function was altered from its Listing 2-1 (and Listing 1-2) form. Here is its function definition (again):

```
static int
echo_write(struct cdev *dev, struct uio *uio, int ioflag)
{
        int error = 0;
        int amount;

        amount = ❶MIN(❷uio->uio_resid,
          ❸(echo_message->buffer_size - 1 - uio->uio_offset > 0) ?
            echo_message->buffer_size - 1 - uio->uio_offset : 0);
        if (amount == 0)
                return (error);

        error = ❹uiomove(❺echo_message->buffer, ❻amount, ❼uio);
        if (error != 0) {
                uprintf("Write failed.\n");
                return (error);
        }

        echo_message->buffer[amount] = '\0';
        echo_message->length = amount;

        return (error);
}
```

This version of echo_write uses ❹ uiomove (as described in Chapter 1) instead of copyin. Note that uiomove decrements uio->uio_resid (by one) and increments uio->uio_offset (by one) for each byte copied. This lets multiple calls to uiomove effortlessly copy a chunk of data.

You'll recall that uio->uio_resid and uio->uio_offset denote the number of bytes remaining to be transferred and an offset into the data (that is, the character string), respectively.

This function starts by ❶ determining the number of bytes to copy—either the ❷ amount the user sent or ❸ whatever the buffer can accommodate. Then it ❹ transfers that ❻ amount from ❼ user space to ❺ kernel space.

The remainder of this function should be self-explanatory.

echo_set_buffer_size Function

As its name implies, the echo_set_buffer_size function takes an integer to resize the memory buffer echo_message->buffer. Here is its function definition (again):

```
static int
echo_set_buffer_size(int size)
{
        int error = 0;

     ❶if (❷echo_message->buffer_size == ❸size)
            ❹return (error);

        if (size >= 128 && size <= 512) {
                echo_message->buffer = ❺realloc(echo_message->buffer, size,
                    M_ECHO, M_WAITOK);
            ❻echo_message->buffer_size = size;

            ❼if (echo_message->length >= size) {
                    ❽echo_message->length = size - 1;
                    ❾echo_message->buffer[size - 1] = '\0';
                }
        } else
                error = EINVAL;

        return (error);
}
```

This function can be split into three parts. The first part ❶ confirms that the ❷ current and ❸ proposed buffer sizes are distinct (or else ❹ nothing needs to occur).

The second part ❺ changes the size of the memory buffer. Then it ❻ records the new buffer size. Note that if the data stored in the buffer is longer than the proposed buffer size, the resize operation (that is, realloc) will truncate that data.

The third part comes about only ❼ if the data stored in the buffer was truncated. It begins by ❽ correcting the stored data's length. Then it ❾ null-terminates the data.

echo_ioctl Function

The echo_ioctl function is the d_ioctl function for Listing 3-1. Here is its function definition (again):

```
static int
echo_ioctl(struct cdev *dev, u_long cmd, caddr_t ❶data, int fflag,
    struct thread *td)
{
        int error = 0;

        switch (cmd) {
    ❷case ECHO_CLEAR_BUFFER:
                ❸memset(echo_message->buffer, '\0',
                    echo_message->buffer_size);
                ❹echo_message->length = 0;
                uprintf("Buffer cleared.\n");
                break;
    ❺case ECHO_SET_BUFFER_SIZE:
                error = ❻echo_set_buffer_size(*(int *)❼data);
                if (error == 0)
                        uprintf("Buffer resized.\n");
                break;
        default:
                error = ENOTTY;
                break;
        }

        return (error);
}
```

This function can perform one of two ioctl-based operations. The first ❷ clears the memory buffer. It begins by ❸ zeroing the buffer. Then it ❹ sets the data length to 0.

The second ❺ resizes the memory buffer by calling ❻ echo_set_buffer_size. Note that this operation requires an ❼ argument: the proposed buffer size. This argument is obtained from user space through ❶ data.

NOTE   *Remember that you must cast data before it can be dereferenced.*

echo_modevent Function

As you know, the echo_modevent function is the module event handler. Like echo_write, this function had to be altered to accommodate adding in echo_ioctl. Here is its function definition (again):

```
static int
echo_modevent(module_t mod __unused, int event, void *arg __unused)
{
        int error = 0;
```

```
switch (event) {
case MOD_LOAD:
        echo_message = ❶malloc(sizeof(echo_t), M_ECHO, M_WAITOK);
        echo_message->buffer_size = 256;
        echo_message->buffer = ❷malloc(echo_message->buffer_size,
            M_ECHO, M_WAITOK);
        echo_dev = make_dev(&echo_cdevsw, 0, UID_ROOT, GID_WHEEL,
            0600, "echo");
        uprintf("Echo driver loaded.\n");
        break;
case MOD_UNLOAD:
        destroy_dev(echo_dev);
        free(echo_message->buffer, M_ECHO);
        free(echo_message, M_ECHO);
        uprintf("Echo driver unloaded.\n");
        break;
default:
        error = EOPNOTSUPP;
        break;
}

    return (error);
}
```

This version of echo_modevent allocates memory for the ❶ echo structure and ❷ memory buffer individually—that's the only change. Previously, the memory buffer couldn't be resized. So, individual memory allocations were unnecessary.

Don't Panic

Now that we've walked through Listing 3-1, let's give it a try:

```
$ sudo kldload ./echo-3.0.ko
Echo driver loaded.
$ su
Password:
# echo "DON'T PANIC" > /dev/echo
Opening echo device.
Closing echo device.
# cat /dev/echo
Opening echo device.
DON'T PANIC
Closing echo device.
```

Apparently it works. But how do we invoke echo_ioctl?

Invoking ioctl

To invoke a d_ioctl function, you'd use the ioctl(2) system call.

```
#include <sys/ioctl.h>

int
ioctl(int d, unsigned long request, ...);
```

The d argument, which stands for *descriptor*, expects a file descriptor for a
device node. The request argument is the ioctl command to be issued (for
example, ECHO_CLEAR_BUFFER). The remaining argument (...) is a pointer to
the data that'll be passed to the d_ioctl function.

Listing 3-2 presents a command-line utility designed to invoke the
echo_ioctl function in Listing 3-1:

```
#include <sys/types.h>
#include <sys/ioctl.h>

#include <err.h>
#include <fcntl.h>
#include <limits.h>
#include <stdio.h>
#include <stdlib.h>
#include <unistd.h>

❶ #define ECHO_CLEAR_BUFFER       _IO('E', 1)
❷ #define ECHO_SET_BUFFER_SIZE    _IOW('E', 2, int)

static enum {UNSET, CLEAR, SETSIZE} action = UNSET;


/*
 * The usage statement: echo_config -c | -s size
 */

static void
usage()
{
        /*
         * Arguments for this program are "either-or." That is,
         * 'echo_config -c' and 'echo_config -s size' are valid; however,
         * 'echo_config -c -s size' is invalid.
         */

        fprintf(stderr, "usage: echo_config -c | -s size\n");
        exit(1);
}


/*
 * This program clears or resizes the memory buffer
 * found in /dev/echo.
 */

int
main(int argc, char *argv[])
```

```c
{
        int ch, fd, i, size;
        char *p;

        /*
         * Parse the command-line argument list to determine
         * the correct course of action.
         *
         *      -c:     clear the memory buffer
         *      -s size: resize the memory buffer to size.
         */

        while ((ch = getopt(argc, argv, "cs:")) != -1)
                switch (ch) {
                case 'c':
                        if (action != UNSET)
                                usage();
                        action = CLEAR;
                        break;
                case 's':
                        if (action != UNSET)
                                usage();
                        action = SETSIZE;
                        size = (int)strtol(optarg, &p, 10);
                        if (*p)
                                errx(1, "illegal size -- %s", optarg);
                        break;
                default:
                        usage();
                }

        /*
         * Perform the chosen action.
         */

        if (action == CLEAR) {
                fd = ❸open("/dev/echo", O_RDWR);
                if (fd < 0)
                        err(1, "open(/dev/echo)");

                i = ❹ioctl(fd, ECHO_CLEAR_BUFFER, ❺NULL);
                if (i < 0)
                        err(1, "ioctl(/dev/echo)");

                close (fd);
        } else if (action == SETSIZE) {
                fd = ❻open("/dev/echo", O_RDWR);
                if (fd < 0)
                        err(1, "open(/dev/echo)");

                i = ❼ioctl(fd, ECHO_SET_BUFFER_SIZE, &size);
                if (i < 0)
                        err(1, "ioctl(/dev/echo)");

                close (fd);
```

```
        } else
                usage();

        return (0);
}
```

Listing 3-2: echo_config.c

Listing 3-2 is a fairly standard command-line utility. As such, I won't cover its program structure. Instead, I'll concentrate on how it invokes echo_ioctl.

This program begins by redefining ❶ ECHO_CLEAR_BUFFER and ❷ ECHO_SET_BUFFER_SIZE.[2] To issue an ioctl command, Listing 3-2 starts by ❸ ❻ opening /dev/echo. Then it ❹ ❼ calls ioctl(2) with the appropriate arguments.

Note that since ECHO_CLEAR_BUFFER doesn't transmit any data, ❺ NULL is passed as the third argument to ioctl(2).

The following shows the results from executing Listing 3-2 to clear the memory buffer:

```
$ sudo cat /dev/echo
Opening echo device.
DON'T PANIC
Closing echo device.
$ sudo ./echo_config -c
Opening echo device.
Buffer cleared.
Closing echo device.
$ sudo cat /dev/echo
Opening echo device.
Closing echo device.
```

The following shows the results from executing Listing 3-2 to resize the memory buffer:

```
$ sudo ./echo_config -s 128
Opening echo device.
Buffer resized.
Closing echo device.
```

sysctl

As mentioned earlier, the sysctl interface is used to dynamically change or examine the kernel's parameters, which includes device drivers. For example, some drivers let you enable (or disable) debug options using sysctls.

NOTE *This book was written under the assumption that you know how to work with sysctls; if you don't, see the sysctl(8) manual page.*

---

2. This step could have been avoided by defining those ioctl commands in a header file.

Unlike with previous topics, I'm going to take a holistic approach to explain sysctl. That is, I'm going to show an example first, and then I'll describe the sysctl functions. I found this to be the easiest way to grok implementing sysctls.

Implementing sysctls, Part 1

Listing 3-3 is a complete KLD (based on code written by Andrzej Bialecki) that creates multiple sysctls.

```
#include <sys/param.h>
#include <sys/module.h>
#include <sys/kernel.h>
#include <sys/systm.h>
#include <sys/sysctl.h>

static long  a = 100;
static int   b = 200;
static char *c = "Are you suggesting coconuts migrate?";

static struct sysctl_ctx_list clist;
static struct sysctl_oid *poid;

static int
❶ sysctl_pointless_procedure(SYSCTL_HANDLER_ARGS)
{
        char *buf = "Not at all. They could be carried.";
        return (sysctl_handle_string(oidp, buf, strlen(buf), req));
}

static int
pointless_modevent(module_t mod __unused, int event, void *arg __unused)
{
        int error = 0;

        switch (event) {
        case MOD_LOAD:
                ❷sysctl_ctx_init(&clist);

                poid = ❸SYSCTL_ADD_NODE(&clist,
                    SYSCTL_STATIC_CHILDREN(/* tree top */), OID_AUTO,
                    "example", CTLFLAG_RW, 0, "new top-level tree");
                if (poid == NULL) {
                        uprintf("SYSCTL_ADD_NODE failed.\n");
                        return (EINVAL);
                }
                ❹SYSCTL_ADD_LONG(&clist, SYSCTL_CHILDREN(poid), OID_AUTO,
                    "long", CTLFLAG_RW, &a, "new long leaf");
                ❺SYSCTL_ADD_INT(&clist, SYSCTL_CHILDREN(poid), OID_AUTO,
                    "int", CTLFLAG_RW, &b, 0, "new int leaf");

                poid = ❻SYSCTL_ADD_NODE(&clist, SYSCTL_CHILDREN(poid),
                    OID_AUTO, "node", CTLFLAG_RW, 0,
```

```
                             "new tree under example");
                    if (poid == NULL) {
                            uprintf("SYSCTL_ADD_NODE failed.\n");
                            return (EINVAL);
                    }
                 ❼SYSCTL_ADD_PROC(&clist, SYSCTL_CHILDREN(poid), OID_AUTO,
                    "proc", CTLFLAG_RD, 0, 0, sysctl_pointless_procedure,
                    "A", "new proc leaf");

                    poid = ❽SYSCTL_ADD_NODE(&clist,
                        SYSCTL_STATIC_CHILDREN(_debug), OID_AUTO, "example",
                        CTLFLAG_RW, 0, "new tree under debug");
                    if (poid == NULL) {
                            uprintf("SYSCTL_ADD_NODE failed.\n");
                            return (EINVAL);
                    }
                 ❾SYSCTL_ADD_STRING(&clist, SYSCTL_CHILDREN(poid), OID_AUTO,
                    "string", CTLFLAG_RD, c, 0, "new string leaf");

                    uprintf("Pointless module loaded.\n");
                    break;
            case MOD_UNLOAD:
                    if (❿sysctl_ctx_free(&clist)) {
                            uprintf("sysctl_ctx_free failed.\n");
                            return (ENOTEMPTY);
                    }
                    uprintf("Pointless module unloaded.\n");
                    break;
            default:
                    error = EOPNOTSUPP;
                    break;
            }

            return (error);
    }

    static moduledata_t pointless_mod = {
            "pointless",
            pointless_modevent,
            NULL
    };

    DECLARE_MODULE(pointless, pointless_mod, SI_SUB_EXEC, SI_ORDER_ANY);
```

Listing 3-3: pointless.c

On module load, Listing 3-3 starts by ❷ initializing a sysctl context named clist. Generally speaking, *sysctl contexts* are responsible for keeping track of dynamically created sysctls—this is why clist gets passed to every SYSCTL_ADD_* call.

The first ❸ SYSCTL_ADD_NODE call creates a new top-level category named example. The ❹ SYSCTL_ADD_LONG call creates a new sysctl named long that handles a long variable. Notice that SYSCTL_ADD_LONG's second argument is

`SYSCTL_CHILDREN(poid)`[3] and that poid contains the return value from `SYSCTL_ADD_NODE`. Thus, `long` is placed under example, like so:

```
example.long
```

The ❺ `SYSCTL_ADD_INT` call creates a new sysctl named int that handles an integer variable. For reasons identical to those for `SYSCTL_ADD_LONG`, int is placed under example:

```
example.long
example.int
```

The second ❻ `SYSCTL_ADD_NODE` call creates a new subcategory named node, which is placed under example, like so:

```
example.long
example.int
example.node
```

The ❼ `SYSCTL_ADD_PROC` call creates a new sysctl named proc that employs a ❶ function to handle its read and write requests; in this case, the function simply prints some flavor text. You'll note that `SYSCTL_ADD_PROC`'s second argument is also `SYSCTL_CHILDREN(poid)`. But poid now contains the return value from the second `SYSCTL_ADD_NODE` call. So, proc is placed under node:

```
example.long
example.int
example.node.proc
```

The third ❽ `SYSCTL_ADD_NODE` call creates a new subcategory named example. As you can see, its second argument is `SYSCTL_STATIC_CHILDREN(_debug)`,[4] which puts example under debug (which is a static top-level category).

```
debug.example
example.long
example.int
example.node.proc
```

The ❾ `SYSCTL_ADD_STRING` call creates a new sysctl named string that handles a character string. For obvious reasons, string is placed under debug.example:

```
debug.example.string
example.long
example.int
example.node.proc
```

---

3. The `SYSCTL_CHILDREN` macro is described on page 47.

4. The `SYSCTL_STATIC_CHILDREN` macro is described on page 47.

On module unload, Listing 3-3 simply passes clist to ❿ sysctl_ctx_free to destroy every sysctl created during module load.

The following shows the results from loading Listing 3-3:

```
$ sudo kldload ./pointless.ko
Pointless module loaded.
$ sysctl -A | grep example
debug.example.string: Are you suggesting coconuts migrate?
example.long: 100
example.int: 200
example.node.proc: Not at all. They could be carried.
```

Now, let's discuss in detail the different functions and macros used in Listing 3-3.

sysctl Context Management Routines

As mentioned previously, sysctl contexts manage dynamically created sysctls. A sysctl context is initialized via the sysctl_ctx_init function.

```
#include <sys/types.h>
#include <sys/sysctl.h>

int
sysctl_ctx_init(struct sysctl_ctx_list *clist);
```

After a sysctl context is initialized, it can be passed to the various SYSCTL_ADD_* macros. These macros will update the sysctl context with pointers to the newly created sysctls.

Conversely, the sysctl_ctx_free function takes a sysctl context and destroys every sysctl that it has a pointer to.

```
#include <sys/types.h>
#include <sys/sysctl.h>

int
sysctl_ctx_free(struct sysctl_ctx_list *clist);
```

If a sysctl cannot be destroyed, all the sysctls that were associated with the sysctl context are reinstated.

Creating Dynamic sysctls

The FreeBSD kernel provides the following 10 macros for creating sysctls during runtime:

```
#include <sys/types.h>
#include <sys/sysctl.h>
```

```
struct sysctl_oid *
SYSCTL_ADD_OID(struct sysctl_ctx_list *ctx,
    struct sysctl_oid_list *parent, int number, const char *name,
    int kind, void *arg1, int arg2, int (*handler) (SYSCTL_HANDLER_ARGS),
    const char *format, const char *descr);

struct sysctl_oid *
SYSCTL_ADD_NODE(struct sysctl_ctx_list *ctx,
    struct sysctl_oid_list *parent, int number, const char *name,
    int access, int (*handler) (SYSCTL_HANDLER_ARGS), const char *descr);

struct sysctl_oid *
SYSCTL_ADD_STRING(struct sysctl_ctx_list *ctx,
    struct sysctl_oid_list *parent, int number, const char *name,
    int access, char *arg, int len, const char *descr);

struct sysctl_oid *
SYSCTL_ADD_INT(struct sysctl_ctx_list *ctx,
    struct sysctl_oid_list *parent, int number, const char *name,
    int access, int *arg, int len, const char *descr);

struct sysctl_oid *
SYSCTL_ADD_UINT(struct sysctl_ctx_list *ctx,
    struct sysctl_oid_list *parent, int number, const char *name,
    int access, unsigned int *arg, int len, const char *descr);

struct sysctl_oid *
SYSCTL_ADD_LONG(struct sysctl_ctx_list *ctx,
    struct sysctl_oid_list *parent, int number, const char *name,
    int access, long *arg, const char *descr);

struct sysctl_oid *
SYSCTL_ADD_ULONG(struct sysctl_ctx_list *ctx,
    struct sysctl_oid_list *parent, int number, const char *name,
    int access, unsigned long *arg, const char *descr);

struct sysctl_oid *
SYSCTL_ADD_OPAQUE(struct sysctl_ctx_list *ctx,
    struct sysctl_oid_list *parent, int number, const char *name,
    int access, void *arg, int len, const char *format,
    const char *descr);

struct sysctl_oid *
SYSCTL_ADD_STRUCT(struct sysctl_ctx_list *ctx,
    struct sysctl_oid_list *parent, int number, const char *name,
    int access, void *arg, STRUCT_NAME, const char *descr);

struct sysctl_oid *
SYSCTL_ADD_PROC(struct sysctl_ctx_list *ctx,
    struct sysctl_oid_list *parent, int number, const char *name,
    int access, void *arg, int len,
    int (*handler) (SYSCTL_HANDLER_ARGS), const char *format,
    const char *descr);
```

The `SYSCTL_ADD_OID` macro creates a new sysctl that can handle any data type. If successful, a pointer to the sysctl is returned; otherwise, `NULL` is returned.

The other `SYSCTL_ADD_*` macros are alternatives to `SYSCTL_ADD_OID` that create a sysctl that can handle a specific data type. These macros are explained in Table 3-2.

Table 3-2: SYSCTL_ADD_* Macros

Macro	Description
SYSCTL_ADD_NODE	Creates a new node (or category) to which child nodes may be added
SYSCTL_ADD_STRING	Creates a new sysctl that handles a null-terminated character string
SYSCTL_ADD_INT	Creates a new sysctl that handles an integer variable
SYSCTL_ADD_UINT	Creates a new sysctl that handles an unsigned integer variable
SYSCTL_ADD_LONG	Creates a new sysctl that handles a long variable
SYSCTL_ADD_ULONG	Creates a new sysctl that handles an unsigned long variable
SYSCTL_ADD_OPAQUE	Creates a new sysctl that handles a chunk of opaque data; the size of this data is specified by the len argument
SYSCTL_ADD_STRUCT	Creates a new sysctl that handles a structure
SYSCTL_ADD_PROC	Creates a new sysctl that uses a function to handle its read and write requests; this "handler function" is normally used to process the data before importing or exporting it

In most cases, you should use a `SYSCTL_ADD_*` macro instead of the generic `SYSCTL_ADD_OID` macro.

The arguments for the `SYSCTL_ADD_*` macros are described in Table 3-3.

Table 3-3: SYSCTL_ADD_* Arguments

Argument	Description
ctx	Expects a pointer to a sysctl context
parent	Expects a pointer to the parent sysctl's list of children; more on this later
number	Expects the sysctl's number; this should always be set to OID_AUTO
name	Expects the sysctl's name
access	Expects an access flag; *access flags* specify whether the sysctl is read-only (CTLFLAG_RD) or read-write (CTLFLAG_RW)
arg	Expects a pointer to the data that the sysctl will manage (or NULL)
len	Set this to 0 unless you're calling SYSCTL_ADD_OPAQUE
handler	Expects a pointer to the function that will handle the sysctl's read and write requests (or 0)
format	Expects a format name; *format names* identify the type of data that the sysctl will manage; the complete list of format names is: "N" for node, "A" for char *, "I" for int, "IU" for unsigned int, "L" for long, "LU" for unsigned long, and "S,foo" for struct foo
descr	Expects a textual description of the sysctl; this description is printed by sysctl -d

A sysctl created by a SYSCTL_ADD_* macro must be connected to a parent sysctl. This is done by passing SYSCTL_STATIC_CHILDREN or SYSCTL_CHILDREN as the parent argument.

SYSCTL_STATIC_CHILDREN Macro

The SYSCTL_STATIC_CHILDREN macro is passed as parent when connecting to a static node. A *static node* is part of the base system.

```
#include <sys/types.h>
#include <sys/sysctl.h>

struct sysctl_oid_list *
SYSCTL_STATIC_CHILDREN(struct sysctl_oid_list OID_NAME);
```

This macro takes the name of the parent sysctl preceded by an underscore. And all dots must be replaced by an underscore. So to connect to hw.usb, you would use _hw_usb.

If SYSCTL_STATIC_CHILDREN(/* no argument */) is passed as parent to SYSCTL_ADD_NODE, a new top-level category will be created.

SYSCTL_CHILDREN Macro

The SYSCTL_CHILDREN macro is passed as parent when connecting to a dynamic node. A *dynamic node* is created by a SYSCTL_ADD_NODE call.

```
#include <sys/types.h>
#include <sys/sysctl.h>

struct sysctl_oid_list *
SYSCTL_CHILDREN(struct sysctl_oid *oidp);
```

This macro takes as its sole argument the pointer returned by a SYSCTL_ADD_NODE call.

Implementing sysctls, Part 2

Now that you know how to create sysctls during runtime, let's do some actual device control (as opposed to quoting Monty Python).

Listing 3-4 is a revision of Listing 3-1 that employs a sysctl to resize the memory buffer.

NOTE   *To save space, the functions* echo_open, echo_close, echo_write, *and* echo_read *aren't listed here, as they haven't been changed.*

```
#include <sys/param.h>
#include <sys/module.h>
#include <sys/kernel.h>
#include <sys/systm.h>
```

```
#include <sys/conf.h>
#include <sys/uio.h>
#include <sys/malloc.h>
#include <sys/ioccom.h>
#include <sys/sysctl.h>

MALLOC_DEFINE(M_ECHO, "echo_buffer", "buffer for echo driver");

#define ECHO_CLEAR_BUFFER       _IO('E', 1)

static d_open_t          echo_open;
static d_close_t         echo_close;
static d_read_t          echo_read;
static d_write_t         echo_write;
static d_ioctl_t         echo_ioctl;

static struct cdevsw echo_cdevsw = {
        .d_version =    D_VERSION,
        .d_open =       echo_open,
        .d_close =      echo_close,
        .d_read =       echo_read,
        .d_write =      echo_write,
        .d_ioctl =      echo_ioctl,
        .d_name =       "echo"
};

typedef struct echo {
        int buffer_size;
        char *buffer;
        int length;
} echo_t;

static echo_t *echo_message;
static struct cdev *echo_dev;

static struct sysctl_ctx_list clist;
static struct sysctl_oid *poid;

static int
echo_open(struct cdev *dev, int oflags, int devtype, struct thread *td)
{
...
}

static int
echo_close(struct cdev *dev, int fflag, int devtype, struct thread *td)
{
...
}

static int
echo_write(struct cdev *dev, struct uio *uio, int ioflag)
{
...
}
```

```
static int
echo_read(struct cdev *dev, struct uio *uio, int ioflag)
{
...
}

static int
echo_ioctl(struct cdev *dev, u_long cmd, caddr_t data, int fflag,
    struct thread *td)
{
        int error = 0;

        switch (cmd) {
        case ECHO_CLEAR_BUFFER:
                memset(echo_message->buffer, '\0',
                    echo_message->buffer_size);
                echo_message->length = 0;
                uprintf("Buffer cleared.\n");
                break;
        default:
                error = ENOTTY;
                break;
        }

        return (error);
}

static int
sysctl_set_buffer_size(SYSCTL_HANDLER_ARGS)
{
        int error = 0;
        int size = echo_message->buffer_size;

        error = sysctl_handle_int(oidp, &size, 0, req);
        if (error || !req->newptr || echo_message->buffer_size == size)
                return (error);

        if (size >= 128 && size <= 512) {
                echo_message->buffer = realloc(echo_message->buffer, size,
                    M_ECHO, M_WAITOK);
                echo_message->buffer_size = size;

                if (echo_message->length >= size) {
                        echo_message->length = size - 1;
                        echo_message->buffer[size - 1] = '\0';
                }
        } else
                error = EINVAL;

        return (error);
}

static int
echo_modevent(module_t mod __unused, int event, void *arg __unused)
```

```
{
        int error = 0;

        switch (event) {
        case MOD_LOAD:
                echo_message = malloc(sizeof(echo_t), M_ECHO, M_WAITOK);
                echo_message->buffer_size = 256;
                echo_message->buffer = malloc(echo_message->buffer_size,
                    M_ECHO, M_WAITOK);
                sysctl_ctx_init(&clist);
                poid = SYSCTL_ADD_NODE(&clist,
                    SYSCTL_STATIC_CHILDREN(/* tree top */), OID_AUTO,
                    "echo", CTLFLAG_RW, 0, "echo root node");
                SYSCTL_ADD_PROC(&clist, SYSCTL_CHILDREN(poid), OID_AUTO,
                    "buffer_size", CTLTYPE_INT | CTLFLAG_RW,
                    ❶&echo_message->buffer_size, 0, ❷sysctl_set_buffer_size,
                    "I", "echo buffer size");
                echo_dev = make_dev(&echo_cdevsw, 0, UID_ROOT, GID_WHEEL,
                    0600, "echo");
                uprintf("Echo driver loaded.\n");
                break;
        case MOD_UNLOAD:
                destroy_dev(echo_dev);
                sysctl_ctx_free(&clist);
                free(echo_message->buffer, M_ECHO);
                free(echo_message, M_ECHO);
                uprintf("Echo driver unloaded.\n");
                break;
        default:
                error = EOPNOTSUPP;
                break;
        }

        return (error);
}

DEV_MODULE(echo, echo_modevent, NULL);
```

Listing 3-4: echo-4.0.c

On module load, Listing 3-4 creates a sysctl named echo.buffer_size that manages the ❶ size of the memory buffer. Moreover, this sysctl uses a ❷ handler function named sysctl_set_buffer_size to resize the memory buffer.

sysctl_set_buffer_size Function

As stated above, the sysctl_set_buffer_size function resizes the memory buffer. Before I describe this function, let's identify its arguments.

```
static int
sysctl_set_buffer_size(❶SYSCTL_HANDLER_ARGS)
```

The constant ❶ SYSCTL_HANDLER_ARGS is defined in <sys/sysctl.h> like so:

```
#define SYSCTL_HANDLER_ARGS struct sysctl_oid ❶*oidp, void ❷*arg1, \
        int ❸arg2, struct sysctl_req ❹*req
```

Here, ❶ oidp points to the sysctl, ❷ arg1 points to the data that the sysctl manages, ❸ arg2 is the length of the data, and ❹ req depicts the sysctl request.

Now, keeping these arguments in mind, let's examine the function sysctl_set_buffer_size.

```
static int
sysctl_set_buffer_size(SYSCTL_HANDLER_ARGS)
{
        int error = 0;
   ❶int size = echo_message->buffer_size;

        error = ❷sysctl_handle_int(oidp, ❸&size, 0, req);
   ❹if (❺error || ❻!req->newptr || echo_message->buffer_size == size)
                return (error);

        if (size >= 128 && size <= 512) {
                echo_message->buffer = realloc(echo_message->buffer, size,
                        M_ECHO, M_WAITOK);
                echo_message->buffer_size = size;

                if (echo_message->length >= size) {
                        echo_message->length = size - 1;
                        echo_message->buffer[size - 1] = '\0';
                }
        } else
                error = EINVAL;

        return (error);
}
```

This function first sets ❶ size to the current buffer size. Afterward, ❷ sysctl_handle_int is called to obtain the new sysctl value (that is, the proposed buffer size) from user space.

Note that the ❸ second argument to sysctl_handle_int is &size. See, this function takes a pointer to the original sysctl value and overwrites it with the new sysctl value.

This ❹ if statement ensures that the new sysctl value was obtained successfully. It works by verifying that sysctl_handle_int returned ❺ error free and that ❻ req->newptr is valid.

The remainder of sysctl_set_buffer_size is identical to echo_set_buffer_size, which was described on page 35.

Don't Panic

Now, let's give Listing 3-4 a try:

```
$ sudo kldload ./echo-4.0.ko
Echo driver loaded.
$ sudo sysctl echo.buffer_size=128
echo.buffer_size: 256 -> 128
```

Success!

Conclusion

This chapter has described the traditional methods for device communication and control: sysctl and ioctl. Generally, sysctls are employed to adjust parameters, and ioctls are used for everything else—that's why ioctls are the catchall of I/O operations. Note that if you find yourself creating a device node just for ioctl requests, you should probably use sysctls instead.

Incidentally, be aware that it's fairly trivial to write user-mode programs that interact with drivers. Thus, your drivers—*not* your user-mode programs (for example, Listing 3-2)—should always validate user input.

4

THREAD SYNCHRONIZATION

This chapter deals with the problem of data and state corruption caused by concurrent threads. When multiple threads executing on different CPUs simultaneously modify the same data structure, that structure can be corrupted. Similarly, when a thread gets interrupted and another thread manipulates the data that the first thread was manipulating, that data can be corrupted (Baldwin, 2002).

Fortunately, FreeBSD provides a set of synchronization primitives to deal with these issues. Before I describe what synchronization primitives do, you'll need an in-depth understanding of the abovementioned concurrency issues, also known as synchronization problems. To that end, let's analyze a few.

A Simple Synchronization Problem

Consider the following scenario in which two threads increment the same global variable. On *i386*, this operation might utilize the following processor instructions:

```
movl    count,%eax      # Move the value of count into a register (eax).
addl    $0x1,%eax       # Add 1 to the value in the register.
movl    %eax,count      # Move the value of the register into count.
```

Imagine that count is currently 0 and that the first thread manages to load the current value of count into %eax (that is, it completes the first instruction) just before the second thread preempts it. As part of the thread switch, FreeBSD saves the value of %eax, which is 0, into the outgoing thread's context. Now, suppose that the second thread manages to complete all three instructions, thereby incrementing count from 0 to 1. If the first thread preempts the second thread, FreeBSD will restore its thread context, which includes setting %eax to 0. The first thread, which resumes execution at the second instruction, will now proceed to add 1 to %eax and then store the result in count. At this point, count equals 1 when it should equal 2. Thus, because of a synchronization problem, we lost an update. This can also occur when the two threads are executing concurrently but just slightly out of step (that is, one thread begins executing the first instruction when the other thread begins executing the second instruction).

A More Complex Synchronization Problem

Listing 4-1 is a complete character driver that lets you manipulate a doubly linked list through its d_ioctl function. You can add or remove an item from the list, determine whether an item is on the list, or print every item on the list. Listing 4-1 also contains some synchronization problems.

NOTE *Take a quick look at this code and try to identify the synchronization problems.*

```
#include <sys/param.h>
#include <sys/module.h>
#include <sys/kernel.h>
#include <sys/systm.h>

#include <sys/conf.h>
#include <sys/uio.h>
#include <sys/malloc.h>
#include <sys/ioccom.h>
#include <sys/queue.h>
#include "race_ioctl.h"

MALLOC_DEFINE(M_RACE, "race", "race object");

struct race_softc {
        ❶LIST_ENTRY(race_softc) list;
```

```
        ❷int unit;
};

static ❸LIST_HEAD(, race_softc) race_list =
    ❹LIST_HEAD_INITIALIZER(&race_list);

static struct race_softc *     race_new(void);
static struct race_softc *     race_find(int unit);
static void                    race_destroy(struct race_softc *sc);
static d_ioctl_t               race_ioctl;

❺ static struct cdevsw race_cdevsw = {
        .d_version =    D_VERSION,
        .d_ioctl =      race_ioctl,
        .d_name =       ❻RACE_NAME
};

static struct cdev *race_dev;

static int
❼ race_ioctl(struct cdev *dev, u_long cmd, caddr_t data, int fflag,
    struct thread *td)
{
        struct race_softc *sc;
        int error = 0;

        switch (cmd) {
        case RACE_IOC_ATTACH:
                sc = race_new();
                *(int *)data = sc->unit;
                break;
        case RACE_IOC_DETACH:
                sc = race_find(*(int *)data);
                if (sc == NULL)
                        return (ENOENT);
                race_destroy(sc);
                break;
        case RACE_IOC_QUERY:
                sc = race_find(*(int *)data);
                if (sc == NULL)
                        return (ENOENT);
                break;
        case RACE_IOC_LIST:
                uprintf("  UNIT\n");
                LIST_FOREACH(sc, &race_list, list)
                        uprintf("  %d\n", sc->unit);
                break;
        default:
                error = ENOTTY;
                break;
        }

        return (error);
}
```

```c
static struct race_softc *
race_new(void)
{
        struct race_softc *sc;
        int unit, max = -1;

        LIST_FOREACH(sc, &race_list, list) {
                if (sc->unit > max)
                        max = sc->unit;
        }
        unit = max + 1;

        sc = (struct race_softc *)malloc(sizeof(struct race_softc), M_RACE,
            M_WAITOK | M_ZERO);
        sc->unit = unit;
        LIST_INSERT_HEAD(&race_list, sc, list);

        return (sc);
}

static struct race_softc *
race_find(int unit)
{
        struct race_softc *sc;

        LIST_FOREACH(sc, &race_list, list) {
                if (sc->unit == unit)
                        break;
        }

        return (sc);
}

static void
race_destroy(struct race_softc *sc)
{
        LIST_REMOVE(sc, list);
        free(sc, M_RACE);
}

static int
race_modevent(module_t mod __unused, int event, void *arg __unused)
{
        int error = 0;

        switch (event) {
        case MOD_LOAD:
                race_dev = make_dev(&race_cdevsw, 0, UID_ROOT, GID_WHEEL,
                    0600, RACE_NAME);
                uprintf("Race driver loaded.\n");
                break;
```

```
            case MOD_UNLOAD:
                    destroy_dev(race_dev);
                    uprintf("Race driver unloaded.\n");
                    break;
            case MOD_QUIESCE:
                    if (!LIST_EMPTY(&race_list))
                            error = EBUSY;
                    break;
            default:
                    error = EOPNOTSUPP;
                    break;
            }

            return (error);
}

DEV_MODULE(race, race_modevent, NULL);
```

Listing 4-1: race.c

Before I identify Listing 4-1's synchronization problems, let's walk through it. Listing 4-1 begins by ❸ defining and ❹ initializing a doubly linked list of race_softc structures named race_list. Each race_softc structure contains a (unique) ❷ unit number and a ❶ structure that maintains a pointer to the previous and next race_softc structure in race_list.

Next, Listing 4-1's ❺ character device switch table is defined. The constant ❻ RACE_NAME is defined in the race_ioctl.h header as follows:

```
#define RACE_NAME               "race"
```

Note how Listing 4-1's character device switch table doesn't define d_open and d_close. Recall, from Chapter 1, that if a d_foo function is undefined the corresponding operation is unsupported. However, d_open and d_close are unique; when they're undefined the kernel will automatically define them as follows:

```
int
nullop(void)
{

        return (0);
}
```

This ensures that every registered character device can be opened and closed.

NOTE *Drivers commonly forgo defining a d_open and d_close function when they don't need to prepare their devices for I/O—like Listing 4-1.*

Next, Listing 4-1's d_ioctl function, named ❼ race_ioctl, is defined. This function is like the main function for Listing 4-1. It uses three helper functions to do its work:

- race_new
- race_find
- race_destroy

Before I describe race_ioctl, I'll describe these functions first.

race_new Function

The race_new function creates a new race_softc structure, which is then inserted at the head of race_list. Here is the function definition for race_new (again):

```
static struct race_softc *
race_new(void)
{
        struct race_softc *sc;
        int unit, max = -1;

        ❶LIST_FOREACH(sc, &race_list, list) {
                if (sc->unit > max)
                        ❷max = sc->unit;
        }
        unit = ❸max + 1;

        sc = (struct race_softc *)❹malloc(sizeof(struct race_softc), M_RACE,
            M_WAITOK | M_ZERO);
        sc->unit = ❺unit;
        ❻LIST_INSERT_HEAD(&race_list, sc, list);

        ❼return (sc);
}
```

This function first ❶ iterates through race_list looking for the largest unit number, which it stores in ❷ max. Next, unit is set to ❸ max plus one. Then race_new ❹ allocates memory for a new race_softc structure, assigns it the unit number ❺ unit, and ❻ inserts it at the head of race_list. Lastly, race_new ❼ returns a pointer to the new race_softc structure.

race_find Function

The race_find function takes a unit number and finds the associated race_softc structure on race_list.

```
static struct race_softc *
race_find(int unit)
{
        struct race_softc *sc;

        LIST_FOREACH(sc, &race_list, list) {
```

```
                    if (sc->unit == unit)
                            break;
        }

        return (sc);
}
```

If race_find is successful, a pointer to the race_softc structure is returned; otherwise, NULL is returned.

race_destroy Function

The race_destroy function destroys a race_softc structure on race_list. Here is its function definition (again):

```
static void
race_destroy(❶struct race_softc *sc)
{
        ❷LIST_REMOVE(sc, list);
        ❸free(sc, M_RACE);
}
```

This function takes a ❶ pointer to a race_softc structure and ❷ removes that structure from race_list. Then it ❸ frees the allocated memory for that structure.

race_ioctl Function

Before I walk through race_ioctl, an explanation of its ioctl commands, which are defined in race_ioctl.h, is needed.

```
#define RACE_IOC_ATTACH        _IOR('R', 0, int)
#define RACE_IOC_DETACH        _IOW('R', 1, int)
#define RACE_IOC_QUERY         _IOW('R', 2, int)
#define RACE_IOC_LIST          _IO('R', 3)
```

As you can see, three of race_ioctl's ioctl commands transfer an integer value. As you'll see, this integer value is a unit number.

Here is the function definition for race_ioctl (again):

```
static int
race_ioctl(struct cdev *dev, u_long cmd, caddr_t data, int fflag,
    struct thread *td)
{
        struct race_softc *sc;
        int error = 0;

        switch (cmd) {
        ❶case RACE_IOC_ATTACH:
                sc = ❷race_new();
                ❸*(int *)data = sc->unit;
                break;
```

```
❹case RACE_IOC_DETACH:
        sc = race_find(*(int *)data);
        if (sc == NULL)
                return (ENOENT);
        race_destroy(sc);
        break;
❺case RACE_IOC_QUERY:
        sc = race_find(*(int *)data);
        if (sc == NULL)
                return (ENOENT);
        break;
❻case RACE_IOC_LIST:
        uprintf("  UNIT\n");
        LIST_FOREACH(sc, &race_list, list)
                uprintf("  %d\n", sc->unit);
        break;
    default:
        error = ENOTTY;
        break;
    }

    return (error);
}
```

This function can perform one of four ioctl-based operations. The first, ❶ RACE_IOC_ATTACH, ❷ creates a new race_softc structure, which is then inserted at the head of race_list. Afterward, the unit number of the new race_softc structure is ❸ returned.

The second operation, ❹ RACE_IOC_DETACH, removes a user-specified race_softc structure from race_list.

The third operation, ❺ RACE_IOC_QUERY, determines whether a user-specified race_softc structure is on race_list.

Lastly, the fourth operation, ❻ RACE_IOC_LIST, prints the unit number of every race_softc structure on race_list.

race_modevent Function

The race_modevent function is the module event handler for Listing 4-1. Here is its function definition (again):

```
static int
race_modevent(module_t mod __unused, int event, void *arg __unused)
{
    int error = 0;

    switch (event) {
    case MOD_LOAD:
        race_dev = make_dev(&race_cdevsw, 0, UID_ROOT, GID_WHEEL,
            0600, RACE_NAME);
        uprintf("Race driver loaded.\n");
        break;
```

```
        case MOD_UNLOAD:
                destroy_dev(race_dev);
                uprintf("Race driver unloaded.\n");
                break;
❶case MOD_QUIESCE:
                ❷if (!LIST_EMPTY(&race_list))
                        error = EBUSY;
                break;
        default:
                error = EOPNOTSUPP;
                break;
        }

        return (error);
}
```

As you can see, this function includes a new case: ❶ MOD_QUIESCE.

NOTE   *Because MOD_LOAD and MOD_UNLOAD are extremely rudimentary and because you've seen
similar code elsewhere, I'll omit discussing them.*

When one issues the kldunload(8) command, MOD_QUIESCE is run before
MOD_UNLOAD. If MOD_QUIESCE returns an error, MOD_UNLOAD does not get executed.
In other words, MOD_QUIESCE verifies that it is safe to unload your module.

NOTE   *The kldunload -f command ignores every error returned by MOD_QUIESCE. So you can
always unload a module, but it may not be the best idea.*

Here, MOD_QUIESCE ❷ guarantees that race_list is empty (before Listing 4-1
is unloaded). This is done to prevent memory leaks from any potentially
unclaimed race_softc structures.

The Root of the Problem

Now that we've walked through Listing 4-1, let's run it and see if we can identify its synchronization problems.
    Listing 4-2 presents a command-line utility designed to invoke the race_ioctl
function in Listing 4-1:

```
#include <sys/types.h>
#include <sys/ioctl.h>

#include <err.h>
#include <fcntl.h>
#include <limits.h>
#include <stdio.h>
#include <stdlib.h>
#include <unistd.h>
#include "../race/race_ioctl.h"

static enum {UNSET, ATTACH, DETACH, QUERY, LIST} action = UNSET;
```

```
/*
 * The usage statement: race_config -a | -d unit | -q unit | -l
 */

static void
usage()
{
        /*
         * Arguments for this program are "either-or." For example,
         * 'race_config -a' or 'race_config -d unit' are valid; however,
         * 'race_config -a -d unit' is invalid.
         */

        fprintf(stderr, "usage: race_config -a | -d unit | -q unit | -l\n");
        exit(1);
}


/*
 * This program manages the doubly linked list found in /dev/race. It
 * allows you to add or remove an item, query the existence of an item,
 * or print every item on the list.
 */

int
main(int argc, char *argv[])
{
        int ch, fd, i, unit;
        char *p;

        /*
         * Parse the command line argument list to determine
         * the correct course of action.
         *
         *      -a:      add an item.
         *      -d unit: detach an item.
         *      -q unit: query the existence of an item.
         *      -l:      list every item.
         */

        while ((ch = getopt(argc, argv, "ad:q:l")) != -1)
                switch (ch) {
                case 'a':
                        if (action != UNSET)
                                usage();
                        action = ATTACH;
                        break;
                case 'd':
                        if (action != UNSET)
                                usage();
                        action = DETACH;
                        unit = (int)strtol(optarg, &p, 10);
                        if (*p)
                                errx(1, "illegal unit -- %s", optarg);
                        break;
```

```
            case 'q':
                    if (action != UNSET)
                            usage();
                    action = QUERY;
                    unit = (int)strtol(optarg, &p, 10);
                    if (*p)
                            errx(1, "illegal unit -- %s", optarg);
                    break;
            case 'l':
                    if (action != UNSET)
                            usage();
                    action = LIST;
                    break;
            default:
                    usage();
            }

    /*
     * Perform the chosen action.
     */

    if (action == ATTACH) {
            fd = open("/dev/" RACE_NAME, O_RDWR);
            if (fd < 0)
                    err(1, "open(/dev/%s)", RACE_NAME);

            i = ioctl(fd, RACE_IOC_ATTACH, &unit);
            if (i < 0)
                    err(1, "ioctl(/dev/%s)", RACE_NAME);
            printf("unit: %d\n", unit);

            close (fd);
    } else if (action == DETACH) {
            fd = open("/dev/" RACE_NAME, O_RDWR);
            if (fd < 0)
                    err(1, "open(/dev/%s)", RACE_NAME);

            i = ioctl(fd, RACE_IOC_DETACH, &unit);
            if (i < 0)
                    err(1, "ioctl(/dev/%s)", RACE_NAME);

            close (fd);
    } else if (action == QUERY) {
            fd = open("/dev/" RACE_NAME, O_RDWR);
            if (fd < 0)
                    err(1, "open(/dev/%s)", RACE_NAME);

            i = ioctl(fd, RACE_IOC_QUERY, &unit);
            if (i < 0)
                    err(1, "ioctl(/dev/%s)", RACE_NAME);

            close (fd);
```

```
        } else if (action == LIST) {
                fd = open("/dev/" RACE_NAME, O_RDWR);
                if (fd < 0)
                        err(1, "open(/dev/%s)", RACE_NAME);

                i = ioctl(fd, RACE_IOC_LIST, NULL);
                if (i < 0)
                        err(1, "ioctl(/dev/%s)", RACE_NAME);

                close (fd);
        } else
                usage();

        return (0);
}
```

Listing 4-2: race_config.c

NOTE *Listing 4-2 is a bog-standard command-line utility. As such, I won't cover its program structure.*

The following shows an example execution of Listing 4-2:

```
$ sudo kldload ./race.ko
Race driver loaded.
$ sudo ./race_config -a & sudo ./race_config -a &
[1] 2378
[2] 2379
$ unit: 0
unit: 0
```

Above, two threads simultaneously add a race_softc structure to race_list, which results in two race_softc structures with the "unique" unit number 0—this is a problem, yes?

Here's another example:

```
$ sudo kldload ./race.ko
Race driver loaded.
$ sudo ./race_config -a & sudo kldunload race.ko &
[1] 2648
[2] 2649
$ unit: 0
Race driver unloaded.

[1]-  Done                    sudo ./race_config -a
[2]+  Done                    sudo kldunload race.ko
$ dmesg | tail -n 1
Warning: memory type race leaked memory on destroy (1 allocations, 16 bytes
leaked).
```

Above, one thread adds a race_softc structure to race_list while another thread unloads *race.ko*, which causes a memory leak. Recall that MOD_QUIESCE is supposed to prevent this, but it didn't. Why?

The problem, in both examples, is a race condition. *Race conditions* are errors caused by a sequence of events. In the first example, both threads check race_list simultaneously, discover that it is empty, and assign 0 as the unit number. In the second example, MOD_QUIESCE returns error-free, a race_softc structure is then added to race_list, and finally MOD_UNLOAD completes.

NOTE *One characteristic of race conditions is that they're hard to reproduce. Ergo, the results were doctored in the preceding examples. That is, I caused the threads to context switch at specific points to achieve the desired outcome. Under normal conditions, it would have taken literally millions of attempts before those race conditions would occur, and I didn't want to spend that much time.*

Preventing Race Conditions

Race conditions are prevented using locks. *Locks*, also known as *synchronization primitives*, are used to serialize the execution of two or more threads. For example, the race conditions in Listing 4-1, which are caused by concurrent access to race_list, can be prevented by using a lock to serialize access to race_list. Before a thread can access race_list, it must first acquire the foo lock. Only one thread can hold foo at a time. If a thread cannot acquire foo, it cannot access race_list and must wait for the current owner to relinquish foo. This protocol guarantees that at any moment in time only one thread can access race_list, which eliminates Listing 4-1's race conditions.

There are several different types of locks in FreeBSD, each having its own characteristics (for example, some locks can be held by more than one thread). The remainder of this chapter describes the different types of locks available in FreeBSD and how to use them.

Mutexes

Mutex locks (mutexes) ensure that at any moment in time, only one thread can access a shared object. Mutex is an amalgamation of mutual and exclusion.

NOTE *The foo lock described in the previous section was a mutex lock.*

FreeBSD provides two types of mutex locks: spin mutexes and sleep mutexes.

Spin Mutexes

Spin mutexes are simple spin locks. If a thread attempts to acquire a spin lock that is being held by another thread, it will "spin" and wait for the lock to be released. *Spin*, in this case, means to loop infinitely on the CPU. This spinning can result in deadlock if a thread that is holding a spin lock is interrupted or if it context switches, and all subsequent threads attempt to acquire that lock. Consequently, while holding a spin mutex all interrupts are blocked on the local processor and a context switch cannot be performed.

Spin mutexes should be held only for short periods of time and should be used only to protect objects related to nonpreemptive interrupts and low-level scheduling code (McKusick and Neville-Neil, 2005). Ordinarily, you'll never use spin mutexes.

Sleep Mutexes

Sleep mutexes are the most commonly used lock. If a thread attempts to acquire a sleep mutex that is being held by another thread, it will context switch (that is, sleep) and wait for the mutex to be released. Because of this behavior, sleep mutexes are not susceptible to the deadlock described above.

Sleep mutexes support priority propagation. When a thread sleeps on a sleep mutex and its priority is higher than the sleep mutex's current owner, the current owner will inherit the priority of this thread (Baldwin, 2002). This characteristic prevents a lower priority thread from blocking a higher priority thread.

NOTE   *Sleeping (for example, calling a *sleep function, which is discussed in Chapter 5) while holding a mutex is never safe and must be avoided; otherwise, there are numerous assertions that will fail and the kernel will panic (McKusick and Neville-Neil, 2005).*

Mutex Management Routines

The FreeBSD kernel provides the following seven functions for working with mutexes:

```
#include <sys/param.h>
#include <sys/lock.h>
#include <sys/mutex.h>

void
mtx_init(struct mtx ❶*mutex, const char ❷*name, const char ❸*type,
    int ❹opts);

void
mtx_lock(struct mtx ❺*mutex);

void
mtx_lock_spin(struct mtx ❻*mutex);

int
mtx_trylock(struct mtx ❼*mutex);

void
mtx_unlock(struct mtx *mutex);

void
mtx_unlock_spin(struct mtx ❽*mutex);
```

```
void
mtx_destroy(struct mtx ❾*mutex);
```

The `mtx_init` function initializes the mutex ❶ mutex. The ❷ name argument is used during debugging to identify `mutex`. The ❸ type argument is used during lock-order verification by `witness(4)`. If type is `NULL`, name is used instead.

NOTE *You'll typically pass `NULL` as type.*

The ❹ opts argument modifies `mtx_init`'s behavior. Valid values for opts are shown in Table 4-1.

Table 4-1: mtx_init Symbolic Constants

Constant	Description
MTX_DEF	Initializes mutex as a sleep mutex; this bit or MTX_SPIN must be present
MTX_SPIN	Initializes mutex as a spin mutex; this bit or MTX_DEF must be present
MTX_RECURSE	Specifies that mutex is a recursive lock; more on recursive locks later
MTX_QUIET	Instructs the system to *not* log the operations done on this lock
MTX_NOWITNESS	Causes witness(4) to ignore this lock
MTX_DUPOK	Causes witness(4) to ignore duplicates of this lock
MTX_NOPROFILE	Instructs the system to *not* profile this lock

Threads acquire sleep mutexes by calling `mtx_lock`. If another thread is currently holding ❺ mutex, the caller will sleep until `mutex` is available.

Threads acquire spin mutexes by calling `mtx_lock_spin`. If another thread is currently holding ❻ mutex, the caller will spin until `mutex` is available. Note that all interrupts are blocked on the local processor during the spin, and they remain disabled following the acquisition of `mutex`.

A thread can recursively acquire ❼ mutex (with no ill effects) if `MTX_RECURSE` was passed to ❹ opts. A recursive lock is useful if it'll be acquired at two or more levels. For example:

```
static void
foo()
{
...
        mtx_lock(&mutex);
...
        foo();
...
        mtx_unlock(&mutex);
...
}
```

By using a recursive lock, lower levels don't need to check if `mutex` has been acquired by a higher level. They can simply acquire and release `mutex` as needed (McKusick and Neville-Neil, 2005).

NOTE *I would avoid recursive mutexes. You'll learn why in "Avoid Recursing on Exclusive Locks" on page 81.*

The mtx_trylock function is identical to mtx_lock except that if another thread is currently holding ❼ mutex, it returns 0 (that is, the caller does not sleep).

Threads release sleep mutexes by calling mtx_unlock. Note that recursive locks "remember" the number of times they've been acquired. Consequently, each successful lock acquisition must have a corresponding lock release.

Threads release spin mutexes by calling mtx_unlock_spin. The mtx_unlock_spin function also restores the interrupt state to what it was before ❽ mutex was acquired.

The mtx_destroy function destroys the mutex ❾ mutex. Note that mutex can be held when it is destroyed. However, mutex cannot be held recursively or have other threads waiting for it when it is destroyed or else the kernel will panic (McKusick and Neville-Neil, 2005).

Implementing Mutexes

Listing 4-3 is a revision of Listing 4-1 that uses a mutex to serialize access to race_list.

NOTE *To save space, the functions race_ioctl, race_new, race_find, and race_destroy aren't listed here, as they haven't been changed.*

```
#include <sys/param.h>
#include <sys/module.h>
#include <sys/kernel.h>
#include <sys/systm.h>

#include <sys/conf.h>
#include <sys/uio.h>
#include <sys/malloc.h>
#include <sys/ioccom.h>
#include <sys/queue.h>
#include <sys/lock.h>
#include <sys/mutex.h>
#include "race_ioctl.h"

MALLOC_DEFINE(M_RACE, "race", "race object");

struct race_softc {
        LIST_ENTRY(race_softc) list;
        int unit;
};

static LIST_HEAD(, race_softc) race_list = LIST_HEAD_INITIALIZER(&race_list);
❶ static struct mtx race_mtx;

static struct race_softc *    race_new(void);
static struct race_softc *    race_find(int unit);
```

```
    static void                    race_destroy(struct race_softc *sc);
    static d_ioctl_t               race_ioctl_mtx;
    static d_ioctl_t               race_ioctl;

    static struct cdevsw race_cdevsw = {
            .d_version =    D_VERSION,
        ❷.d_ioctl =        race_ioctl_mtx,
            .d_name =       RACE_NAME
    };

    static struct cdev *race_dev;

    static int
❸ race_ioctl_mtx(struct cdev *dev, u_long cmd, caddr_t data, int fflag,
        struct thread *td)
    {
            int error;

        ❹mtx_lock(&race_mtx);
            error = ❺race_ioctl(dev, cmd, data, fflag, td);
        ❻mtx_unlock(&race_mtx);

            return (error);
    }

    static int
    race_ioctl(struct cdev *dev, u_long cmd, caddr_t data, int fflag,
        struct thread *td)
    {
    ...
    }

    static struct race_softc *
    race_new(void)
    {
    ...
    }

    static struct race_softc *
    race_find(int unit)
    {
    ...
    }

    static void
    race_destroy(struct race_softc *sc)
    {
    ...
    }

    static int
    race_modevent(module_t mod __unused, int event, void *arg __unused)
    {
            int error = 0;
            struct race_softc *sc, *sc_temp;
```

```
        switch (event) {
        case MOD_LOAD:
                mtx_init(&race_mtx, "race config lock", NULL, ❼MTX_DEF);
                race_dev = make_dev(&race_cdevsw, 0, UID_ROOT, GID_WHEEL,
                    0600, RACE_NAME);
                uprintf("Race driver loaded.\n");
                break;
        case MOD_UNLOAD:
                destroy_dev(race_dev);
                mtx_lock(&race_mtx);
                if (!LIST_EMPTY(&race_list)) {
                        LIST_FOREACH_SAFE(sc, &race_list, list, sc_temp) {
                                LIST_REMOVE(sc, list);
                                free(sc, M_RACE);
                        }
                }

                mtx_unlock(&race_mtx);
                mtx_destroy(&race_mtx);
                uprintf("Race driver unloaded.\n");
                break;
        case MOD_QUIESCE:
                mtx_lock(&race_mtx);
                if (!LIST_EMPTY(&race_list))
                        error = EBUSY;
                mtx_unlock(&race_mtx);
                break;
        default:
                error = EOPNOTSUPP;
                break;
        }

        return (error);
}

DEV_MODULE(race, race_modevent, NULL);
```

Listing 4-3: race_mtx.c

This driver ❶ declares a mutex named race_mtx, which gets initialized as
a ❼ sleep mutex in the module event handler.

NOTE   *As you'll see, a mutex is not the ideal solution for Listing 4-1. However, for now, I just
want to cover how to use mutexes.*

In Listing 4-1, the main source of concurrent access to race_list is the
race_ioctl function. This should be obvious, because race_ioctl manages
race_list.

Listing 4-3 remedies the race conditions caused by race_ioctl by serializing
its execution via the ❸ race_ioctl_mtx function. race_ioctl_mtx is defined as
the ❷ d_ioctl function. It begins by ❹ acquiring race_mtx. Then ❺ race_ioctl
is called and subsequently race_mtx is ❻ released.

As you can see, it takes just three lines (or one mutex) to serialize the execution of race_ioctl.

race_modevent Function

The race_modevent function is the module event handler for Listing 4-3. Here is its function definition (again):

```
static int
race_modevent(module_t mod __unused, int event, void *arg __unused)
{
        int error = 0;
        struct race_softc *sc, *sc_temp;

        switch (event) {
        case MOD_LOAD:
                ❶mtx_init(&race_mtx, "race config lock", NULL, ❷MTX_DEF);
                    race_dev = ❸make_dev(&race_cdevsw, 0, UID_ROOT, GID_WHEEL,
                        0600, RACE_NAME);
                    uprintf("Race driver loaded.\n");
                    break;
        case MOD_UNLOAD:
                ❹destroy_dev(race_dev);
                    mtx_lock(&race_mtx);
                ❺if (!LIST_EMPTY(&race_list)) {
                            LIST_FOREACH_SAFE(sc, &race_list, list, sc_temp) {
                                    LIST_REMOVE(sc, list);
                                    ❻free(sc, M_RACE);
                            }
                    }
                    mtx_unlock(&race_mtx);
                ❼mtx_destroy(&race_mtx);
                    uprintf("Race driver unloaded.\n");
                    break;
        case MOD_QUIESCE:
                ❽mtx_lock(&race_mtx);
                ❾if (!LIST_EMPTY(&race_list))
                            error = EBUSY;
                ❿mtx_unlock(&race_mtx);
                    break;
        default:
                    error = EOPNOTSUPP;
                    break;
        }

        return (error);
}
```

On module load, this function ❶ initializes race_mtx as a ❷ sleep mutex. Then it ❸ creates Listing 4-3's device node: race.

On MOD_QUIESCE, this function ❽ acquires race_mtx, ❾ confirms that race_list is empty, and then ❿ releases race_mtx.

On module unload, this function first calls ❹ destroy_dev to destroy the race device node.

NOTE   *The destroy_dev function does not return until every d_foo function currently executing completes. Consequently, one should not hold a lock while calling destroy_dev; otherwise, you could deadlock your driver or panic your system.*

Next, race_modevent ❺ confirms that race_list is still empty. See, after the execution of MOD_QUIESCE, a race_softc structure could have been added to race_list. So, race_list is checked again and every race_softc structure found is ❻ released. Once this is done, race_mtx is ❼ destroyed.

As you can see, every time race_list was accessed, mtx_lock(&race_mtx) was called first. This was necessary in order to serialize access to race_list throughout Listing 4-3.

Don't Panic

Now that we've examined Listing 4-3, let's give it a try:

```
$ sudo kldload ./race_mtx.ko
Race driver loaded.
$ sudo ./race_config -a & sudo ./race_config -a &
[1] 923
[2] 924
$ unit: 0
unit: 1

...

$ sudo kldload ./race_mtx.ko
Race driver loaded.
$ sudo ./race_config -a & sudo kldunload race_mtx.ko &
[1] 933
[2] 934
$ Race driver unloaded.
race_config: open(/dev/race): No such file or directory

[1]-  Exit 1              sudo ./race_config -a
[2]+  Done                sudo kldunload race_mtx.ko
```

Unsurprisingly, it works. Yet using a mutex has introduced a new problem. See, the function definition for race_new contains this line:

```
sc = (struct race_softc *)malloc(sizeof(struct race_softc), M_RACE,
    ❶M_WAITOK | M_ZERO);
```

Here, ❶ M_WAITOK means that it's okay to sleep. But it's *never* okay to sleep while holding a mutex. Recall that sleeping while holding a mutex causes the kernel to panic.

There are two solutions to this problem: First, change `M_WAITOK` to `M_NOWAIT`. Second, use a lock that can be held while sleeping. As the first solution changes the functionality of Listing 4-1 (that is, currently, `race_new` never fails), let's go with the second.

Shared/Exclusive Locks

Shared/exclusive locks (sx locks) are locks that threads can hold while asleep. As the name implies, multiple threads can have a *shared hold* on an sx lock, but only one thread can have an *exclusive hold* on an sx lock. When a thread has an exclusive hold on an sx lock, other threads cannot have a shared hold on that lock.

sx locks do not support priority propagation and are inefficient compared to mutexes. The main reason for using sx locks is that threads can sleep while holding one.

Shared/Exclusive Lock Management Routines

The FreeBSD kernel provides the following 14 functions for working with sx locks:

```
#include <sys/param.h>
#include <sys/lock.h>
#include <sys/sx.h>

void
sx_init(struct sx ❶*sx, const char ❷*description);

void
sx_init_flags(struct sx *sx, const char *description, int ❸opts);

void
sx_slock(struct sx *sx);

void
sx_xlock(struct sx *sx);

int
sx_slock_sig(struct sx *sx);

int
sx_xlock_sig(struct sx *sx);

int
sx_try_slock(struct sx *sx);

int
sx_try_xlock(struct sx *sx);

void
sx_sunlock(struct sx *sx);
```

```
void
sx_xunlock(struct sx *sx);

void
sx_unlock(struct sx *sx);

int
sx_try_upgrade(struct sx *sx);

void
sx_downgrade(struct sx *sx);

void
sx_destroy(struct sx ❹*sx);
```

The sx_init function initializes the sx lock ❶ sx. The ❷ description argument is used during debugging to identify sx.

The sx_init_flags function is an alternative to sx_init. The ❸ opts argument modifies sx_init_flags's behavior. Valid values for opts are shown in Table 4-2.

Table 4-2: sx_init_flags Symbolic Constants

Constant	Description
SX_NOADAPTIVE	If this bit is passed and the kernel is compiled without options NO_ADAPTIVE_SX, then threads holding sx will spin instead of sleeping.
SX_RECURSE	Specifies that sx is a recursive lock
SX_QUIET	Instructs the system to *not* log the operations done on this lock
SX_NOWITNESS	Causes witness(4) to ignore this lock
SX_DUPOK	Causes witness(4) to ignore duplicates of this lock
SX_NOPROFILE	Instructs the system to *not* profile this lock

Threads acquire a shared hold on sx by calling sx_slock. If another thread currently has an exclusive hold on sx, the caller will sleep until sx is available.

Threads acquire an exclusive hold on sx by calling sx_xlock. If any threads currently have a shared or exclusive hold on sx, the caller will sleep until sx is available.

The sx_slock_sig and sx_xlock_sig functions are identical to sx_slock and sx_xlock except that when the caller sleeps it can be woken up by signals. If this occurs, a nonzero value is returned.

NOTE *Normally, threads sleeping on locks cannot be woken up early.*

The sx_try_slock and sx_try_xlock functions are identical to sx_slock and sx_xlock except that if sx cannot be acquired, they return 0 (that is, the caller does not sleep).

Threads release a shared hold on sx by calling sx_sunlock, and they release an exclusive hold by calling sx_xunlock.

The sx_unlock function is a front end to sx_sunlock and sx_xunlock. This function is used when the hold state on sx is unknown.

Threads can upgrade a shared hold to an exclusive hold by calling sx_try_upgrade. If the hold cannot be immediately upgraded, 0 is returned. Threads can downgrade an exclusive hold to a shared hold by calling sx_downgrade.

The sx_destroy function destroys the sx lock ❹ sx. Note that sx cannot be held when it is destroyed.

Implementing Shared/Exclusive Locks

Listing 4-4 is a revision of Listing 4-3 that uses an sx lock instead of a mutex.

NOTE *To save space, the functions race_ioctl, race_new, race_find, and race_destroy aren't listed here, as they haven't been changed.*

```
#include <sys/param.h>
#include <sys/module.h>
#include <sys/kernel.h>
#include <sys/systm.h>

#include <sys/conf.h>
#include <sys/uio.h>
#include <sys/malloc.h>
#include <sys/ioccom.h>
#include <sys/queue.h>
#include <sys/lock.h>
❶ #include <sys/sx.h>
#include "race_ioctl.h"

MALLOC_DEFINE(M_RACE, "race", "race object");

struct race_softc {
        LIST_ENTRY(race_softc) list;
        int unit;
};

static LIST_HEAD(, race_softc) race_list = LIST_HEAD_INITIALIZER(&race_list);
❷ static struct sx race_sx;

static struct race_softc *     race_new(void);
static struct race_softc *     race_find(int unit);
static void                    race_destroy(struct race_softc *sc);
static d_ioctl_t               race_ioctl_sx;
static d_ioctl_t               race_ioctl;

static struct cdevsw race_cdevsw = {
        .d_version =    D_VERSION,
        .d_ioctl =      race_ioctl_sx,
        .d_name =       RACE_NAME
};
```

```
static struct cdev *race_dev;

static int
race_ioctl_sx(struct cdev *dev, u_long cmd, caddr_t data, int fflag,
    struct thread *td)
{
        int error;

    ❸sx_xlock(&race_sx);
        error = race_ioctl(dev, cmd, data, fflag, td);
    ❹sx_xunlock(&race_sx);

        return (error);
}

static int
race_ioctl(struct cdev *dev, u_long cmd, caddr_t data, int fflag,
    struct thread *td)
{
...
}

static struct race_softc *
race_new(void)
{
...
}

static struct race_softc *
race_find(int unit)
{
...
}

static void
race_destroy(struct race_softc *sc)
{
...
}

static int
race_modevent(module_t mod __unused, int event, void *arg __unused)
{
        int error = 0;
        struct race_softc *sc, *sc_temp;

        switch (event) {
        case MOD_LOAD:
            ❺sx_init(&race_sx, "race config lock");
                race_dev = make_dev(&race_cdevsw, 0, UID_ROOT, GID_WHEEL,
                    0600, RACE_NAME);
                uprintf("Race driver loaded.\n");
                break;
```

```
       case MOD_UNLOAD:
             destroy_dev(race_dev);
          ❻sx_xlock(&race_sx);
             if (!LIST_EMPTY(&race_list)) {
                   LIST_FOREACH_SAFE(sc, &race_list, list, sc_temp) {
                         LIST_REMOVE(sc, list);
                         free(sc, M_RACE);
                   }
             }

          ❼sx_xunlock(&race_sx);
          ❽sx_destroy(&race_sx);
             uprintf("Race driver unloaded.\n");
             break;
       case MOD_QUIESCE:
          ❾sx_xlock(&race_sx);
             if (!LIST_EMPTY(&race_list))
                   error = EBUSY;
          ❿sx_xunlock(&race_sx);
             break;
       default:
             error = EOPNOTSUPP;
             break;
       }

       return (error);
}

DEV_MODULE(race, race_modevent, NULL);
```

Listing 4-4: race_sx.c

Listing 4-4 is identical to Listing 4-3 except that every mutex management function has been replaced by its sx lock equivalent.

NOTE   *The numbered balls in Listing 4-4 highlight the differences.*

Here are the results from interacting with Listing 4-4:

```
$ sudo kldload ./race_sx.ko
Race driver loaded.
$ sudo ./race_config -a & sudo ./race_config -a &
[1] 800
[2] 801
$ unit: 0
unit: 1


...


$ sudo kldload ./race_sx.ko
Race driver loaded.
$ sudo ./race_config -a & sudo kldunload race_sx.ko &
[1] 811
[2] 812
$ unit: 0
```

```
kldunload: can't unload file: Device busy

[1]-  Done                      sudo ./race_config -a
[2]+  Exit 1                     sudo kldunload race_sx.ko
```

Naturally, everything works, and no new problems were introduced.

Reader/Writer Locks

Reader/writer locks (rw locks) are basically mutexes with sx lock semantics. Like
sx locks, threads can hold rw locks as a *reader*, which is identical to a shared
hold, or as a *writer*, which is identical to an exclusive hold. Like mutexes,
rw locks support priority propagation and threads cannot hold them while
sleeping (or the kernel will panic).

rw locks are used when you need to protect an object that is mostly going
to be read from instead of written to.

Reader/Writer Lock Management Routines

The FreeBSD kernel provides the following 11 functions for working with rw
locks:

```
#include <sys/param.h>
#include <sys/lock.h>
#include <sys/rwlock.h>

void
rw_init(struct rwlock ❶*rw, const char ❷*name);

void
rw_init_flags(struct rwlock *rw, const char *name, int ❸opts);

void
rw_rlock(struct rwlock *rw);

void
rw_wlock(struct rwlock *rw);

int
rw_try_rlock(struct rwlock *rw);

int
rw_try_wlock(struct rwlock *rw);

void
rw_runlock(struct rwlock *rw);

void
rw_wunlock(struct rwlock *rw);

int
rw_try_upgrade(struct rwlock *rw);
```

```
void
rw_downgrade(struct rwlock *rw);

void
rw_destroy(struct rwlock ❹*rw);
```

The `rw_init` function initializes the rw lock ❶ rw. The ❷ name argument is used during debugging to identify rw.

The `rw_init_flags` function is an alternative to `rw_init`. The ❸ opts argument modifies `rw_init_flags`'s behavior. Valid values for opts are shown in Table 4-3.

Table 4-3: rw_init_flags Symbolic Constants

Constant	Description
RW_RECURSE	Specifies that rw is a recursive lock
RW_QUIET	Instructs the system to *not* log the operations done on this lock
RW_NOWITNESS	Causes witness(4) to ignore this lock
RW_DUPOK	Causes witness(4) to ignore duplicates of this lock
RW_NOPROFILE	Instructs the system to *not* profile this lock

Threads acquire a shared hold on rw by calling `rw_rlock`. If another thread currently has an exclusive hold on rw, the caller will sleep until rw is available.

Threads acquire an exclusive hold on rw by calling `rw_wlock`. If any threads currently have a shared or exclusive hold on rw, the caller will sleep until rw is available.

The `rw_try_rlock` and `rw_try_wlock` functions are identical to `rw_rlock` and `rw_wlock` except that if rw cannot be acquired, they return 0 (that is, the caller does not sleep).

Threads release a shared hold on rw by calling `rw_runlock`, and they release an exclusive hold by calling `rw_wunlock`.

Threads can upgrade a shared hold to an exclusive hold by calling `rw_try_upgrade`. If the hold cannot be immediately upgraded, 0 is returned. Threads can downgrade an exclusive hold to a shared hold by calling `rw_downgrade`.

The `rw_destroy` function destroys the rw lock ❹ rw. Note that rw cannot be held when it is destroyed.

At this point, you should be comfortable with locks—there's really nothing to them. So, I'm going to omit discussing an example that uses rw locks.

Condition Variables

Condition variables synchronize the execution of two or more threads based upon the value of an object. In contrast, locks synchronize threads by controlling their access to objects.

Condition variables are used in conjunction with locks to "block" threads until a condition is true. It works like this: A thread first acquires the foo lock. Then it examines the condition. If the condition is false, it sleeps on the bar condition variable. While asleep on bar, threads relinquish foo. A thread that causes the condition to be true wakes up the threads sleeping on bar. Threads woken up in this manner reacquire foo before proceeding.

Condition Variable Management Routines

The FreeBSD kernel provides the following 11 functions for working with condition variables:

```
#include <sys/param.h>
#include <sys/proc.h>
#include <sys/condvar.h>

void
cv_init(struct cv ❶*cvp, const char ❷*d);

const char *
cv_wmesg(struct cv ❸*cvp);

void
cv_wait(struct cv ❹*cvp, ❺lock);

void
cv_wait_unlock(struct cv ❻*cvp, ❼lock);

int
cv_wait_sig(struct cv *cvp, lock);

int
cv_timedwait(struct cv *cvp, lock, int ❽timo);

int
cv_timedwait_sig(struct cv *cvp, lock, int timo);

void
cv_signal(struct cv *cvp);

void
cv_broadcast(struct cv *cvp);

void
cv_broadcastpri(struct cv *cvp, int ❾pri);

void
cv_destroy(struct cv ❿*cvp);
```

The cv_init function initializes the condition variable ❶ cvp. The ❷ d argument describes cvp.

The cv_wmesg function gets the ❷ description of ❸ cvp. This function is primarily used in error reporting.

Threads sleep on ❹ cvp by calling cv_wait. The ❺ lock argument demands a sleep mutex, sx lock, or rw lock. Threads must hold lock before calling cv_wait. Threads must not sleep on cvp with lock held recursively.

The cv_wait_unlock function is a variant of cv_wait. When threads wake up from sleeping on ❻ cvp, they forgo reacquiring ❼ lock.

The cv_wait_sig function is identical to cv_wait except that when the caller is asleep it can be woken up by signals. If this occurs, the error code EINTR or ERESTART is returned.

NOTE   *Normally, threads sleeping on condition variables cannot be woken up early.*

The cv_timedwait function is identical to cv_wait except that the caller sleeps at most ❽ timo / hz seconds. If the sleep times out, the error code EWOULDBLOCK is returned.

The cv_timedwait_sig function is like cv_wait_sig and cv_timedwait. The caller can be woken up by signals and sleeps at most timo / hz seconds.

Threads wake up one thread sleeping on cvp by calling cv_signal, and they wake up every thread sleeping on cvp by calling cv_broadcast.

The cv_broadcastpri function is identical to cv_broadcast except that all threads woken up have their priority raised to ❾ pri. Threads with a priority higher than pri do not have their priority lowered.

The cv_destroy function destroys the condition variable ❿ cvp.

NOTE   *We'll walk through an example that uses condition variables in Chapter 5.*

General Guidelines

Here are some general guidelines for lock usage. Note that these aren't hard-and-fast rules, just things to keep in mind.

Avoid Recursing on Exclusive Locks

When an exclusive hold or lock is acquired, the holder usually assumes that it has exclusive access to the objects the lock protects. Unfortunately, recursive locks can break this assumption in some cases. As an example, suppose function F1 uses a recursive lock L to protect object O. If function F2 acquires L, modifies O, leaving it in an inconsistent state, and then calls F1, F1 will recursively acquire L and falsely assume that O is in a consistent state.[1]

One solution to this problem is to use a nonrecursive lock and to rewrite F1 so that it does not acquire L. Instead, L must be acquired before calling F1.

---

1. This paragraph is adapted from *Locking in the Multithreaded FreeBSD Kernel* by John H. Baldwin (2002).

Avoid Holding Exclusive Locks for Long Periods of Time

Exclusive locks reduce concurrency and should be released as soon as possible. Note that it is better to hold a lock for a short period of time when it is not needed than to release the lock only to reacquire it (Baldwin, 2002). This is because the operations to acquire and release a lock are relatively expensive.

Conclusion

This chapter dealt with the problem of data and state corruption caused by concurrent threads. In short, whenever an object is accessible by multiple threads, its access must be managed.

5

DELAYING EXECUTION

Often, drivers need to delay their execution in order to give their device(s), the kernel, or a user the time to accomplish some task. In this chapter, I'll detail the different functions available for achieving these delays. In the process, I'll also describe asynchronous code execution.

Voluntary Context Switching, or Sleeping

Voluntary context switching, or *sleeping*, is done when a driver thread must await the availability of a resource or the arrival of an event; for example, a driver thread should sleep after it requests data from an input device, such as a terminal (McKusick and Neville-Neil, 2005). A driver thread sleeps by calling a *sleep function.

```
#include <sys/param.h>
#include <sys/systm.h>
#include <sys/proc.h>
```

```
int
tsleep(void *chan, int priority, const char *wmesg, int timo);

void
wakeup(void *chan);

void
wakeup_one(void *chan);

void
pause(const char *wmesg, int timo);

#include <sys/param.h>
#include <sys/lock.h>
#include <sys/mutex.h>

int
mtx_sleep(void *chan, struct mtx *mtx, int priority, const char *wmesg,
    int timo);

#include <sys/param.h>
#include <sys/systm.h>
#include <sys/proc.h>

int
msleep_spin(void *chan, struct mtx *mtx, const char *wmesg, int timo);

#include <sys/param.h>
#include <sys/lock.h>
#include <sys/sx.h>

int
sx_sleep(void *chan, struct sx *sx, int priority, const char *wmesg,
    int timo);

#include <sys/param.h>
#include <sys/lock.h>
#include <sys/rwlock.h>

int
rw_sleep(void *chan, struct rwlock *rw, int priority, const char *wmesg,
    int timo);
```

A thread voluntarily context switches (or sleeps) by calling tsleep. The arguments for tsleep are common to the other *sleep functions and are described in the next few paragraphs.

The chan argument is the channel (that is to say, an arbitrary address) that uniquely identifies the event that the thread is waiting for.

The priority argument is the priority for the thread when it resumes. If priority is 0, the current thread priority is used. If PCATCH is OR'ed into priority, signals are checked before and after sleeping.

The `wmesg` argument expects a concise description of the sleeping thread. This description is displayed by user-mode utilities, such as `ps(1)`, and has no real impact on performance.

The `timo` argument specifies the sleep timeout. If `timo` is nonzero, the thread will sleep for at most `timo` / `hz` seconds. Afterward, `tsleep` returns the error code `EWOULDBLOCK`.

The `wakeup` function wakes up every thread asleep on the channel `chan`. Generally speaking, threads woken from sleep should re-evaluate the conditions they slept on.

The `wakeup_one` function is a variant of `wakeup` that only gets up the first thread that it finds asleep on `chan`. The assumption is that when the awakened thread is done, it calls `wakeup_one` to wake up another thread that's asleep on `chan`; this succession of `wakeup_one` calls continues until every thread asleep on `chan` has been awakened (McKusick and Neville-Neil, 2005). This reduces the load in cases when numerous threads are asleep on `chan`, but only one thread can do anything meaningful when made runnable.

The `pause` function puts the calling thread to sleep for `timo` / `hz` seconds. This thread cannot be awoken by `wakeup`, `wakeup_one`, or signals.

The remaining *sleep functions—`mtx_sleep`, `msleep_spin`, `sx_sleep`, and `rw_sleep`—are variants of `tsleep` that take a particular lock. This lock is dropped before the thread sleeps and is reacquired before the thread awakes; if `PDROP` is OR'ed into priority, this lock is not reacquired.

Note that the `msleep_spin` function does not have a priority argument. Consequently, it cannot assign a new thread priority, catch signals via `PCATCH`, or drop its spin mutex via `PDROP`.

Implementing Sleeps and Condition Variables

Listing 5-1 (which is based on code written by John Baldwin) is a KLD designed to demonstrate sleeps and condition variables. It works by obtaining "events" from a sysctl; each event is then passed to a thread, which performs a specific task based on the event it received.

NOTE *Take a quick look at this code and try to discern some of its structure. If you don't understand all of it, don't worry; an explanation follows.*

```
#define INVARIANTS
#define INVARIANT_SUPPORT

#include <sys/param.h>
#include <sys/module.h>
#include <sys/kernel.h>
#include <sys/systm.h>

#include <sys/kthread.h>
#include <sys/proc.h>
#include <sys/sched.h>
#include <sys/unistd.h>
```

```
          #include <sys/lock.h>
          #include <sys/mutex.h>
          #include <sys/condvar.h>
          #include <sys/sysctl.h>

❶ #define MAX_EVENT 1

❷ static struct proc *kthread;
❸ static int event;
❹ static struct cv event_cv;
❺ static struct mtx event_mtx;

          static struct sysctl_ctx_list clist;
          static struct sysctl_oid *poid;

          static void
❻ sleep_thread(void *arg)
          {
                  int ev;

                  for (;;) {
                          mtx_lock(&event_mtx);
                          while ((ev = event) == 0)
                                  cv_wait(&event_cv, &event_mtx);
                          event = 0;
                          mtx_unlock(&event_mtx);

                          switch (ev) {
                          case -1:
                                  kproc_exit(0);
                                  break;
                          case 0:
                                  break;
                          case 1:
                                  printf("sleep... is alive and well.\n");
                                  break;
                          default:
                                  panic("event %d is bogus\n", event);
                          }
                  }
          }

          static int
❼ sysctl_debug_sleep_test(SYSCTL_HANDLER_ARGS)
          {
                  int error, i = 0;

                  error = sysctl_handle_int(oidp, &i, 0, req);
                  if (error == 0 && req->newptr != NULL) {
                          if (i >= 1 && i <= MAX_EVENT) {
                                  mtx_lock(&event_mtx);
                                  KASSERT(event == 0, ("event %d was unhandled",
                                          event));
                                  event = i;
                                  cv_signal(&event_cv);
```

```
                             mtx_unlock(&event_mtx);
                    } else
                             error = EINVAL;
            }

            return (error);
    }

    static int
❽ load(void *arg)
    {
            int error;
            struct proc *p;
            struct thread *td;

            error = kproc_create(sleep_thread, NULL, &p, RFSTOPPED, 0, "sleep");
            if (error)
                    return (error);

            event = 0;
            mtx_init(&event_mtx, "sleep event", NULL, MTX_DEF);
            cv_init(&event_cv, "sleep");

            td = FIRST_THREAD_IN_PROC(p);
            thread_lock(td);
            TD_SET_CAN_RUN(td);
            sched_add(td, SRQ_BORING);
            thread_unlock(td);
            kthread = p;

            sysctl_ctx_init(&clist);
            poid = SYSCTL_ADD_NODE(&clist, SYSCTL_STATIC_CHILDREN(_debug),
                OID_AUTO, "sleep", CTLFLAG_RD, 0, "sleep tree");
            SYSCTL_ADD_PROC(&clist, SYSCTL_CHILDREN(poid), OID_AUTO, "test",
                CTLTYPE_INT | CTLFLAG_RW, 0, 0, sysctl_debug_sleep_test, "I",
                "");

            return (0);
    }

    static int
❾ unload(void *arg)
    {
            sysctl_ctx_free(&clist);
            mtx_lock(&event_mtx);
            event = -1;
            cv_signal(&event_cv);
            mtx_sleep(kthread, &event_mtx, PWAIT, "sleep", 0);
            mtx_unlock(&event_mtx);
            mtx_destroy(&event_mtx);
            cv_destroy(&event_cv);

            return (0);
    }
```

```
         static int
 ⑩ sleep_modevent(module_t mod __unused, int event, void *arg)
         {
                 int error = 0;

                 switch (event) {
                 case MOD_LOAD:
                         error = load(arg);
                         break;
                 case MOD_UNLOAD:
                         error = unload(arg);
                         break;
                 default:
                         error = EOPNOTSUPP;
                         break;
                 }

                 return (error);
         }

         static moduledata_t sleep_mod = {
                 "sleep",
                 sleep_modevent,
                 NULL
         };

         DECLARE_MODULE(sleep, sleep_mod, SI_SUB_SMP, SI_ORDER_ANY);
```

Listing 5-1: sleep.c

Near the beginning of Listing 5-1, a constant named ❶ MAX_EVENT is
defined as 1, and a struct proc pointer named ❷ kthread is declared. For
now, ignore these two objects; I'll discuss them later.

Next, there are two variable declarations: an integer named ❸ event and a
condition variable named ❹ event_cv. These variables are used to synchronize
Listing 5-1's threads. Obviously, the ❺ event_mtx mutex is used to protect event.

The remaining parts—❻ sleep_thread, ❼ sysctl_debug_sleep_test, ❽ load,
❾ unload, and ⑩ sleep_modevent—require a more in-depth explanation and
are therefore described in their own sections.

To make things easier to follow, I'll describe the abovementioned parts
in the order they execute, rather than in the order they appear. Thus, I'll
begin with Listing 5-1's module event handler.

sleep_modevent Function

The sleep_modevent function is the module event handler for Listing 5-1. Here
is its function definition (again):

```
         static int
         sleep_modevent(module_t mod __unused, int event, void *arg)
         {
                 int error = 0;
```

```
        switch (event) {
        case MOD_LOAD:
                error = ❶load(arg);
                break;
        case MOD_UNLOAD:
                error = ❷unload(arg);
                break;
        default:
                error = EOPNOTSUPP;
                break;
        }

        return (error);
}
```

On module load, this function simply calls the ❶ load function. On module unload, it calls the ❷ unload function.

load Function

The load function initializes this KLD. Here is its function definition (again):

```
static int
load(void *arg)
{
        int error;
        struct proc *p;
        struct thread *td;

        error = ❶kproc_create(❷sleep_thread, NULL, ❸&p, ❹RFSTOPPED, 0,
            "sleep");
        if (error)
                return (error);

        ❺event = 0;
        mtx_init(❻&event_mtx, "sleep event", NULL, MTX_DEF);
        cv_init(❼&event_cv, "sleep");

        td = FIRST_THREAD_IN_PROC(p);
        thread_lock(td);
        TD_SET_CAN_RUN(td);
        ❽sched_add(td, SRQ_BORING);
        thread_unlock(td);
        ❾kthread = p;

        sysctl_ctx_init(&clist);
        poid = SYSCTL_ADD_NODE(&clist, SYSCTL_STATIC_CHILDREN(_debug),
            OID_AUTO, "sleep", CTLFLAG_RD, 0, "sleep tree");
        SYSCTL_ADD_PROC(&clist, SYSCTL_CHILDREN(poid), OID_AUTO, "test",
            CTLTYPE_INT | CTLFLAG_RW, 0, 0, ❿sysctl_debug_sleep_test, "I",
            "");

        return (0);
}
```

This function can be split into four parts. The first ❶ creates a kernel process to execute the function ❷ sleep_thread. A handle to this process is saved in ❸ p. The constant ❹ RFSTOPPED puts the process in the stopped state. The second part initializes the ❺ event, ❻ event_mtx, and ❼ event_cv variables. The third part ❽ schedules the new process to execute sleep_thread. It also saves the process handle in ❾ kthread.

NOTE   *Processes are executed at thread granularity, which is why this code is thread centric.*

The fourth part creates a sysctl named debug.sleep.test, which uses a handler function named ❿ sysctl_debug_sleep_test.

sleep_thread Function

The sleep_thread function receives events from the sysctl_debug_sleep_test function. It then performs a specific task based on the event received. Here is its function definition (again):

```
static void
sleep_thread(void *arg)
{
        int ev;

  ❶for (;;) {
          ❷mtx_lock(&event_mtx);
          ❸while ((ev = event) == 0)
                  ❹cv_wait(&event_cv, &event_mtx);
          ❺event = 0;
          ❻mtx_unlock(&event_mtx);

          ❼switch (ev) {
          ❽case -1:
                  ❾kproc_exit(0);
                  break;
          case 0:
                  break;
          case 1:
                  printf("sleep... is alive and well.\n");
                  break;
          default:
                  panic("event %d is bogus\n", event);
          }
    }
}
```

As you can see, the execution of sleep_thread is contained within a ❶ forever loop. This loop begins by ❷ acquiring event_mtx. Next, the value of event is ❸ saved in ev. If event is equal to 0, sleep_thread ❹ waits on event_cv. See, event is only 0 if sleep_thread has yet to receive an event. If an event has been received, sleep_thread ❺ sets event to 0 to prevent reprocessing it. Next, event_mtx is ❻ released. Finally, the received event is processed by a ❼ switch statement. Note that if the received event is ❽ -1, sleep_thread ❾ self-terminates via kproc_exit.

sysctl_debug_sleep_test Function

The sysctl_debug_sleep_test function obtains events from the sysctl debug.sleep.test. It then passes those events to the sleep_thread function.

```
static int
sysctl_debug_sleep_test(SYSCTL_HANDLER_ARGS)
{
        int error, i = 0;

        error = ❶sysctl_handle_int(oidp, ❷&i, 0, req);
     ❸if (error == 0 && req->newptr != NULL) {
            ❹if (i >= 1 && i <= MAX_EVENT) {
                ❺mtx_lock(&event_mtx);
                ❻KASSERT(event == 0, ("event %d was unhandled",
                        event));
                ❼event = i;
                ❽cv_signal(&event_cv);
                  mtx_unlock(&event_mtx);
            } else
                  error = EINVAL;
        }

        return (error);
}
```

This function begins by ❶ obtaining an event from debug.sleep.test and ❷ storing it in i. The following ❸ if statement ensures that the event was obtained successfully. Next, a ❹ range check is performed on i. If i is in the allowable range, event_mtx is ❺ acquired and event is ❻ queried to ensure that it equals 0.

NOTE   *If event does not equal 0, something has gone horribly wrong. And if INVARIANTS is enabled, the kernel panics.*

Finally, event is ❼ set to i and sleep_thread is ❽ unblocked to process it.

unload Function

The unload function shuts down this KLD. Here is its function definition (again):

```
static int
unload(void *arg)
{
      ❶sysctl_ctx_free(&clist);
        mtx_lock(&event_mtx);
      ❷event = -1;
      ❸cv_signal(&event_cv);
```

```
❹mtx_sleep(❺kthread, &event_mtx, PWAIT, "sleep", 0);
  mtx_unlock(&event_mtx);
❻mtx_destroy(&event_mtx);
❼cv_destroy(&event_cv);

    return (0);
}
```

This function begins by ❶ tearing down the sysctl debug.sleep.test. After-ward, event is ❷ set to -1 and sleep_thread is ❸ unblocked to process it.

Recall that if event is -1, sleep_thread self-terminates via kproc_exit. Note that kproc_exit executes wakeup on its caller's process handle before return-ing. This is why unload ❹ sleeps on the channel ❺ kthread, because it contains sleep_thread's process handle.

NOTE *Recall that load saved sleep_thread's process handle in kthread.*

As unload sleeps (at ❹) until sleep_thread exits, it cannot destroy ❻ event_mtx and ❼ event_cv while they're still in use.

Don't Panic

Here are the results from loading and unloading Listing 5-1:

```
$ sudo kldload ./sleep.ko
$ sudo sysctl debug.sleep.test=1
debug.sleep.test: 0 -> 0
$ dmesg | tail -n 1
sleep... is alive and well.
$ sudo kldunload ./sleep.ko
$
```

Naturally, it works. Now, let's look at some other ways to delay execution.

Kernel Event Handlers

Event handlers allow drivers to register one or more functions to be called when an event occurs. As an example, before halting the system, every function that is registered with the event handler shutdown_final is called. Table 5-1 describes every event handler that is available.

Table 5-1: Kernel Event Handlers

Event Handler	Description
acpi_sleep_event	Registered functions are called when the system is sent to sleep.
acpi_wakeup_event	Registered functions are called when the system is woken up.
dev_clone	Registered functions are called when a solicited item under /dev does not exist; in other words, these functions create device nodes on demand.

Table 5-1: Kernel Event Handlers (continued)

Event Handler	Description
ifaddr_event	Registered functions are called when an address is set up on a network interface.
if_clone_event	Registered functions are called when a network interface is cloned.
ifnet_arrival_event	Registered functions are called when a new network interface appears.
ifnet_departure_event	Registered functions are called when a network interface is taken down.
power_profile_change	Registered functions are called when the system's power profile changes.
process_exec	Registered functions are called when a process issues an exec operation.
process_exit	Registered functions are called when a process exits.
process_fork	Registered functions are called when a process forks.
shutdown_pre_sync	Registered functions are called when the system is shut down before any filesystems are synchronized.
shutdown_post_sync	Registered functions are called when the system is shut down after every filesystem is synchronized.
shutdown_final	Registered functions are called before halting the system.
vm_lowmem	Registered functions are called when virtual memory is low.
watchdog_list	Registered functions are called when the watchdog timer is reinitialized.

The FreeBSD kernel provides the following three macros for working with event handlers:

```
#include <sys/eventhandler.h>

❶ eventhandler_tag
EVENTHANDLER_REGISTER(❷name, ❸func, ❹arg, ❺priority);

EVENTHANDLER_DEREGISTER(❻name, ❼tag);

EVENTHANDLER_INVOKE(❽name, ...);
```

The EVENTHANDLER_REGISTER macro registers the function ❸ func with the event handler ❷ name. If successful, an ❶ eventhandler_tag is returned. When func is called, ❹ arg will be its first argument. Functions registered with name are called in order of ❺ priority. priority can be 0 (which is the highest priority) to 20000 (which is the lowest priority).

NOTE *Generally, I use the constant* EVENTHANDLER_PRI_ANY, *which equals* 10000, *for priority.*

The EVENTHANDLER_DEREGISTER macro deletes the function associated with ❼ tag from the event handler ❻ name (where tag is an ❶ eventhandler_tag).

The EVENTHANDLER_INVOKE macro executes every function registered with the event handler ❽ name. Note that you'll never call EVENTHANDLER_INVOKE, because each event handler has threads dedicated to do just that.

NOTE *We'll walk through an example that uses event handlers in Chapter 6.*

Callouts

Callouts allow drivers to asynchronously execute a function after a specified amount of time (or at regular intervals). These functions are known as *callout functions*.

The FreeBSD kernel provides the following seven functions for working with callouts:

```
#include <sys/types.h>
#include <sys/systm.h>

typedef void timeout_t (void *);

void
callout_init(struct callout ❶*c, int ❷mpsafe);

void
callout_init_mtx(struct callout *c, struct mtx ❸*mtx, int ❹flags);

void
callout_init_rw(struct callout *c, struct rwlock ❺*rw, int ❻flags);

int
callout_stop(struct callout *c);

int
callout_drain(struct callout *c);

int
callout_reset(struct callout ❼*c, int ❽ticks, timeout_t ❾*func,
    void ❿*arg);

int
callout_schedule(struct callout *c, int ticks);
```

The callout_init function initializes the callout structure ❶ c. The ❷ mpsafe argument denotes whether the callout function is "multiprocessor safe." Valid values for this argument are shown in Table 5-2.

Table 5-2: callout_init Symbolic Constants

Constant	Description
0	The callout function is *not* multiprocessor safe; the Giant mutex is acquired before executing the callout function, and it's dropped after the callout function returns.
CALLOUT_MPSAFE	The callout function is multiprocessor safe; in other words, race conditions are dealt with by the callout function itself.

NOTE   *Here, Giant is acquired and dropped by the callout subsystem. Giant primarily protects legacy code and should not be used by contemporary code.*

The callout_init_mtx function is an alternative to callout_init. The mutex ❸ mtx is acquired before executing the callout function and it's dropped after the callout function returns (mtx is acquired and dropped by the callout subsystem). After callout_init_mtx returns, mtx is associated with the callout structure c and its callout function.

The ❹ flags argument modifies callout_init_mtx's behavior. Table 5-3 displays its only valid value.

Table 5-3: callout_init_mtx Symbolic Constants

Constant	Description
CALLOUT_RETURNUNLOCKED	Indicates that the callout function will drop mtx itself; in other words, mtx is not dropped after the callout function returns, but during.

The callout_init_rw function is an alternative to callout_init. The rw lock ❺ rw is acquired, as a writer, before executing the callout function and it's dropped after the callout function returns (rw is acquired and dropped by the callout subsystem). After callout_init_rw returns, rw is associated with the callout structure c and its callout function.

The ❻ flags argument modifies callout_init_rw's behavior. Table 5-4 displays its only valid value.

Table 5-4: callout_init_rw Symbolic Constants

Constant	Description
CALLOUT_SHAREDLOCK	Causes rw to be acquired as a reader

The callout_stop function cancels a callout function that's currently pending. If successful, a nonzero value is returned. If 0 is returned, the callout function is either currently executing or it has already finished executing.

You must exclusively hold the lock associated with the callout function that you're trying to stop before calling callout_stop.

The callout_drain function is identical to callout_stop except that if the callout function is currently executing, it waits for the callout function to finish before returning. If the callout function that you're trying to stop requires a lock and you're exclusively holding that lock while calling callout_drain, deadlock will result.

The callout_reset function schedules the function ❾ func to be executed, one time, after ❽ ticks / hz seconds; negative values for ticks are converted to 1. When func is called, ❿ arg will be its first and only argument. After callout_reset returns, func is the callout function for the callout structure ❼ c.

The callout_reset function can also reschedule a pending callout function to execute at a new time.

NOTE *You must exclusively hold the lock associated with the callout or callout function that you're trying to establish or reschedule before calling* callout_reset.

The callout_schedule function reschedules a pending callout function to execute at a new time. This function is simply a convenience wrapper for callout_reset.

NOTE *You must exclusively hold the lock associated with the callout function that you're trying to reschedule before calling* callout_schedule.

Callouts and Race Conditions

Because callout functions execute asynchronously, it's possible for a callout function to be called while another thread attempts to stop or reschedule it; thus creating a race condition. Fortunately, there are two simple solutions available for solving this problem:

Use callout_init_mtx, callout_init_rw, or callout_init(foo, 0)
Callout functions associated with a lock are exempt from the race condition described above—as long as the associated lock is held before calling the callout management functions.

Use callout_drain to permanently cancel a callout function
Use callout_drain instead of callout_stop to permanently cancel a callout function. See, by waiting for the callout function to finish, you can't destroy any objects that it might need.

NOTE *We'll walk through an example that uses callouts in Chapter 6.*

Taskqueues

Taskqueues allow drivers to schedule the asynchronous execution of one or more functions at a later time. These functions are known as *tasks*. Taskqueues are primarily used for deferred work.

NOTE *Taskqueues are like callouts except that you can't specify the time to execute your functions.*

Taskqueues work by having tasks queued on them. Intermittently, these tasks get executed.

Global Taskqueues

FreeBSD runs and maintains four global taskqueues:

taskqueue_swi

The taskqueue_swi taskqueue executes its tasks in the context of an interrupt. Interrupt handlers typically defer their computationally expensive work to this taskqueue. This taskqueue lets interrupt handlers finish sooner, thereby reducing the amount of time spent with interrupts disabled. Interrupt handlers are discussed in detail in Chapter 8.

taskqueue_swi_giant

The taskqueue_swi_giant taskqueue is identical to taskqueue_swi except that it acquires the Giant mutex before executing its tasks. Contemporary code should avoid this taskqueue.

taskqueue_thread

The taskqueue_thread taskqueue is the general-purpose taskqueue. It executes its tasks in the context of a kernel thread (which is the same context that drivers execute in). You can use this taskqueue when you have code that executes without a thread context (such as an interrupt handler) that needs to execute code that requires a thread context.

taskqueue_fast

The taskqueue_fast taskqueue is identical to taskqueue_thread except that it acquires a spin mutex before executing its tasks. Use this taskqueue when your tasks cannot sleep.

Taskqueue Management Routines

The FreeBSD kernel provides the following macro and functions for working with taskqueues:

```
#include <sys/param.h>
#include <sys/kernel.h>
#include <sys/malloc.h>
#include <sys/queue.h>
#include <sys/taskqueue.h>

typedef void (*task_fn_t)(void *context, int pending);

struct task {
        STAILQ_ENTRY(task)    ta_link;       /* Link for queue. */
        u_short             ❶ta_pending;     /* # of times queued. */
        u_short               ta_priority;   /* Task priority. */
        task_fn_t             ta_func;       /* Task handler function. */
        void                  *ta_context;   /* Argument for handler. */
};
```

```
TASK_INIT(struct task ❷*task, int ❸priority, task_fn_t ❹*func,
    void ❺*context);

int
taskqueue_enqueue(struct taskqueue ❻*queue, struct task ❼*task);

void
taskqueue_run(struct taskqueue ❽*queue);

void
taskqueue_drain(struct taskqueue ❾*queue, struct task ❿*task);
```

The TASK_INIT macro initializes the task structure ❷ task. The ❸ priority argument is task's position on a taskqueue. The ❹ func argument is the function to be executed (one time). When func is called, ❺ context will be its first argument and the value of ❶ ta_pending will be its second.

The taskqueue_enqueue function puts ❼ task on the taskqueue ❻ queue right before the first task structure that has a lower priority value. If taskqueue_enqueue gets called to put task on queue again, task's ta_pending value is incremented—another copy of task is *not* put on queue.

The taskqueue_run function executes every task on the taskqueue ❽ queue in the order of the task's priority value. After each task finishes, its task structure is removed from queue. Then its ta_pending value is zeroed and wakeup is called on its task structure. Note that you'll never call taskqueue_run, because each taskqueue has threads dedicated to do just that.

The taskqueue_drain function waits for ❿ task, which is on ❾ queue, to finish executing.

NOTE *We'll walk through an example that uses taskqueues in Chapter 6.*

Conclusion

This chapter covered the four different methods for delaying execution:

Sleeping Sleeping is done when you must wait for something to occur before you can proceed.

Event Handlers Event handlers let you register one or more functions to be executed when an event occurs.

Callouts Callouts let you perform asynchronous code execution. Callouts are used to execute your functions at a specific time.

Taskqueues Taskqueues also let you perform asynchronous code execution. Taskqueues are used for deferred work.

6

CASE STUDY:
VIRTUAL NULL MODEM

This chapter is the first of several case studies that'll guide you through a real-world device driver. The purpose of these case studies is to expose you to genuine driver code—warts and all—and to consolidate the information presented in earlier chapters.

In this chapter, we'll go through nmdm(4), the virtual null modem terminal. This driver creates two tty(4) devices that are connected by a virtual modem cable. In other words, the output of one tty(4) device is the input for the other tty(4) device, and vice versa. I chose to profile nmdm(4) because it uses event handlers, callouts, and taskqueues, all of which were described, but not demonstrated, in Chapter 5.

Prerequisites

Before I can walk you through nmdm(4), you'll need to grok the following functions:

```
#include <sys/tty.h>

struct tty *
tty_alloc_mutex(struct ttydevsw *tsw, void *softc, struct mtx *mtx);

void
tty_makedev(struct tty *tp, struct ucred *cred, const char *fmt, ...);

void *
tty_softc(struct tty *tp);
```

The tty_alloc_mutex function creates a TTY device. The tsw argument expects a pointer to a TTY device switch table, which is like a character device switch table, but for TTY devices. The softc argument is the software context (or instance variables) for the TTY device. The mtx argument specifies the mutex that'll protect the TTY device.

NOTE *At some point in the near future, the tty_alloc_mutex function is supposed to be deprecated and removed.*

The tty_makedev function creates a TTY device node under */dev*. The tp argument expects a pointer to a TTY device (for example, the return value from tty_alloc_mutex). The cred argument is the credentials for the device node. If cred is NULL, UID_ROOT and GID_WHEEL are used. The fmt argument specifies the name for the device node.

The tty_softc function returns the software context of the TTY device tp.

Code Analysis

Listing 6-1 provides a terse, source-level overview of nmdm(4).

```
#include <sys/param.h>
#include <sys/module.h>
#include <sys/kernel.h>
#include <sys/systm.h>

#include <sys/tty.h>
#include <sys/conf.h>
#include <sys/eventhandler.h>
#include <sys/limits.h>
#include <sys/serial.h>
#include <sys/malloc.h>
#include <sys/queue.h>
#include <sys/taskqueue.h>
#include <sys/lock.h>
#include <sys/mutex.h>
```

```c
MALLOC_DEFINE(M_NMDM, "nullmodem", "nullmodem data structures");

struct nmdm_part {
        struct tty              *np_tty;
        struct nmdm_part        *np_other;
        struct task             np_task;
        struct callout          np_callout;
        int                     np_dcd;
        int                     np_rate;
        u_long                  np_quota;
        int                     np_credits;
        u_long                  np_accumulator;

#define QS 8                    /* Quota shift. */
};

struct nmdm_softc {
        struct nmdm_part        ns_partA;
        struct nmdm_part        ns_partB;
        struct mtx              ns_mtx;
};

static tsw_outwakeup_t          nmdm_outwakeup;
static tsw_inwakeup_t           nmdm_inwakeup;
static tsw_param_t              nmdm_param;
static tsw_modem_t              nmdm_modem;

static struct ttydevsw nmdm_class = {
        .tsw_flags =            TF_NOPREFIX,
        .tsw_outwakeup =        nmdm_outwakeup,
        .tsw_inwakeup =         nmdm_inwakeup,
        .tsw_param =            nmdm_param,
        .tsw_modem =            nmdm_modem
};

static int nmdm_count = 0;

static void
nmdm_timeout(void *arg)
{
...
}

static void
nmdm_task_tty(void *arg, int pending __unused)
{
...
}

static struct nmdm_softc *
nmdm_alloc(unsigned long unit)
{
...
}
```

```
static void
nmdm_clone(void *arg, struct ucred *cred, char *name, int len,
    struct cdev **dev)
{
...
}

static void
nmdm_outwakeup(struct tty *tp)
{
...
}

static void
nmdm_inwakeup(struct tty *tp)
{
...
}

static int
bits_per_char(struct termios *t)
{
...
}

static int
nmdm_param(struct tty *tp, struct termios *t)
{
...
}

static int
nmdm_modem(struct tty *tp, int sigon, int sigoff)
{
...
}

static int
nmdm_modevent(module_t mod __unused, int event, void *arg __unused)
{
...
}

DEV_MODULE(nmdm, nmdm_modevent, NULL);
```

Listing 6-1: nmdm.c

Listing 6-1 is provided as a convenience; as I go through the code for nmdm(4) you can refer to it to see how nmdm(4)'s functions and structures are laid out.

To make things easier to understand, I'll detail the functions and structures in nmdm(4) in the order I would've written them (instead of in the order they appear). To that end, we'll begin with the module event handler.

nmdm_modevent Function

The nmdm_modevent function is the module event handler for nmdm(4). Here is its function definition:

```
static int
nmdm_modevent(module_t mod __unused, int event, void *arg __unused)
{
        static eventhandler_tag tag;

        switch (event) {
        case MOD_LOAD:
                tag = ❶EVENTHANDLER_REGISTER(❷dev_clone, ❸nmdm_clone, 0,
                    1000);
                if (tag == NULL)
                        return (ENOMEM);
                break;
        case MOD_SHUTDOWN:
                break;
        case MOD_UNLOAD:
                ❹if (nmdm_count != 0)
                        ❺return (EBUSY);
                ❻EVENTHANDLER_DEREGISTER(dev_clone, tag);
                break;
        default:
                return (EOPNOTSUPP);
        }

        return (0);
}
```

On module load, this function ❶ registers the function ❸ nmdm_clone with the event handler ❷ dev_clone.

NOTE *The dev_clone event handler was described in Table 5-1 on page 92.*

Recall that functions registered with dev_clone are called when a solicited item under /dev does not exist. So when a nmdm(4) device node is accessed for the first time, nmdm_clone will be called to create the device node on the fly. Interestingly, this on-the-fly device creation lets one create an unlimited number of nmdm(4) device nodes.

On module unload, this function begins by ❹ checking the value of nmdm_count.

NOTE *The variable nmdm_count is declared near the beginning of Listing 6-1 as an integer initialized to 0.*

nmdm_count counts the number of active nmdm(4) device nodes. If it equals 0, nmdm_clone is ❻ removed from the event handler dev_clone; otherwise, EBUSY (which stands for *error: device busy*) is ❺ returned.

nmdm_clone Function

As mentioned in the previous section, `nmdm_clone` creates `nmdm(4)` device nodes on the fly. Note that all `nmdm(4)` device nodes are created in pairs named `nmdm%lu%c`, where `%lu` is the unit number and `%c` is either A or B. Here is the function definition for `nmdm_clone`:

```
static void
nmdm_clone(void *arg, struct ucred *cred, char *name, int len,
    struct cdev **dev)
{
        unsigned long unit;
        char *end;
        struct nmdm_softc *ns;

    ❶if (*dev != NULL)
              return;
    ❷if (strncmp(name, "nmdm", 4) != 0)
              return;

        /* Device name must be "nmdm%lu%c", where %c is "A" or "B". */
        name += 4;
        unit = ❸strtoul(name, &end, 10);
    ❹if (unit == ULONG_MAX || name == end)
              return;
    ❺if ((end[0] != 'A' && end[0] != 'B') || end[1] != '\0')
              return;

        ns = ❻nmdm_alloc(unit);

        if (end[0] == 'A')
              ❼*dev = ns->ns_partA.np_tty->t_dev;
        else
              ❽*dev = ns->ns_partB.np_tty->t_dev;
}
```

This function first ❶ checks the value of *dev (which is a character device pointer). If *dev does not equal NULL, which implies that a device node already exists, nmdm_clone exits (because no nodes need to be created). Next, nmdm_clone ❷ ensures that the first four characters in name are equal to nmdm; otherwise it exits (because the solicited device node is for another driver). Then the fifth character in name, which should be a unit number, is ❸ converted to an unsigned long and stored in unit. The following ❹ if statement checks that the conversion was a success. Afterward, nmdm_clone ❺ ensures that following the unit number (in name) is the letter A or B; otherwise it exits. Now, having confirmed that the solicited device node is indeed for this driver, ❻ nmdm_alloc is called to actually create the device nodes. Finally, *dev is set to the solicited device node (either ❼ nmdm%luA or ❽ nmdm%luB).

Note that since nmdm_clone is registered with dev_clone, its function prototype must conform to the type expected by dev_clone, which is defined in <sys/conf.h>.

nmdm_alloc Function

As mentioned in the previous section, `nmdm_alloc` actually creates `nmdm(4)`'s device nodes. Before I describe this function, an explanation of `nmdm_class` is needed.

NOTE   *The data structure `nmdm_class` is declared near the beginning of Listing 6-1 as a TTY device switch table.*

```
static struct ttydevsw nmdm_class = {
        .tsw_flags =            ❶TF_NOPREFIX,
        .tsw_outwakeup =        nmdm_outwakeup,
        .tsw_inwakeup =         nmdm_inwakeup,
        .tsw_param =            nmdm_param,
        .tsw_modem =            nmdm_modem
};
```

The flag ❶ TF_NOPREFIX means *don't prefix tty to the device name.* The other definitions are the operations that `nmdm_class` supports. These operations will be described as we encounter them.

Now that you're familiar with `nmdm_class`, let's walk through `nmdm_alloc`.

```
static struct nmdm_softc *
nmdm_alloc(unsigned long unit)
{
        struct nmdm_softc *ns;

    ❶atomic_add_int(&nmdm_count, 1);

        ns = ❷malloc(sizeof(*ns), M_NMDM, M_WAITOK | M_ZERO);
    ❸mtx_init(&ns->ns_mtx, "nmdm", NULL, MTX_DEF);

        /* Connect the pairs together. */
    ❹ns->ns_partA.np_other = &ns->ns_partB;
    ❺TASK_INIT(&ns->ns_partA.np_task, 0, nmdm_task_tty, &ns->ns_partA);
    ❻callout_init_mtx(&ns->ns_partA.np_callout, &ns->ns_mtx, 0);

    ❼ns->ns_partB.np_other = &ns->ns_partA;
    ❽TASK_INIT(&ns->ns_partB.np_task, 0, nmdm_task_tty, &ns->ns_partB);
    ❾callout_init_mtx(&ns->ns_partB.np_callout, &ns->ns_mtx, 0);

        /* Create device nodes. */
        ns->ns_partA.np_tty = tty_alloc_mutex(&nmdm_class, &ns->ns_partA,
            &ns->ns_mtx);
        tty_makedev(ns->ns_partA.np_tty, NULL, "nmdm%luA", unit);

        ns->ns_partB.np_tty = tty_alloc_mutex(&nmdm_class, &ns->ns_partB,
            &ns->ns_mtx);
        tty_makedev(ns->ns_partB.np_tty, NULL, "nmdm%luB", unit);

        return (ns);
}
```

This function can be split into four parts. The first ❶ increments nmdm_count by one via the atomic_add_int function. As its name implies, atomic_add_int is atomic. Consequently, we don't need a lock to protect nmdm_count when we increment it.

The second part ❷ allocates memory for a new nmdm_softc structure. After that, its mutex is ❸ initialized. Besides a mutex, nmdm_softc contains two additional member variables: ns_partA and ns_partB. These variables are nmdm_part structures and will maintain data relating to nmdm%luA or nmdm%luB.

NOTE   *struct nmdm_softc is defined near the beginning of Listing 6-1.*

The third part ❹ ❼ connects the member variables ns_partA and ns_partB, so that given ns_partA we can find ns_partB, and vice versa. The third part also initializes ns_partA's and ns_partB's ❺ ❽ task and ❻ ❾ callout structures.

Finally, the fourth part creates nmdm(4)'s device nodes (that is, nmdm%luA and nmdm%luB).

nmdm_outwakeup Function

The nmdm_outwakeup function is defined in nmdm_class as the tsw_outwakeup operation. It is executed when output from nmdm%luA or nmdm%luB is available. Here is its function definition:

```
static void
nmdm_outwakeup(struct tty *tp)
{
        struct nmdm_part *np = tty_softc(tp);

        /* We can transmit again, so wake up our side. */
        ❶taskqueue_enqueue(❷taskqueue_swi, ❸&np->np_task);
}
```

This function ❶ queues ns_partA's or ns_partB's ❸ task structure on ❷ taskqueue_swi (that is to say, it defers processing the output from nmdm%luA and nmdm%luB).

nmdm_task_tty Function

The nmdm_task_tty function transfers data from nmdm%luA to nmdm%luB, and vice versa. This function is queued on taskqueue_swi by nmdm_outwakeup (for verification, see the third argument to TASK_INIT in nmdm_alloc). Here is its function definition:

```
static void
nmdm_task_tty(void *arg, int pending __unused)
{
        struct tty *tp, *otp;
        struct nmdm_part *np = arg;
        char c;
```

```
        tp = np->np_tty;
        tty_lock(tp);

        otp = np->np_other->np_tty;
        KASSERT(otp != NULL, ("nmdm_task_tty: null otp"));
        KASSERT(otp != tp, ("nmdm_task_tty: otp == tp"));

  ❶if (np->np_other->np_dcd) {
          ❷if (!tty_opened(tp)) {
                  ❸np->np_other->np_dcd = 0;
                  ❹ttydisc_modem(otp, 0);
              }
  ❺} else {
          ❻if (tty_opened(tp)) {
                  np->np_other->np_dcd = 1;
                  ttydisc_modem(otp, 1);
              }
        }

        while (❼ttydisc_rint_poll(otp) > 0) {
              if (np->np_rate && !np->np_quota)
                      break;
              if (❽ttydisc_getc(tp, &c, 1) != 1)
                      break;
              np->np_quota--;
          ❾ttydisc_rint(otp, c, 0);
        }
        ttydisc_rint_done(otp);

        tty_unlock(tp);
}
```

NOTE   *In this function's explanation, "our TTY" refers to the TTY device (that is, nmdm%luA or nmdm%luB) that queued this function on taskqueue_swi.*

This function is composed of two parts. The first changes the connection state between the two TTYs to match the status of our TTY. If our TTY is ❷ closed and the other TTY's Data Carrier Detect (DCD) flag is ❶ on, we ❸ turn off that flag and ❹ switch off their carrier signal. On the other hand, if our TTY has been ❻ opened and the other TTY's DCD flag is ❺ off, we turn on that flag and switch on their carrier signal. In short, this part ensures that if our TTY is closed (that is, there is no data to transfer), the other TTY will not have a carrier signal, and if our TTY has been opened (that is, there is data to transfer), the other TTY will have a carrier signal. A carrier signal indicates a connection. In other words, loss of the carrier equates to termination of the connection.

The second part transfers data from our TTY's output queue to the other TTY's input queue. This part first ❼ polls the other TTY to determine whether it can accept data. Then one character is ❽ removed from our TTY's output queue and ❾ placed in the other TTY's input queue. These steps are repeated until the transfer is complete.

nmdm_inwakeup Function

The `nmdm_inwakeup` function is defined in `nmdm_class` as the `tsw_inwakeup` operation. It is called when input for `nmdm%luA` or `nmdm%luB` can be received again.
That is, when `nmdm%luA`'s or `nmdm%luB`'s input queue is full and then space
becomes available, this function is executed. Here is its function definition:

```
static void
nmdm_inwakeup(struct tty *tp)
{
        struct nmdm_part *np = tty_softc(tp);

        /* We can receive again, so wake up the other side. */
    ❶taskqueue_enqueue(❷taskqueue_swi, ❸&np->np_other->np_task);
}
```

NOTE   *In this function's explanation, "our TTY" refers to the TTY device (that is, nmdm%luA or
nmdm%luB) that executed this function.*

This function ❶ queues the other TTY's ❸ task structure on ❷
`taskqueue_swi`. In other words, when input for our TTY can be received
again, our TTY tells the other TTY to transfer data to it.

nmdm_modem Function

The `nmdm_modem` function is defined in `nmdm_class` as the `tsw_modem` operation.
This function sets or gets the modem control line state. Here is its function
definition:

```
static int
nmdm_modem(struct tty *tp, int sigon, int sigoff)
{
        struct nmdm_part *np = tty_softc(tp);
        int i = 0;

        /* Set modem control lines. */
    ❶if (sigon || sigoff) {
            ❷if (sigon & SER_DTR)
                    ❸np->np_other->np_dcd = 1;
            ❹if (sigoff & SER_DTR)
                    ❺np->np_other->np_dcd = 0;

        ❻ttydisc_modem(np->np_other->np_tty, np->np_other->np_dcd);

            return (0);
        /* Get state of modem control lines. */
        } else {
            ❼if (np->np_dcd)
                    ❽i |= SER_DCD;
            ❾if (np->np_other->np_dcd)
                    ❿i |= SER_DTR;
```

```
                    return (i);
            }
    }
```

NOTE   *In this function's explanation, "our TTY" refers to the TTY device (that is, nmdm%luA or nmdm%luB) that executed this function.*

This function sets the modem control lines when the sigon (signal on) or the sigoff (signal off) argument is ❶ nonzero. If sigon ❷ contains the Data Terminal Ready (DTR) flag, the other TTY's DCD flag is ❸ turned on. If sigoff ❹ contains the DTR flag, the other TTY's DCD flag is ❺ turned off. The other TTY's carrier signal is ❻ turned on or off alongside its DCD flag.

If the preceding discussion didn't make any sense to you, this should help: A null modem connects the DTR output of each serial port to the DCD input of the other. The DTR output is kept off until a program accesses the serial port and turns it on; the other serial port will sense this as its DCD input turning on. Thus, the DCD input is used to detect the readiness of the other side. This is why when our TTY's DTR is sigon'd or sigoff'd, the other TTY's DCD flag and carrier signal are also turned on or off.

This function gets the modem control line state when sigon and sigoff are 0. If our TTY's DCD flag is ❼ on, SER_DCD is ❽ returned. If the other TTY's DCD flag is ❾ on, indicating that our TTY's DTR flag is on, SER_DTR is ❿ returned.

nmdm_param Function

The nmdm_param function is defined in nmdm_class as the tsw_param operation. This function sets up nmdm_task_tty to be executed at regular intervals. That is, it sets nmdm%luA to periodically transfer data to nmdm%luB, and vice versa. This periodic data transfer requires flow control to prevent one side from overrunning the other with data. Flow control works by halting the sender when the receiver can't keep up.

Here is the function definition for nmdm_param:

```
static int
nmdm_param(struct tty *tp, struct termios *t)
{
        struct nmdm_part *np = tty_softc(tp);
        struct tty *otp;
        int bpc, rate, speed, i;

        otp = np->np_other->np_tty;

    ❶if (!((t->c_cflag | otp->t_termios.c_cflag) & CDSR_OFLOW)) {
            np->np_rate = 0;
            np->np_other->np_rate = 0;
            return (0);
    }

    ❷bpc = imax(bits_per_char(t), bits_per_char(&otp->t_termios));
```

```
            for (i = 0; i < 2; i++) {
                    /* Use the slower of their transmit or our receive rate. */
                ❸speed = imin(otp->t_termios.c_ospeed, t->c_ispeed);
                    if (speed == 0) {
                            np->np_rate = 0;
                            np->np_other->np_rate = 0;
                            return (0);
                    }

                    speed <<= QS;               /* bits per second, scaled. */
                    speed /= bpc;               /* char per second, scaled. */
                    rate = (hz << QS) / speed;  /* hz per callout. */
                    if (rate == 0)
                            rate = 1;

                    speed *= rate;
                    speed /= hz;                /* (char/sec)/tick, scaled. */

                ❹np->np_credits = speed;
                    np->np_rate = ❺rate;
                    callout_reset(&np->np_callout, ❻rate, ❼nmdm_timeout, np);

                    /* Swap pointers for second pass--to update the other end. */
                    np = np->np_other;
                    t = &otp->t_termios;
                    otp = tp;
            }

            return (0);
    }
```

This function can be split into three parts. The first ❶ determines
whether flow control is disabled. If it is, ns_partA's and ns_partB's np_rate
variable is zeroed and nmdm_param exits. The np_rate variable is the rate at
which nmdm_task_tty will be executed. This rate can differ for nmdm%luA and
nmdm%luB.

The second part calculates the ❺ value for np_rate. This calculation takes
into consideration the ❸ speed of nmdm%luA and nmdm%luB and the ❷ number of
bits per character. The second part also determines the ❹ maximum number of characters to transfer per execution of nmdm_task_tty.

Lastly, the third part causes ❼ nmdm_timeout to execute one time after
❻ rate / hz seconds. The nmdm_timeout function queues nmdm_task_tty on
taskqueue_swi.

The second and third parts are executed twice, once for nmdm%luA and
once for nmdm%luB.

nmdm_timeout Function

As indicated in the previous section, the nmdm_timeout function queues nmdm_task_tty on taskqueue_swi at regular intervals. Here is its function definition:

```
static void
nmdm_timeout(void *arg)
{
        struct nmdm_part *np = arg;

    ❶if (np->np_rate == 0)
            return;

    /*
     * Do a simple Floyd-Steinberg dither to avoid FP math.
     * Wipe out unused quota from last tick.
     */
    np->np_accumulator += np->np_credits;
    np->np_quota = ❷np->np_accumulator >> QS;
    np->np_accumulator &= ((1 << QS) - 1);

    ❸taskqueue_enqueue(❹taskqueue_swi, &np->np_task);
    ❺callout_reset(&np->np_callout, ❻np->np_rate, ❼nmdm_timeout, np);
}
```

This function first ❶ checks the value of np_rate. If it equals 0, nmdm_timeout exits. Next, ns_partA's or ns_partB's np_quota variable is assigned the ❷ maximum number of characters to transfer (if you return to "nmdm_task_tty Function" on page 106, it should be obvious how np_quota is used). Once this is done, nmdm_task_tty is ❸ queued on ❹ taskqueue_swi and ❼ nmdm_timeout is ❺ rescheduled to execute after ❻ np_rate / hz seconds.

The nmdm_param and nmdm_timeout functions are used to emulate the TTYs' baud rate. Without these two functions, data transfers would be slower.

bits_per_char Function

The bits_per_char function returns the number of bits used to represent a single character for a given TTY. This function is used only in nmdm_param. Here is its function definition:

```
static int
bits_per_char(struct termios *t)
{
        int bits;

    ❶bits = 1;                   /* start bit. */
    ❷switch (t->c_cflag & CSIZE) {
```

```
            case CS5:
                    bits += 5;
                    break;
            case CS6:
                    bits += 6;
                    break;
            case CS7:
                    bits += 7;
                    break;
            case CS8:
                    bits += 8;
                    break;
        }
❸bits++;                             /* stop bit. */
❹if (t->c_cflag & PARENB)
            bits++;
❺if (t->c_cflag & CSTOPB)
            bits++;

        return (❻bits);
}
```

Notice that the ❻ return value takes into account the ❷ variable character size, ❶ start bit, ❸ stop bit, ❹ parity enabled bit, and ❺ second stop bit.

Don't Panic

Now that we've walked through nmdm(4), let's give it a try:

```
$ sudo kldload ./nmdm.ko
$ sudo /usr/libexec/getty std.9600 nmdm0A &
[1] 936
$ sudo cu -l /dev/nmdm0B
Connected

FreeBSD/i386 (wintermute.phub.net.cable.rogers.com) (nmdm0A)

login:
```

Excellent. We're able to connect to nmdm0A, which is running getty(8), from nmdm0B.

Conclusion

This chapter described the entire code base of nmdm(4), the virtual null modem terminal driver. If you noticed the complete lack of locking in this driver and are alarmed, don't be. The ns_mtx mutex, which gets initialized in nmdm_alloc, is implicitly acquired by the TTY subsystem before nmdm_outwakeup, nmdm_inwakeup, nmdm_modem, and nmdm_param are called. In short, every operation between nmdm%luA and nmdm%luB is serialized.

7

NEWBUS AND RESOURCE ALLOCATION

Until now, we've examined only pseudo-devices, which provide a superb introduction to driver writing. However, most drivers need to interact with real hardware. This chapter shows you how to write drivers that do just that.

I'll start by introducing *Newbus*, which is the infrastructure used in FreeBSD to manage the hardware devices on the system (McKusick and Neville-Neil, 2005). I'll then describe the basics of a Newbus driver, and I'll conclude this chapter by talking about hardware resource allocation.

Autoconfiguration and Newbus Drivers

Autoconfiguration is the procedure carried out by FreeBSD to enable the hardware devices on a machine (McKusick and Neville-Neil, 2005). It works by systematically probing a machine's I/O buses in order to identify their child devices. For each identified device, an appropriate Newbus driver is assigned to configure and initialize it. Note that it's possible for a device to be unidentifiable or unsupported. As a result, no Newbus driver will be assigned.

A *Newbus driver* is any driver in FreeBSD that controls a device that is bound to an I/O bus (that is, roughly every driver that is not a pseudo-device driver).

In general, three components are common to all Newbus drivers:

- The device_foo functions
- A device method table
- A DRIVER_MODULE macro call

device_foo Functions

The device_foo functions are, more or less, the operations executed by a Newbus driver during autoconfiguration. Table 7-1 briefly introduces each device_foo function.

Table 7-1: device_foo Functions

Function	Description
device_identify	Add new device to I/O bus
device_probe	Probe for specific device(s)
device_attach	Attach to device
device_detach	Detach from device
device_shutdown	Shut down device
device_suspend	Device suspend requested
device_resume	Resume has occurred

The device_identify function adds a new device (instance) to an I/O bus. This function is used only by buses that cannot directly identify their children. Recall that autoconfiguration begins by identifying the child devices on each I/O bus. Modern buses can directly identify the devices that are connected to them. Older buses, such as ISA, have to use the device_identify routine provided by their associated drivers to identify their child devices (McKusick and Neville-Neil, 2005). You'll learn how to associate a driver with an I/O bus shortly.

All identified child devices are passed to every Newbus driver's device_probe function. A device_probe function tells the kernel whether its driver can handle the identified device.

Note that there may be more than one driver that can handle an identified child device. Thus, device_probe's return value is used to specify how well its driver matches the identified device. The device_probe function that returns the highest value denotes the best Newbus driver for the identified device. The following excerpt from <sys/bus.h> shows the constants used to indicate success (that is, a match):

```
#define BUS_PROBE_SPECIFIC      0          /* Only I can use this device. */
#define BUS_PROBE_VENDOR        (-10)      /* Vendor-supplied driver. */
#define BUS_PROBE_DEFAULT       (-20)      /* Base OS default driver. */
#define BUS_PROBE_LOW_PRIORITY  (-40)      /* Older, less desirable driver. */
#define BUS_PROBE_GENERIC       (-100)     /* Generic driver for device. */
#define BUS_PROBE_HOOVER        (-500)     /* Driver for all devices on bus. */
#define BUS_PROBE_NOWILDCARD    (-2000000000) /* No wildcard matches. */
```

As you can see, success codes are values less than or equal to zero. The standard UNIX error codes (that is, positive values) are used as failure codes.

Once the best driver has been found to handle a device, its device_attach function is called. A device_attach function initializes a device and any essential software (for example, device nodes).

The device_detach function disconnects a driver from a device. This function should set the device to a sane state and release any resources that were allocated during device_attach.

A Newbus driver's device_shutdown, device_suspend, and device_resume functions are called when the system is shut down, when its device is suspended, or when its device returns from suspension, respectively. These functions let a driver manage its device as these events occur.

Device Method Table

A device method table, device_method_t, specifies which device_foo functions a Newbus driver implements. It is defined in the <sys/bus.h> header.

Here is an example device method table for a fictitious PCI device:

```
static device_method_t foo_pci_methods[] = {
        /* Device interface. */
        DEVMETHOD(device_probe,         foo_pci_probe),
        DEVMETHOD(device_attach,        foo_pci_attach),
        DEVMETHOD(device_detach,        foo_pci_detach),
        { 0, 0 }
};
```

As you can see, not every device_foo function has to be defined. If a device_foo function is undefined, the corresponding operation is unsupported.

Unsurprisingly, the device_probe and device_attach functions must be defined for every Newbus driver. For drivers on older buses, the device_identify function must also be defined.

DRIVER_MODULE Macro

The `DRIVER_MODULE` macro registers a Newbus driver with the system. This macro is defined in the `<sys/bus.h>` header. Here is its function prototype:

```
#include <sys/param.h>
#include <sys/kernel.h>
#include <sys/bus.h>
#include <sys/module.h>

DRIVER_MODULE(name, busname, driver_t driver, devclass_t devclass,
    modeventhand_t evh, void *arg);
```

The arguments expected by this macro are as follows.

name

The `name` argument is used to identify the driver.

busname

The `busname` argument specifies the driver's I/O bus (for example, isa, pci, usb, and so on).

driver

The `driver` argument expects a filled-out `driver_t` structure. This argument is best understood with an example:

```
static driver_t foo_pci_driver = {
    ❶"foo_pci",
    ❷foo_pci_methods,
    ❸sizeof(struct foo_pci_softc)
};
```

Here, ❶ "foo_pci" is this example driver's official name, ❷ `foo_pci_methods` is its device method table, and ❸ `sizeof(struct foo_pci_softc)` is the size of its software context.

devclass

The `devclass` argument expects an uninitialized `devclass_t` variable, which will be used by the kernel for internal bookkeeping.

evh

The `evh` argument denotes an optional module event handler. Generally, we'll always set evh to 0, because `DRIVER_MODULE` supplies its own module event handler.

arg

The `arg` argument is the void * argument for the module event handler specified by evh. If evh is set to 0, arg must be too.

Tying Everything Together

You now know enough to write your first Newbus driver. Listing 7-1 is a simple Newbus driver (based on code written by Murray Stokely) for a fictitious PCI device.

NOTE *Take a quick look at this code and try to discern some of its structure. If you don't understand all of it, don't worry; an explanation follows.*

```
#include <sys/param.h>
#include <sys/module.h>
#include <sys/kernel.h>
#include <sys/systm.h>

#include <sys/conf.h>
#include <sys/uio.h>
#include <sys/bus.h>

#include <dev/pci/pcireg.h>
#include <dev/pci/pcivar.h>

❶ struct foo_pci_softc {
        ❷device_t        device;
        ❸struct cdev     *cdev;
};

static d_open_t         foo_pci_open;
static d_close_t        foo_pci_close;
static d_read_t         foo_pci_read;
static d_write_t        foo_pci_write;

❹ static struct cdevsw foo_pci_cdevsw = {
        .d_version =    D_VERSION,
        .d_open =       foo_pci_open,
        .d_close =      foo_pci_close,
        .d_read =       foo_pci_read,
        .d_write =      foo_pci_write,
        .d_name =       "foo_pci"
};

❺ static devclass_t foo_pci_devclass;

static int
foo_pci_open(struct cdev *dev, int oflags, int devtype, struct thread *td)
{
        struct foo_pci_softc *sc;

        sc = dev->si_drv1;
        device_printf(sc->device, "opened successfully\n");
        return (0);
}
```

```
static int
foo_pci_close(struct cdev *dev, int fflag, int devtype, struct thread *td)
{
        struct foo_pci_softc *sc;

        sc = dev->si_drv1;
        device_printf(sc->device, "closed\n");
        return (0);
}

static int
foo_pci_read(struct cdev *dev, struct uio *uio, int ioflag)
{
        struct foo_pci_softc *sc;

        sc = dev->si_drv1;
        device_printf(sc->device, "read request = %dB\n", uio->uio_resid);
        return (0);
}

static int
foo_pci_write(struct cdev *dev, struct uio *uio, int ioflag)
{
        struct foo_pci_softc *sc;

        sc = dev->si_drv1;
        device_printf(sc->device, "write request = %dB\n", uio->uio_resid);
        return (0);
}

static struct _pcsid {
        uint32_t        type;
        const char      *desc;
} pci_ids[] = {
        { 0x1234abcd, "RED PCI Widget" },
        { 0x4321fedc, "BLU PCI Widget" },
        { 0x00000000, NULL }
};

static int
foo_pci_probe(device_t dev)
{
        uint32_t type = pci_get_devid(dev);
        struct _pcsid *ep = pci_ids;

        while (ep->type && ep->type != type)
                ep++;
        if (ep->desc) {
                device_set_desc(dev, ep->desc);
                return (BUS_PROBE_DEFAULT);
        }

        return (ENXIO);
}
```

```
static int
foo_pci_attach(device_t dev)
{
        struct foo_pci_softc *sc = device_get_softc(dev);
        int unit = device_get_unit(dev);

        sc->device = dev;
        sc->cdev = ❻make_dev(&foo_pci_cdevsw, unit, UID_ROOT, GID_WHEEL,
            0600, "foo_pci%d", unit);
        sc->cdev->si_drv1 = sc;

        return (0);
}

static int
foo_pci_detach(device_t dev)
{
        struct foo_pci_softc *sc = device_get_softc(dev);

        destroy_dev(sc->cdev);
        return (0);
}

static device_method_t foo_pci_methods[] = {
        /* Device interface. */
        DEVMETHOD(device_probe,         foo_pci_probe),
        DEVMETHOD(device_attach,        foo_pci_attach),
        DEVMETHOD(device_detach,        foo_pci_detach),
        { 0, 0 }
};

static driver_t foo_pci_driver = {
        "foo_pci",
        foo_pci_methods,
        sizeof(struct foo_pci_softc)
};

❼ DRIVER_MODULE(foo_pci, pci, foo_pci_driver, ❽foo_pci_devclass, 0, 0);
```

Listing 7-1: foo_pci.c

This driver begins by defining its ❶ software context, which will maintain a ❷ pointer to its device and the ❸ cdev returned by the ❻ make_dev call.

Next, its ❹ character device switch table is defined. This table contains four d_foo functions named foo_pci_open, foo_pci_close, foo_pci_read, and foo_pci_write. I'll describe these functions in "d_foo Functions" on page 121.

Then a ❺ devclass_t variable is declared. This variable is passed to the ❼ DRIVER_MODULE macro as its ❽ devclass argument.

Finally, the d_foo and device_foo functions are defined. These functions are described in the order they would execute.

foo_pci_probe Function

The foo_pci_probe function is the device_probe implementation for this driver. Before I walk through this function, a description of the pci_ids array (found around the middle of Listing 7-1) is needed.

```
static struct _pcsid {
     ❶uint32_t      type;
     ❷const char    *desc;
} pci_ids[] = {
        { 0x1234abcd, "RED PCI Widget" },
        { 0x4321fedc, "BLU PCI Widget" },
        { 0x00000000, NULL }
};
```

This array is composed of three _pcsid structures. Each _pcsid structure contains a ❶ PCI ID and a ❷ description of the PCI device. As you might have guessed, pci_ids lists the devices that Listing 7-1 supports.

Now that I've described pci_ids, let's walk through foo_pci_probe.

```
static int
foo_pci_probe(device_t ❶dev)
{
        uint32_t type = ❷pci_get_devid(dev);
        struct _pcsid *ep = ❸pci_ids;

     ❹while (ep->type && ep->type != type)
                ep++;
        if (ep->desc) {
             ❺device_set_desc(dev, ep->desc);
             ❻return (BUS_PROBE_DEFAULT);
        }

        return (ENXIO);
}
```

Here, ❶ dev describes an identified device found on the PCI bus. So this function begins by ❷ obtaining the PCI ID of dev. Then it ❹ determines if dev's PCI ID is listed in ❸ pci_ids. If it is, dev's verbose description is ❺ set and the success code BUS_PROBE_DEFAULT is ❻ returned.

NOTE   *The verbose description is printed to the system console when foo_pci_attach executes.*

foo_pci_attach Function

The foo_pci_attach function is the device_attach implementation for this driver. Here is its function definition (again):

```
static int
foo_pci_attach(device_t ❶dev)
{
        struct foo_pci_softc *sc = ❷device_get_softc(dev);
```

```
        int unit = ❸device_get_unit(dev);

        sc->device = ❹dev;
        sc->cdev = ❺make_dev(&foo_pci_cdevsw, unit, UID_ROOT, GID_WHEEL,
            0600, "foo_pci%d", unit);
        sc->cdev->si_drv1 = ❻sc;

        return (0);
}
```

Here, ❶ dev describes a device under this driver's control. Thus, this function starts by getting dev's ❷ software context and ❸ unit number. Then a character device node is ❺ created and the variables sc->device and sc->cdev->si_drv1 are set to ❹ dev and ❻ sc, respectively.

NOTE   *The d_foo functions (described next) use sc->device and cdev->si_drv1 to gain access to dev and sc.*

d_foo Functions

Because every d_foo function in Listing 7-1 just prints a debug message (that is to say, they're all basically the same), I'm only going to walk through one of them: foo_pci_open.

```
static int
foo_pci_open(struct cdev ❶*dev, int oflags, int devtype, struct thread *td)
{
        struct foo_pci_softc *sc;

    ❷sc = dev->si_drv1;
    ❸device_printf(sc->device, "opened successfully\n");
        return (0);
}
```

Here, ❶ dev is the cdev returned by the make_dev call in foo_pci_attach. So, this function first ❷ obtains its software context. Then it ❸ prints a debug message.

foo_pci_detach Function

The foo_pci_detach function is the device_detach implementation for this driver. Here is its function definition (again):

```
static int
foo_pci_detach(device_t ❶dev)
{
        struct foo_pci_softc *sc = ❷device_get_softc(dev);

    ❸destroy_dev(sc->cdev);
        return (0);
}
```

Here, ❶ dev describes a device under this driver's control. Thus, this function simply obtains dev's ❷ software context to ❸ destroy its device node.

Don't Panic

Now that we've discussed Listing 7-1, let's give it a try:

```
$ sudo kldload ./foo_pci.ko
$ kldstat
Id Refs Address    Size    Name
 1    3 0xc0400000 c9f490  kernel
 2    1 0xc3af0000 2000    foo_pci.ko
$ ls -l /dev/foo*
ls: /dev/foo*: ❶No such file or directory
```

Of course, it ❶ fails miserably, because foo_pci_probe is probing for fictitious PCI devices. Before concluding this chapter, one additional topic bears mentioning.

Hardware Resource Management

As part of configuring and operating devices, a driver might need to manage hardware resources, such as interrupt-request lines (IRQs), I/O ports, or I/O memory (McKusick and Neville-Neil, 2005). Naturally, Newbus includes several functions for doing just that.

```
#include <sys/param.h>
#include <sys/bus.h>

#include <machine/bus.h>
#include <sys/rman.h>
#include <machine/resource.h>

struct resource *
bus_alloc_resource(device_t dev, int type, int *rid, u_long start,
    u_long end, u_long count, u_int flags);

struct resource *
bus_alloc_resource_any(device_t dev, int type, int *rid,
    u_int flags);

int
bus_activate_resource(device_t dev, int type, int rid,
    struct resource *r);

int
bus_deactivate_resource(device_t dev, int type, int rid,
    struct resource *r);

int
bus_release_resource(device_t dev, int type, int rid,
    struct resource *r);
```

The `bus_alloc_resource` function allocates hardware resources for a specific device to use. If successful, a `struct resource` pointer is returned; otherwise, `NULL` is returned. This function is normally called during `device_attach`. If it is called during `device_probe`, all allocated resources must be released (via `bus_release_resource`) before returning. Most of the arguments for `bus_alloc_resource` are common to the other hardware resource management functions. These arguments are described in the next few paragraphs.

The `dev` argument is the device that requires ownership of the hardware resource(s). Before allocation, resources are owned by the parent bus.

The `type` argument represents the type of resource `dev` wants allocated. Valid values for this argument are listed in Table 7-2.

Table 7-2: Symbolic Constants for Hardware Resources

Constant	Description
SYS_RES_IRQ	Interrupt-request line
SYS_RES_IOPORT	I/O port
SYS_RES_MEMORY	I/O memory

The `rid` argument expects a resource ID (RID). If `bus_alloc_resource` is successful, a RID is returned in `rid` that may differ from what you passed. You'll learn more about RIDs later.

The `start` and `end` arguments are the start and end addresses of the hardware resource(s). To employ the default bus values, simply pass `0ul` as `start` and `~0ul` as `end`.

The `count` argument denotes the size of the hardware resource(s). If you used the default bus values for `start` and `end`, `count` is used only if it is larger than the default bus value.

The `flags` argument details the characteristics of the hardware resource. Valid values for this argument are listed in Table 7-3.

Table 7-3: bus_alloc_resource Symbolic Constants

Constant	Description
RF_ALLOCATED	Allocate hardware resource, but don't activate it
RF_ACTIVE	Allocate hardware resource and activate resource automatically
RF_SHAREABLE	Hardware resource permits contemporaneous sharing; you should always set this flag, unless the resource cannot be shared
RF_TIMESHARE	Hardware resource permits time-division sharing

The `bus_alloc_resource_any` function is a convenience wrapper for `bus_alloc_resource` that sets `start`, `end`, and `count` to their default bus values.

The `bus_activate_resource` function activates a previously allocated hardware resource. Naturally, resources must be activated before they can be used. Most drivers simply pass `RF_ACTIVE` to `bus_alloc_resource` or `bus_alloc_resource_any` to avoid calling `bus_activate_resource`.

The bus_deactivate_resource function deactivates a hardware resource. This function is primarily used in bus drivers (so we'll never call it).

The bus_release_resource function releases a previously allocated hardware resource. Of course, the resource cannot be in use on release. If successful, 0 is returned; otherwise, the kernel panics.

NOTE *We'll cover an example that employs IRQs in Chapters 8 and 9, and I'll go over an example that requires I/O ports and I/O memory in Chapters 10 and 11.*

Conclusion

This chapter introduced you to the basics of Newbus driver development—working with real hardware. The remainder of this book builds upon the concepts described here to complete your understanding of Newbus.

8

INTERRUPT HANDLING

Hardware devices often have to perform (or deal with) external events, such as spinning disk platters, winding tapes, waiting for I/O, and so on. Most of these external events occur in a timeframe that is much slower than the processor's—that is, if the processor were to wait for the completion (or arrival) of these events, it would be idle for some time. To avoid wasting the processor's valuable time, interrupts are employed. An *interrupt* is simply a signal that a hardware device can send when it wants the processor's attention (Corbet et al., 2005). For the most part, a driver only needs to register a handler function to service its device's interrupts.

Registering an Interrupt Handler

The following functions, declared in <sys/bus.h>, register or tear down an interrupt handler:

```
#include <sys/param.h>
#include <sys/bus.h>
```

```
int
bus_setup_intr(device_t dev, struct resource *r, int flags,
    driver_filter_t filter, driver_intr_t ithread, void *arg,
    void **cookiep);

int
bus_teardown_intr(device_t dev, struct resource *r, void *cookiep);
```

The bus_setup_intr function registers an interrupt handler with an IRQ. This IRQ must be allocated beforehand with bus_alloc_resource, as described in "Hardware Resource Management" on page 122.

The bus_setup_intr function is normally called during device_attach. The arguments for this function are described in the next few paragraphs.

The dev argument is the device whose interrupts are to be handled. This device must have an IRQ.

The r argument demands the return value from the successful bus_alloc_resource call that assigned an IRQ for dev.

The flags argument classifies the interrupt handler and/or the interrupt. Valid values for this argument are defined in the intr_type enumeration, found in <sys/bus.h>. Table 8-1 describes the more commonly used values.

Table 8-1: bus_setup_intr Symbolic Constants

Constant	Description
INTR_MPSAFE	Indicates that the interrupt handler is multiprocessor safe and does not need to be protected by Giant—that is, any race conditions are to be handled by the interrupt handler itself; contemporary code should always pass this flag
INTR_ENTROPY	Indicates that the interrupt is a good source of entropy and may be employed by the entropy device /dev/random

The filter and ithread arguments specify the filter and ithread routines for the interrupt handler. For now, don't worry about these arguments; I'll discuss them in the following section.

The arg argument is the sole argument that gets passed to the interrupt handler. Generally, you'll always set arg to dev's software context.

The cookiep argument expects a pointer to void *. If bus_setup_intr is successful, a cookie is returned in cookiep; this cookie is needed to destroy the interrupt handler.

As you would expect, the bus_teardown_intr function tears down an interrupt handler.

Interrupt Handlers in FreeBSD

Now that you know how to register an interrupt handler, let's discuss how interrupt handlers are implemented.

In FreeBSD, interrupt handlers are composed of a filter routine, an ithread routine, or both. A *filter routine* executes in primary interrupt context (that is, it does not have its own context). Thus, it cannot block or context switch, and it can use only spin mutexes for synchronization. Due to these constraints, filter routines are typically used only with devices that require a nonpreemptive interrupt handler.

A filter routine may either completely handle an interrupt or defer the computationally expensive work to its associated ithread routine, assuming it has one. Table 8-2 details the values that a filter routine can return.

Table 8-2: Filter Routine Return Values

Constant	Description
FILTER_STRAY	Indicates that the filter routine can't handle this interrupt; this value is equivalent to an error code.
FILTER_HANDLED	Indicates that the interrupt has been completely handled; this value is equivalent to a success code.
FILTER_SCHEDULE_THREAD	Schedules the ithread routine to execute; this value can be returned if and only if the filter routine has an associated ithread routine.

An *ithread routine,* unlike a filter routine, executes in its own thread context. You can do whatever you want in an ithread routine, except voluntarily context switch (that is, sleep) or wait on a condition variable. Because filter routines are nonpreemptive, most interrupt handlers in FreeBSD are just ithread routines.

Implementing an Interrupt Handler

Listing 8-1 is a contrived Newbus driver designed to demonstrate interrupt handlers. Listing 8-1 sets up an interrupt handler on the parallel port; on read, it sleeps until it receives an interrupt.

NOTE   *Take a quick look at this code and try to discern some of its structure. If you don't understand all of it, don't worry; an explanation follows.*

```
#include <sys/param.h>
#include <sys/module.h>
#include <sys/kernel.h>
#include <sys/systm.h>

#include <sys/conf.h>
#include <sys/uio.h>
#include <sys/bus.h>
#include <sys/malloc.h>

#include <machine/bus.h>
#include <sys/rman.h>
#include <machine/resource.h>

#include <dev/ppbus/ppbconf.h>
#include "ppbus_if.h"
#include <dev/ppbus/ppbio.h>
```

```
#define PINT_NAME               "pint"
#define BUFFER_SIZE             256

struct pint_data {
        int                     sc_irq_rid;
        struct resource         *sc_irq_resource;
        void                    *sc_irq_cookie;
        device_t                sc_device;
        struct cdev             *sc_cdev;
        short                   sc_state;
#define PINT_OPEN               0x01
        char                    *sc_buffer;
        int                     sc_length;
};

static d_open_t                 pint_open;
static d_close_t                pint_close;
static d_read_t                 pint_read;
static d_write_t                pint_write;

static struct cdevsw pint_cdevsw = {
        .d_version =            D_VERSION,
        .d_open =               pint_open,
        .d_close =              pint_close,
        .d_read =               pint_read,
        .d_write =              pint_write,
        .d_name =               PINT_NAME
};

static devclass_t pint_devclass;

static int
pint_open(struct cdev *dev, int oflags, int devtype, struct thread *td)
{
        struct pint_data *sc = dev->si_drv1;
        device_t pint_device = sc->sc_device;
        device_t ppbus = device_get_parent(pint_device);
        int error;

        ppb_lock(ppbus);

        if (sc->sc_state) {
                ppb_unlock(ppbus);
                return (EBUSY);
        } else
                sc->sc_state |= PINT_OPEN;

        error = ppb_request_bus(ppbus, pint_device, PPB_WAIT | PPB_INTR);
        if (error) {
                sc->sc_state = 0;
                ppb_unlock(ppbus);
                return (error);
        }
```

```
        ppb_wctr(ppbus, 0);
        ppb_wctr(ppbus, IRQENABLE);

        ppb_unlock(ppbus);
        return (0);
}

static int
pint_close(struct cdev *dev, int fflag, int devtype, struct thread *td)
{
        struct pint_data *sc = dev->si_drv1;
        device_t pint_device = sc->sc_device;
        device_t ppbus = device_get_parent(pint_device);

        ppb_lock(ppbus);

        ppb_wctr(ppbus, 0);
        ppb_release_bus(ppbus, pint_device);
        sc->sc_state = 0;

        ppb_unlock(ppbus);
        return (0);
}

static int
pint_write(struct cdev *dev, struct uio *uio, int ioflag)
{
        struct pint_data *sc = dev->si_drv1;
        device_t pint_device = sc->sc_device;
        int amount, error = 0;

        amount = MIN(uio->uio_resid,
            (BUFFER_SIZE - 1 - uio->uio_offset > 0) ?
             BUFFER_SIZE - 1 - uio->uio_offset : 0);
        if (amount == 0)
                return (error);

        error = uiomove(sc->sc_buffer, amount, uio);
        if (error) {
                device_printf(pint_device, "write failed\n");
                return (error);
        }

        sc->sc_buffer[amount] = '\0';
        sc->sc_length = amount;

        return (error);
}

static int
pint_read(struct cdev *dev, struct uio *uio, int ioflag)
{
        struct pint_data *sc = dev->si_drv1;
        device_t pint_device = sc->sc_device;
        device_t ppbus = device_get_parent(pint_device);
```

```
                int amount, error = 0;

                ppb_lock(ppbus);
                error = ppb_sleep(ppbus, pint_device, PPBPRI | PCATCH, PINT_NAME, 0);
                ppb_unlock(ppbus);
                if (error)
                        return (error);

                amount = MIN(uio->uio_resid,
                    (sc->sc_length - uio->uio_offset > 0) ?
                     sc->sc_length - uio->uio_offset : 0);

                error = uiomove(sc->sc_buffer + uio->uio_offset, amount, uio);
                if (error)
                        device_printf(pint_device, "read failed\n");

                return (error);
        }

static void
pint_intr(void *arg)
{
        struct pint_data *sc = arg;
        device_t pint_device = sc->sc_device;

#ifdef INVARIANTS
        device_t ppbus = device_get_parent(pint_device);
        ppb_assert_locked(ppbus);
#endif

        wakeup(pint_device);
}

static void
pint_identify(driver_t *driver, device_t parent)
{
        device_t dev;

        dev = device_find_child(parent, PINT_NAME, -1);
        if (!dev)
                BUS_ADD_CHILD(parent, 0, PINT_NAME, -1);
}

static int
pint_probe(device_t dev)
{
        /* probe() is always OK. */
        device_set_desc(dev, "Interrupt Handler Example");

        return (BUS_PROBE_SPECIFIC);
}

static int
pint_attach(device_t dev)
{
```

```
        struct pint_data *sc = device_get_softc(dev);
        int error, unit = device_get_unit(dev);

        /* Declare our interrupt handler. */
        sc->sc_irq_rid = 0;
        sc->sc_irq_resource = bus_alloc_resource_any(dev, SYS_RES_IRQ,
            &sc->sc_irq_rid, RF_ACTIVE | RF_SHAREABLE);

        /* Interrupts are mandatory. */
        if (!sc->sc_irq_resource) {
                device_printf(dev,
                    "unable to allocate interrupt resource\n");
                return (ENXIO);
        }

        /* Register our interrupt handler. */
        error = bus_setup_intr(dev, sc->sc_irq_resource,
            INTR_TYPE_TTY | INTR_MPSAFE, NULL, pint_intr,
            sc, &sc->sc_irq_cookie);
        if (error) {
                bus_release_resource(dev, SYS_RES_IRQ, sc->sc_irq_rid,
                    sc->sc_irq_resource);
                device_printf(dev, "unable to register interrupt handler\n");
                return (error);
        }

        sc->sc_buffer = malloc(BUFFER_SIZE, M_DEVBUF, M_WAITOK);

        sc->sc_device = dev;
        sc->sc_cdev = make_dev(&pint_cdevsw, unit, UID_ROOT, GID_WHEEL, 0600,
            PINT_NAME "%d", unit);
        sc->sc_cdev->si_drv1 = sc;

        return (0);
}

static int
pint_detach(device_t dev)
{
        struct pint_data *sc = device_get_softc(dev);

        destroy_dev(sc->sc_cdev);

        bus_teardown_intr(dev, sc->sc_irq_resource, sc->sc_irq_cookie);
        bus_release_resource(dev, SYS_RES_IRQ, sc->sc_irq_rid,
            sc->sc_irq_resource);

        free(sc->sc_buffer, M_DEVBUF);

        return (0);
}

static device_method_t pint_methods[] = {
        /* Device interface. */
        DEVMETHOD(device_identify,      pint_identify),
```

```
        DEVMETHOD(device_probe,        pint_probe),
        DEVMETHOD(device_attach,       pint_attach),
        DEVMETHOD(device_detach,       pint_detach),
        { 0, 0 }
};

static driver_t pint_driver = {
        PINT_NAME,
        pint_methods,
        sizeof(struct pint_data)
};

DRIVER_MODULE(pint, ppbus, pint_driver, pint_devclass, 0, 0);
MODULE_DEPEND(pint, ppbus, 1, 1, 1);
```

Listing 8-1: pint.c

To make things easier to understand, I'll describe the functions in Listing 8-1 in the order they were written, instead of in the order they appear. To that end, I'll begin with the pint_identify function.

pint_identify Function

The pint_identify function is the device_identify implementation for this driver. Logically, this function is required because the parallel port cannot identify its children unaided.

Here is the function definition for pint_identify (again):

```
static void
pint_identify(driver_t *driver, device_t parent)
{
        device_t dev;

        dev = ❶device_find_child(parent, ❷PINT_NAME, -1);
        if (!dev)
                ❸BUS_ADD_CHILD(parent, 0, PINT_NAME, -1);
}
```

This function first ❶ determines whether the parallel port has (ever) identified a child device named ❷ PINT_NAME. If it has not, then pint_identify ❸ adds PINT_NAME to the parallel port's list of identified children.

pint_probe Function

The pint_probe function is the device_probe implementation for this driver. Here is its function definition (again):

```
static int
pint_probe(device_t dev)
{
        /* probe() is always OK. */
        device_set_desc(dev, "Interrupt Handler Example");
```

```
❶return (BUS_PROBE_SPECIFIC);
}
```

As you can see, this function always ❶ returns the success code
BUS_PROBE_SPECIFIC, so Listing 8-1 attaches to every device it probes. This
may seem erroneous, but it is the correct behavior, as devices identified by
a device_identify routine, using BUS_ADD_CHILD, are probed only by drivers with
the same name. In this case, the identified device and driver name is PINT_NAME.

pint_attach Function

The pint_attach function is the device_attach implementation for this driver.
Here is its function definition (again):

```
static int
pint_attach(device_t dev)
{
        struct pint_data *sc = device_get_softc(dev);
        int error, unit = device_get_unit(dev);

        /* Declare our interrupt handler. */
        sc->sc_irq_rid = 0;
        sc->sc_irq_resource = ❶bus_alloc_resource_any(dev, SYS_RES_IRQ,
            &sc->sc_irq_rid, RF_ACTIVE | RF_SHAREABLE);

        /* Interrupts are mandatory. */
        if (!sc->sc_irq_resource) {
                device_printf(dev,
                    "unable to allocate interrupt resource\n");
            ❷return (ENXIO);
        }

        /* Register our interrupt handler. */
        error = ❸bus_setup_intr(dev, sc->sc_irq_resource,
            INTR_TYPE_TTY | INTR_MPSAFE, NULL, ❹pint_intr,
            sc, &sc->sc_irq_cookie);
        if (error) {
                bus_release_resource(dev, SYS_RES_IRQ, sc->sc_irq_rid,
                    sc->sc_irq_resource);
                device_printf(dev, "unable to register interrupt handler\n");
                return (error);
        }

        sc->sc_buffer = ❺malloc(BUFFER_SIZE, M_DEVBUF, M_WAITOK);

    ❻sc->sc_device = dev;
        sc->sc_cdev = ❼make_dev(&pint_cdevsw, unit, UID_ROOT, GID_WHEEL,
            0600, PINT_NAME "%d", unit);
    ❽sc->sc_cdev->si_drv1 = sc;

        return (0);
}
```

This function first ❶ allocates an IRQ. If unsuccessful, the error code ENXIO (which stands for *error: device not configured*) is ❷ returned. Next, the ❹ pint_intr function is ❸ set up as the interrupt handler for dev (in this case, the interrupt handler is just an ithread routine). Afterward, a buffer of BUFFER_SIZE bytes is ❺ allocated. Then sc->sc_device is ❻ set to dev, Listing 8-1's character device node is ❼ created, and a pointer to the software context (sc) is ❽ saved in sc->sc_cdev->si_drv1.

pint_detach Function

The pint_detach function is the device_detach implementation for this driver. Here is its function definition (again):

```
static int
pint_detach(device_t dev)
{
        struct pint_data *sc = device_get_softc(dev);

    ❶destroy_dev(sc->sc_cdev);

    ❷bus_teardown_intr(dev, sc->sc_irq_resource, sc->sc_irq_cookie);
    ❸bus_release_resource(dev, SYS_RES_IRQ, sc->sc_irq_rid,
            sc->sc_irq_resource);

    ❹free(sc->sc_buffer, M_DEVBUF);

        return (0);
}
```

This function starts by ❶ destroying Listing 8-1's device node. Once this is done, it ❷ tears down dev's interrupt handler, ❸ releases dev's IRQ, and ❹ frees the allocated memory.

pint_open Function

The pint_open function is defined in pint_cdevsw (that is, Listing 8-1's character device switch table) as the d_open operation. Recall that d_open operations prepare the device for I/O.

Here is the function definition for pint_open (again):

```
static int
pint_open(struct cdev *dev, int oflags, int devtype, struct thread *td)
{
        struct pint_data *sc = dev->si_drv1;
        device_t pint_device = sc->sc_device;
        device_t ppbus = device_get_parent(pint_device);
        int error;

    ❶ppb_lock(ppbus);

    ❷if (sc->sc_state) {
                ppb_unlock(ppbus);
```

```
        ❸return (EBUSY);
    } else
        ❹sc->sc_state |= PINT_OPEN;

    error = ❺ppb_request_bus(ppbus, pint_device, PPB_WAIT | PPB_INTR);
    if (error) {
        sc->sc_state = 0;
        ppb_unlock(ppbus);
        return (error);
    }

❻ppb_wctr(ppbus, 0);
❼ppb_wctr(ppbus, IRQENABLE);

    ppb_unlock(ppbus);
    return (0);
}
```

This function first ❶ acquires the parallel port mutex. Then the value of sc->sc_state is ❷ examined. If it does not equal 0, which indicates that another process has opened the device, the error code EBUSY is ❸ returned; otherwise, pint_open ❹ "opens" the device. Opening the device, in this case, means setting sc->sc_state to PINT_OPEN. Afterward, the ppb_request_bus function is ❺ called to mark pint_device as the owner of the parallel port. Naturally, pint_device is our device (that is, it points to dev from pint_attach).

NOTE   *Owning the parallel port lets a device transfer data to and from it.*

Finally, before ❼ enabling interrupts, pint_open ❻ clears the parallel port's control register.

pint_close Function

The pint_close function is defined in pint_cdevsw as the d_close operation. Here is its function definition (again):

```
static int
pint_close(struct cdev *dev, int fflag, int devtype, struct thread *td)
{
        struct pint_data *sc = dev->si_drv1;
        device_t pint_device = sc->sc_device;
        device_t ppbus = device_get_parent(pint_device);

    ❶ppb_lock(ppbus);

    ❷ppb_wctr(ppbus, 0);
    ❸ppb_release_bus(ppbus, pint_device);
    ❹sc->sc_state = 0;

        ppb_unlock(ppbus);
        return (0);
}
```

This function first ❶ acquires the parallel port mutex. Then interrupts on the parallel port are ❷ disabled (for all intents and purposes, clearing the control register, which is what the above code does, disables interrupts). Next, the `ppb_release_bus` function is ❸ called to relinquish ownership of the parallel port. Finally, `sc->sc_state` is ❹ zeroed, so that another process can open this device.

pint_write Function

The `pint_write` function is defined in `pint_cdevsw` as the `d_write` operation. This function acquires a character string from user space and stores it.

Here is the function definition for `pint_write` (again):

```
static int
pint_write(struct cdev *dev, struct uio *uio, int ioflag)
{
        struct pint_data *sc = dev->si_drv1;
        device_t pint_device = sc->sc_device;
        int amount, error = 0;

        amount = MIN(uio->uio_resid,
            (BUFFER_SIZE - 1 - uio->uio_offset > 0) ?
            BUFFER_SIZE - 1 - uio->uio_offset : 0);
        if (amount == 0)
                return (error);

        error = uiomove(sc->sc_buffer, amount, uio);
        if (error) {
                device_printf(pint_device, "write failed\n");
                return (error);
        }

        sc->sc_buffer[amount] = '\0';
        sc->sc_length = amount;

        return (error);
}
```

This function is fundamentally identical to the `echo_write` function described on page 34. Consequently, I won't walk through it again here.

pint_read Function

The `pint_read` function is defined in `pint_cdevsw` as the `d_read` operation. This function sleeps on entry. It also returns the stored character string to user space.

Here is the function definition for `pint_read` (again):

```
static int
pint_read(struct cdev *dev, struct uio *uio, int ioflag)
{
```

```
        struct pint_data *sc = dev->si_drv1;
        device_t pint_device = sc->sc_device;
        device_t ppbus = device_get_parent(pint_device);
        int amount, error = 0;

    ❶ppb_lock(ppbus);
        error = ❷ppb_sleep(ppbus, ❸pint_device, PPBPRI | PCATCH,
            PINT_NAME, 0);
        ppb_unlock(ppbus);
        if (error)
                return (error);

        amount = MIN(uio->uio_resid,
            (sc->sc_length - uio->uio_offset > 0) ?
            sc->sc_length - uio->uio_offset : 0);

        error = uiomove(sc->sc_buffer + uio->uio_offset, amount, uio);
        if (error)
                device_printf(pint_device, "read failed\n");

        return (error);
}
```

This function begins by ❶ acquiring the parallel port mutex. Then it ❷ sleeps on the channel ❸ pint_device.

NOTE   *The ppb_sleep function releases the parallel port mutex before sleeping. Of course, it also reacquires the parallel port mutex before returning to its caller.*

The remnants of this function are basically identical to the echo_read function described on page 13, so we won't discuss them again here.

pint_intr Function

The pint_intr function is the interrupt handler for Listing 8-1. Here is its function definition (again):

```
static void
pint_intr(void *arg)
{
        struct pint_data *sc = arg;
        device_t pint_device = sc->sc_device;

#ifdef INVARIANTS
        device_t ppbus = device_get_parent(pint_device);
        ppb_assert_locked(ppbus);
#endif

    ❶wakeup(pint_device);
}
```

As you can see, this function simply ❶ wakes up every thread sleeping on pint_device.

NOTE *Parallel port interrupt handlers are unique, because they get invoked with the parallel port mutex already held. Conversely, normal interrupt handlers need to explicitly acquire their own locks.*

Don't Panic

Now that we've walked through Listing 8-1, let's give it a try:

```
$ sudo kldload ./pint.ko
$ su
Password:
# echo "DON'T PANIC" > /dev/pint0
# cat /dev/pint0 &
[1] 954
# ps | head -n 1 && ps | grep "cat"
  PID  TT  STAT      TIME COMMAND
  954  v1  I       0:00.03 cat /dev/pint0
```

Apparently it works. But how do we generate an interrupt to test our interrupt handler?

Generating Interrupts on the Parallel Port

Once interrupts are enabled, the parallel port generates an interrupt whenever the electrical signal at pin 10, dubbed the *ACK bit*, changes from low to high (Corbet et al., 2005).

To toggle the electrical signal at pin 10, I connected pin 10 to pin 9 (using a resistor) and then I executed the program shown in Listing 8-2.

```
#include <sys/types.h>
#include <machine/cpufunc.h>

#include <err.h>
#include <fcntl.h>
#include <stdio.h>
#include <stdlib.h>
#include <unistd.h>

❶ #define BASE_ADDRESS    0x378

int
main(int argc, char *argv[])
{
        int fd;

        fd = open("/dev/io", O_RDWR);
        if (fd < 0)
                err(1, "open(/dev/io)");

        outb(BASE_ADDRESS, ❷0x00);
        outb(BASE_ADDRESS, ❸0xff);
        outb(BASE_ADDRESS, 0x00);
```

```
        close(fd);
        return (0);
}
```

Listing 8-2: tint.c

Here, ❶ BASE_ADDRESS denotes the base address of the parallel port. On most contemporary PCs, 0x378 is the base address of the parallel port. However, you can check your machine's BIOS to be sure.

This program changes the electrical signal at pin 9 of the parallel port from ❷ low to ❸ high.

NOTE *If you're curious, pin 9 is the most significant bit of the parallel data byte (Corbet et al., 2005).*

Here are the results from executing Listing 8-2:

```
# echo "DON'T PANIC" > /dev/pint0
# cat /dev/pint0 &
[1] 1056
# ./tint
DON'T PANIC
```

Conclusion

This chapter focused primarily on implementing an interrupt handler. In Chapter 9, we'll build upon the concepts and code described here to write a nontrivial, interrupt-driven driver.

9

CASE STUDY: PARALLEL PORT PRINTER DRIVER

This chapter is the second case study in this book. In this chapter, we'll go through lpt(4), the parallel port printer driver. lpt(4), by default, is configured to be interrupt-driven, which gives us an opportunity to go through a nontrivial interrupt handler. Aside from this, I chose to profile lpt(4) because it uses almost every topic described in the previous chapters. It's also relatively short.

NOTE   *To improve readability, some of the variables and functions presented in this chapter have been renamed and restructured from their counterparts in the FreeBSD source.*

Code Analysis

Listing 9-1 provides a terse, source-level overview of lpt(4).

```
#include <sys/param.h>
#include <sys/module.h>
```

```
#include <sys/kernel.h>
#include <sys/systm.h>

#include <sys/conf.h>
#include <sys/uio.h>
#include <sys/bus.h>
#include <sys/malloc.h>
#include <sys/syslog.h>

#include <machine/bus.h>
#include <sys/rman.h>
#include <machine/resource.h>

#include <dev/ppbus/ppbconf.h>
#include "ppbus_if.h"
#include <dev/ppbus/ppbio.h>
#include <dev/ppbus/ppb_1284.h>

#include <dev/ppbus/lpt.h>
#include <dev/ppbus/lptio.h>

#define LPT_NAME        "lpt"           /* official driver name.       */
#define LPT_INIT_READY  4               /* wait up to 4 seconds.       */
#define LPT_PRI         (PZERO + 8)     /* priority.                   */
#define BUF_SIZE        1024            /* sc_buf size.                */
#define BUF_STAT_SIZE   32              /* sc_buf_stat size.           */

struct lpt_data {
        short               sc_state;
        char                sc_primed;
        struct callout      sc_callout;
        u_char              sc_ticks;
        int                 sc_irq_rid;
        struct resource     *sc_irq_resource;
        void                *sc_irq_cookie;
        u_short             sc_irq_status;
        void                *sc_buf;
        void                *sc_buf_stat;
        char                *sc_cp;
        device_t            sc_dev;
        struct cdev         *sc_cdev;
        struct cdev         *sc_cdev_bypass;
        char                sc_flags;
        u_char              sc_control;
        short               sc_transfer_count;
};

/* bits for sc_state. */
#define LP_OPEN         (1 << 0)        /* device is open.             */
#define LP_ERROR        (1 << 2)        /* error received from printer. */
#define LP_BUSY         (1 << 3)        /* printer is busy writing.    */
#define LP_TIMEOUT      (1 << 5)        /* timeout enabled.            */
#define LP_INIT         (1 << 6)        /* initializing in lpt_open.   */
#define LP_INTERRUPTED  (1 << 7)        /* write call was interrupted. */
#define LP_HAVEBUS      (1 << 8)        /* driver owns the bus.        */
```

```c
/* bits for sc_ticks. */
#define LP_TOUT_INIT    10              /* initial timeout: 1/10 sec.   */
#define LP_TOUT_MAX     1               /* max timeout: 1/1 sec.        */

/* bits for sc_irq_status. */
#define LP_HAS_IRQ      0x01            /* we have an IRQ available.    */
#define LP_USE_IRQ      0x02            /* our IRQ is in use.           */
#define LP_ENABLE_IRQ   0x04            /* enable our IRQ on open.      */
#define LP_ENABLE_EXT   0x10            /* enable extended mode.        */

/* bits for sc_flags. */
#define LP_NO_PRIME     0x10            /* don't prime the printer.     */
#define LP_PRIME_OPEN   0x20            /* prime on every open.         */
#define LP_AUTO_LF      0x40            /* automatic line feed.         */
#define LP_BYPASS       0x80            /* bypass printer ready checks. */

/* masks to interrogate printer status. */
#define LP_READY_MASK   (LPS_NERR | LPS_SEL | LPS_OUT | LPS_NBSY)
#define LP_READY        (LPS_NERR | LPS_SEL |            LPS_NBSY)

/* used in polling code. */
#define LPS_INVERT      (LPS_NERR | LPS_SEL |            LPS_NACK | LPS_NBSY)
#define LPS_MASK        (LPS_NERR | LPS_SEL | LPS_OUT | LPS_NACK | LPS_NBSY)
#define NOT_READY(bus)  ((ppb_rstr(bus) ^ LPS_INVERT) & LPS_MASK)
#define MAX_SPIN        20             /* wait up to 20 usec.          */
#define MAX_SLEEP       (hz * 5)       /* timeout while waiting.       */

static d_open_t                 lpt_open;
static d_close_t                lpt_close;
static d_read_t                 lpt_read;
static d_write_t                lpt_write;
static d_ioctl_t                lpt_ioctl;

static struct cdevsw lpt_cdevsw = {
        .d_version =            D_VERSION,
        .d_open =               lpt_open,
        .d_close =              lpt_close,
        .d_read =               lpt_read,
        .d_write =              lpt_write,
        .d_ioctl =              lpt_ioctl,
        .d_name =               LPT_NAME
};

static devclass_t lpt_devclass;

static void
lpt_identify(driver_t *driver, device_t parent)
{
...
}

static int
lpt_request_ppbus(device_t dev, int how)
{
```

```c
...
}

static int
lpt_release_ppbus(device_t dev)
{
...
}

static int
lpt_port_test(device_t ppbus, u_char data, u_char mask)
{
...
}

static int
lpt_detect(device_t dev)
{
...
}

static int
lpt_probe(device_t dev)
{
...
}

static void
lpt_intr(void *arg)
{
...
}

static int
lpt_attach(device_t dev)
{
...
}

static int
lpt_detach(device_t dev)
{
...
}

static void
lpt_timeout(void *arg)
{
...
}

static int
lpt_open(struct cdev *dev, int oflags, int devtype, struct thread *td)
```

```
{
...
}

static int
lpt_close(struct cdev *dev, int fflag, int devtype, struct thread *td)
{
...
}

static int
lpt_read(struct cdev *dev, struct uio *uio, int ioflag)
{
...
}

static int
lpt_push_bytes(struct lpt_data *sc)
{
...
}

static int
lpt_write(struct cdev *dev, struct uio *uio, int ioflag)
{
...
}

static int
lpt_ioctl(struct cdev *dev, u_long cmd, caddr_t data, int fflag,
    struct thread *td)
{
...
}

static device_method_t lpt_methods[] = {
        DEVMETHOD(device_identify,      lpt_identify),
        DEVMETHOD(device_probe,         lpt_probe),
        DEVMETHOD(device_attach,        lpt_attach),
        DEVMETHOD(device_detach,        lpt_detach),
        { 0, 0 }
};

static driver_t lpt_driver = {
        LPT_NAME,
        lpt_methods,
        sizeof(struct lpt_data)
};

DRIVER_MODULE(lpt, ppbus, lpt_driver, lpt_devclass, 0, 0);
MODULE_DEPEND(lpt, ppbus, 1, 1, 1);
```

Listing 9-1: lpt.c

Listing 9-1 is provided as a convenience; as I go through the code for lpt(4) you can refer to it to see how lpt(4)'s functions and structures are laid out.

To make things easier to follow, I'll analyze the functions in lpt(4) in the approximate order they would execute in (rather than in the order they appear). To that end, I'll begin with the lpt_identify function.

lpt_identify Function

The lpt_identify function is the device_identify implementation for lpt(4). Logically, this function is required because the parallel port cannot identify its children unaided.

Here is the function definition for lpt_identify:

```
static void
lpt_identify(driver_t *driver, device_t parent)
{
        device_t dev;

        dev = ❶device_find_child(parent, ❷LPT_NAME, -1);
        if (!dev)
                ❸BUS_ADD_CHILD(parent, 0, LPT_NAME, -1);
}
```

This function first ❶ determines whether the parallel port has (ever) identified a child device named ❷ LPT_NAME. If it has not, then lpt_identify ❸ adds LPT_NAME to the parallel port's list of identified children.

lpt_probe Function

The lpt_probe function is the device_probe implementation for lpt(4). Here is its function definition:

```
static int
lpt_probe(device_t dev)
{
        if (!❶lpt_detect(dev))
                return (ENXIO);

        device_set_desc(dev, "Printer");

        return (BUS_PROBE_SPECIFIC);
}
```

This function simply calls ❶ lpt_detect to detect (that is, probe for) the presence of a printer.

lpt_detect Function

As mentioned in the previous section, lpt_detect detects the presence of a printer. It works by writing to the parallel port's data register. If a printer is present, it can read back the value just written.

Here is the function definition for lpt_detect:

```
static int
lpt_detect(device_t dev)
{
        device_t ppbus = device_get_parent(dev);
❶       static u_char test[18] = {
                0x55,                   /* alternating zeros.   */
                0xaa,                   /* alternating ones.    */
                0xfe, 0xfd, 0xfb, 0xf7,
                0xef, 0xdf, 0xbf, 0x7f, /* walking zero.        */
                0x01, 0x02, 0x04, 0x08,
                0x10, 0x20, 0x40, 0x80  /* walking one.         */
        };
        int i, error, success = 1;      /* assume success.      */

❷       ppb_lock(ppbus);

        error = ❸lpt_request_ppbus(dev, PPB_DONTWAIT);
        if (error) {
                ppb_unlock(ppbus);
                device_printf(dev, "cannot allocate ppbus (%d)!\n", error);
                return (0);
        }

        for (i = 0; i < 18; i++)
                if (!❹lpt_port_test(ppbus, test[i], 0xff)) {
                        success = 0;
                        break;
                }

❺       ppb_wdtr(ppbus, 0);
❻       ppb_wctr(ppbus, 0);

❼       lpt_release_ppbus(dev);
❽       ppb_unlock(ppbus);

        return (success);
}
```

This function first ❷ acquires the parallel port mutex. Next, lpt(4) is ❸ assigned ownership of the parallel port. Then ❹ lpt_port_test is called to write to and read from the parallel port's data register. The values written to this 8-bit register are housed in ❶ test[] and are designed to toggle all 8 bits.

Once this is done, the parallel port's ❺ data and ❻ control registers are cleared, ownership of the parallel port is ❼ relinquished, and the parallel port mutex is ❽ released.

lpt_port_test Function

The lpt_port_test function is called by lpt_detect to determine whether a printer is present. Here is its function definition:

```
static int
lpt_port_test(device_t ppbus, ❶u_char data, u_char mask)
{
        int temp, timeout = 10000;

        data &= mask;
    ❷ppb_wdtr(ppbus, data);

        do {
                DELAY(10);
                temp = ❸ppb_rdtr(ppbus) & mask;
        } while (temp != data && --timeout);

    ❹return (temp == data);
}
```

This function takes an ❶ 8-bit value and ❷ writes it to the parallel port's data register. Then it ❸ reads from that register and ❹ returns whether the value written and read match.

lpt_attach Function

The lpt_attach function is the device_attach implementation for lpt(4). Here is its function definition:

```
static int
lpt_attach(device_t dev)
{
        device_t ppbus = device_get_parent(dev);
        struct lpt_data *sc = device_get_softc(dev);
        int error, unit = device_get_unit(dev);

    ❶sc->sc_primed = 0;
    ❷ppb_init_callout(ppbus, &sc->sc_callout, 0);

        ppb_lock(ppbus);
        error = lpt_request_ppbus(dev, PPB_DONTWAIT);
        if (error) {
                ppb_unlock(ppbus);
                device_printf(dev, "cannot allocate ppbus (%d)!\n", error);
                return (0);
        }
```

```
❸ppb_wctr(ppbus, LPC_NINIT);

    lpt_release_ppbus(dev);
    ppb_unlock(ppbus);

    /* Declare our interrupt handler. */
    sc->sc_irq_rid = 0;
    sc->sc_irq_resource = bus_alloc_resource_any(dev, SYS_RES_IRQ,
        &sc->sc_irq_rid, RF_ACTIVE | RF_SHAREABLE);

    /* Register our interrupt handler. */
    if (sc->sc_irq_resource) {
            error = bus_setup_intr(dev, sc->sc_irq_resource,
                INTR_TYPE_TTY | INTR_MPSAFE, NULL, ❹lpt_intr,
                sc, &sc->sc_irq_cookie);
            if (error) {
                    bus_release_resource(dev, SYS_RES_IRQ,
                        sc->sc_irq_rid, sc->sc_irq_resource);
                    device_printf(dev,
                        "unable to register interrupt handler\n");
                    return (error);
            }

        ❺sc->sc_irq_status = LP_HAS_IRQ | LP_USE_IRQ | LP_ENABLE_IRQ;
            device_printf(dev, "interrupt-driven port\n");
    } else {
            sc->sc_irq_status = 0;
            device_printf(dev, "polled port\n");
    }

❻sc->sc_buf = malloc(BUF_SIZE, M_DEVBUF, M_WAITOK);
❼sc->sc_buf_stat = malloc(BUF_STAT_SIZE, M_DEVBUF, M_WAITOK);

    sc->sc_dev = dev;

    sc->sc_cdev = make_dev(&lpt_cdevsw, unit, UID_ROOT, GID_WHEEL, 0600,
        LPT_NAME "%d", unit);
    sc->sc_cdev->si_drv1 = sc;
    sc->sc_cdev->si_drv2 = 0;

    sc->sc_cdev_bypass = make_dev(&lpt_cdevsw, unit, UID_ROOT, GID_WHEEL,
        0600, LPT_NAME "%d.ctl", unit);
    sc->sc_cdev_bypass->si_drv1 = sc;
    sc->sc_cdev_bypass->si_drv2 = (void *)❽LP_BYPASS;

    return (0);
}
```

This function can be split into five parts. The first ❶ sets sc->sc_primed to 0 to indicate that the printer needs to be primed. It also ❷ initializes lpt(4)'s callout structure. The second part essentially ❸ changes the electrical signal at pin 16, dubbed *nINIT*, from high to low causing the printer to initiate an internal reset.

As most signals are active high, the n *in* nINIT *denotes that the signal is active low.*

The third part registers the function ❹ lpt_intr as the interrupt handler. If successful, the variable sc->sc_irq_status is ❺ assigned LP_HAS_IRQ, LP_USE_IRQ, and LP_ENABLE_IRQ to indicate that the printer is interrupt-driven. The fourth part allocates memory for two buffers: ❻ sc->sc_buf (which will maintain the data to be printed) and ❼ sc->sc_buf_stat (which will maintain the printer's status). Finally, the fifth part creates lpt(4)'s device nodes: lpt%d and lpt%d.ctl, where %d is the unit number. Note that lpt%d.ctl contains the ❽ LP_BYPASS flag, while lpt%d does not. In the d_foo functions, LP_BYPASS is used to tell lpt%d.ctl from lpt%d. As you'll see, the lpt%d device node represents the printer, while lpt%d.ctl is used solely to change the printer's mode of operation (via lpt(4)'s d_ioctl routine).

lpt_detach Function

The lpt_detach function is the device_detach implementation for lpt(4). Here is its function definition:

```
static int
lpt_detach(device_t dev)
{
        device_t ppbus = device_get_parent(dev);
        struct lpt_data *sc = device_get_softc(dev);

❶destroy_dev(sc->sc_cdev_bypass);
❷destroy_dev(sc->sc_cdev);

        ppb_lock(ppbus);
❸lpt_release_ppbus(dev);
        ppb_unlock(ppbus);

❹callout_drain(&sc->sc_callout);

        if (sc->sc_irq_resource) {
❺bus_teardown_intr(dev, sc->sc_irq_resource,
                        sc->sc_irq_cookie);
❻bus_release_resource(dev, SYS_RES_IRQ, sc->sc_irq_rid,
                        sc->sc_irq_resource);
        }

❼free(sc->sc_buf_stat, M_DEVBUF);
❽free(sc->sc_buf, M_DEVBUF);

        return (0);
}
```

This function begins by ❶ ❷ destroying lpt(4)'s device nodes. Once this is done, it ❸ relinquishes ownership of the parallel port, ❹ drains lpt(4)'s callout function, ❺ tears down lpt(4)'s interrupt handler, ❻ releases lpt(4)'s IRQ, and ❼ ❽ frees the allocated memory.

lpt_open Function

The lpt_open function is defined in lpt_cdevsw (that is, lpt(4)'s character device switch table) as the d_open operation. Recall that d_open operations prepare the device for I/O.

Here is the function definition for lpt_open:

```
static int
lpt_open(struct cdev *dev, int oflags, int devtype, struct thread *td)
{
        struct lpt_data *sc = dev->si_drv1;
        device_t lpt_dev = sc->sc_dev;
        device_t ppbus = device_get_parent(lpt_dev);
        int try, error;

        if (!sc)
                return (ENXIO);

        ppb_lock(ppbus);
❶if (sc->sc_state) {
                ppb_unlock(ppbus);
                return (EBUSY);
        } else
                sc->sc_state |= LP_INIT;

❷sc->sc_flags = (uintptr_t)dev->si_drv2;
        if (sc->sc_flags & LP_BYPASS) {
                sc->sc_state = LP_OPEN;
                ppb_unlock(ppbus);
                return (0);
        }

        error = lpt_request_ppbus(lpt_dev, PPB_WAIT | PPB_INTR);
        if (error) {
                sc->sc_state = 0;
                ppb_unlock(ppbus);
                return (error);
        }

        /* Use our IRQ? */
        if (sc->sc_irq_status & LP_ENABLE_IRQ)
                sc->sc_irq_status |= LP_USE_IRQ;
        else
                sc->sc_irq_status &= ~LP_USE_IRQ;

        /* Reset printer. */
        if ((sc->sc_flags & LP_NO_PRIME) == 0)
                if ((sc->sc_flags & LP_PRIME_OPEN) || sc->sc_primed == 0) {
                        ❸ppb_wctr(ppbus, 0);
                        sc->sc_primed++;
                        DELAY(500);
                }
```

```
❹ppb_wctr(ppbus, LPC_SEL | LPC_NINIT);

    /* Wait until ready--printer should be running diagnostics. */
    try = 0;
❺do {
        /* Give up? */
        if (try++ >= (LPT_INIT_READY * 4)) {
                lpt_release_ppbus(lpt_dev);
                sc->sc_state = 0;
                ppb_unlock(ppbus);
                return (EBUSY);
        }

        /* Wait 1/4 second. Give up if we get a signal. */
        if (ppb_sleep(ppbus, lpt_dev, LPT_PRI | PCATCH, "lpt_open",
            hz / 4) != EWOULDBLOCK) {
                lpt_release_ppbus(lpt_dev);
                sc->sc_state = 0;
                ppb_unlock(ppbus);
                return (EBUSY);
        }
} ❻while ((ppb_rstr(ppbus) & LP_READY_MASK) != LP_READY);

❼sc->sc_control = LPC_SEL | LPC_NINIT;
if (sc->sc_flags & LP_AUTO_LF)
        ❽sc->sc_control |= LPC_AUTOL;
if (sc->sc_irq_status & LP_USE_IRQ)
        ❾sc->sc_control |= LPC_ENA;

ppb_wctr(ppbus, sc->sc_control);

sc->sc_state &= ~LP_INIT;
sc->sc_state |= LP_OPEN;
sc->sc_transfer_count = 0;

if (sc->sc_irq_status & LP_USE_IRQ) {
        sc->sc_state |= LP_TIMEOUT;
        sc->sc_ticks = hz / LP_TOUT_INIT;
        callout_reset(&sc->sc_callout, sc->sc_ticks,
            ❿lpt_timeout, sc);
}

lpt_release_ppbus(lpt_dev);
ppb_unlock(ppbus);

return (0);
}
```

This function can be split into six parts. The first ❶ checks the value of
sc->sc_state. If it does not equal 0, which implies that another process has
opened the printer, the error code EBUSY is returned; otherwise, sc->sc_state
is assigned LP_INIT. The second part ❷ checks the value of dev->si_drv2.

If it contains the LP_BYPASS flag, which indicates that the device node is lpt%d.ctl, sc->sc_state is set to LP_OPEN and lpt_open exits. Recall that lpt%d.ctl is used solely to change the printer's mode of operation, hence the minute amount of preparatory work. The third part ❸ primes the printer and then ❹ selects and resets the printer (a printer prepares to receive data when it's selected, which occurs when the electrical signal at pin 17, dubbed *nSELIN*, changes from high to low). The fourth part ❺ waits for the printer to ❻ finish its internal reset. The fifth part ❼ selects and resets the printer, ❽ enables automatic line feed if requested,[1] and ❾ enables interrupts if the printer is interrupt-driven. The fifth part also assigns LP_OPEN to sc->sc_state and zeroes the variable sc->sc_transfer_count.

NOTE *Automatic line feed is enabled when the electrical signal at pin 14, dubbed* nAUTOF, *changes from high to low. As you would expect, this causes the printer to automatically insert a line feed after each line.*

Finally, the sixth part causes ❿ lpt_timeout to execute one time after sc->sc_ticks / hz seconds. The lpt_timeout function is used alongside the interrupt handler lpt_intr. I'll discuss these functions shortly.

lpt_read Function

The lpt_read function retrieves the printer's status. Users can get the printer's status by applying the cat(1) command to the device node lpt%d.

Here is the function definition for lpt_read:

```
static int
lpt_read(struct cdev *dev, struct uio *uio, int ioflag)
{
        struct lpt_data *sc = dev->si_drv1;
        device_t lpt_dev = sc->sc_dev;
        device_t ppbus = device_get_parent(lpt_dev);
        int num, error = 0;

      ❶if (sc->sc_flags & LP_BYPASS)
                return (EPERM);

        ppb_lock(ppbus);
        error = ❷ppb_1284_negociate(ppbus, ❸PPB_NIBBLE, 0);
        if (error) {
                ppb_unlock(ppbus);
                return (error);
        }

        num = 0;
        while (uio->uio_resid) {
                error = ❹ppb_1284_read(ppbus, PPB_NIBBLE, ❺sc->sc_buf_stat,
                    min(BUF_STAT_SIZE, uio->uio_resid), ❻&num);
                if (error)
                        goto end_read;
```

---

1. Curiously enough, it's currently impossible to request automatic line feed.

```
        ❼if (!num)
                goto end_read;

        ppb_unlock(ppbus);
        error = ❽uiomove(❾sc->sc_buf_stat, num, ❿uio);
        ppb_lock(ppbus);
        if (error)
                goto end_read;
    }

end_read:
    ppb_1284_terminate(ppbus);
    ppb_unlock(ppbus);
    return (error);
}
```

This function first ❶ checks the value of sc->sc_flags. If it contains the LP_BYPASS flag, which indicates that the device node is lpt%d.ctl, the error code EPERM (which stands for *error: operation not permitted*) is returned. Next, the function ❷ ppb_1284_negociate is called to put the parallel port interface into ❸ nibble mode.

NOTE   *Nibble mode is the most common way to retrieve data from a printer. Normally, pins 10, 11, 12, 13, and 15 are used by the printer as external status indicators; however, in nibble mode these pins are used to send data to the host (4 bits at a time).*

The remainder of this function transfers data from the printer to user space. The data in this case is the printer's status. Here, ❹ ppb_1284_read transfers data from the printer to ❺ kernel space. The number of bytes transferred is saved in ❻ num. If num ❼ equals 0, lpt_read exits. The ❽ uiomove function then moves the data from ❾ kernel space to ❿ user space.

lpt_write Function

The lpt_write function acquires data from user space and stores it in sc->sc_buf. This data is then sent to the printer to be printed.

Here is the function definition for lpt_write:

```
static int
lpt_write(struct cdev *dev, struct uio *uio, int ioflag)
{
        struct lpt_data *sc = dev->si_drv1;
        device_t lpt_dev = sc->sc_dev;
        device_t ppbus = device_get_parent(lpt_dev);
        register unsigned num;
        int error;

        if (sc->sc_flags & LP_BYPASS)
                return (EPERM);

        ppb_lock(ppbus);
        error = lpt_request_ppbus(lpt_dev, PPB_WAIT | PPB_INTR);
```

```
        if (error) {
                ppb_unlock(ppbus);
                return (error);
        }

❶sc->sc_state &= ~LP_INTERRUPTED;
    while (❷(num = min(BUF_SIZE, uio->uio_resid))) {
            sc->sc_cp = sc->sc_buf;

            ppb_unlock(ppbus);
            error = ❸uiomove(sc->sc_cp, num, uio);
            ppb_lock(ppbus);
            if (error)
                    break;

        ❹sc->sc_transfer_count = num;

        ❺if (sc->sc_irq_status & LP_ENABLE_EXT) {
                error = ❻ppb_write(ppbus, sc->sc_cp,
                    sc->sc_transfer_count, 0);
                switch (error) {
                case 0:
                        sc->sc_transfer_count = 0;
                        break;
                case EINTR:
                        sc->sc_state |= LP_INTERRUPTED;
                        ppb_unlock(ppbus);
                        return (error);
                case EINVAL:
                        log(LOG_NOTICE,
                            "%s: extended mode not available\n",
                            device_get_nameunit(lpt_dev));
                        break;
                default:
                        ppb_unlock(ppbus);
                        return (error);
                }
        } else while ((sc->sc_transfer_count > 0) &&
                    ❼(sc->sc_irq_status & LP_USE_IRQ)) {
                if (!(sc->sc_state & LP_BUSY))
                        ❽lpt_intr(sc);

                if (sc->sc_state & LP_BUSY) {
                        error = ❾ppb_sleep(ppbus, lpt_dev,
                            LPT_PRI | PCATCH, "lpt_write", 0);
                        if (error) {
                                sc->sc_state |= LP_INTERRUPTED;
                                ppb_unlock(ppbus);
                                return (error);
                        }
                }
        }

        if (!(sc->sc_irq_status & LP_USE_IRQ) &&
            (sc->sc_transfer_count)) {
```

```
                           error = ❿lpt_push_bytes(sc);
                           if (error) {
                                   ppb_unlock(ppbus);
                                   return (error);
                           }
                   }
           }
   }

   lpt_release_ppbus(lpt_dev);
   ppb_unlock(ppbus);

   return (error);
}
```

Like lpt_read, this function starts by checking the value of sc->sc_flags.
If it contains the LP_BYPASS flag, the error code EPERM is returned. Next, the
LP_INTERRUPTED flag is ❶ removed from sc->sc_state (as you'll see, LP_INTERRUPTED
is added to sc->sc_state whenever a write operation is interrupted). The following while loop contains the bulk of lpt_write. Note that its ❷ expression
determines the amount of data to ❸ copy from user space to kernel space.
This amount is saved in ❹ sc->sc_transfer_count, which is decremented each
time a byte is sent to the printer.

Now, there are three ways to transfer data from kernel space to the
printer. First, if extended mode is ❺ enabled, lpt_write can ❻ write directly
to the printer.

NOTE   *Extended mode refers to either Enhanced Parallel Port (EPP) or Extended Capabilities*
Port (ECP) mode. EPP and ECP modes are designed to transmit data faster and with
less CPU overhead than normal parallel port communications. Most parallel ports sup-
port one or both of these modes.

Second, if the printer is ❼ interrupt-driven and the LP_BUSY flag is cleared
in sc->sc_state, lpt_write can call ❽ lpt_intr to transfer data to the printer.
Looking at the function definition for lpt_intr in the following section,
you'll see that LP_BUSY is set during lpt_intr's execution, and that LP_BUSY is
not cleared until sc->sc_transfer_count is 0. This prevents lpt_write from issuing another interrupt-driven transfer until the current one completes, which
is why lpt_write ❾ sleeps.

Finally, if the first and second options are unavailable, lpt_write can
issue a polled transfer by calling ❿ lpt_push_bytes, which is described in
"lpt_push_bytes Function" on page 158.

lpt_intr Function

The lpt_intr function is lpt(4)'s interrupt handler. This function transfers
1 byte from sc->sc_buf to the printer and then it exits. When the printer
is ready for another byte, it will send an interrupt. Note that in lpt_intr,
sc->sc_buf is accessed via sc->sc_cp.

Here is the function definition for `lpt_intr`:

```
static void
lpt_intr(void *arg)
{
        struct lpt_data *sc = arg;
        device_t lpt_dev = sc->sc_dev;
        device_t ppbus = device_get_parent(lpt_dev);
        int i, status = 0;

    ❶for (i = 0; i < 100 &&
            ((status = ppb_rstr(ppbus)) & LP_READY_MASK) != LP_READY; i++)
            ;           /* nothing. */

        if ((status & LP_READY_MASK) == LP_READY) {
            ❷sc->sc_state = (sc->sc_state | LP_BUSY) & ~LP_ERROR;
            ❸sc->sc_ticks = hz / LP_TOUT_INIT;

                if (sc->sc_transfer_count) {
                    ❹ppb_wdtr(ppbus, *sc->sc_cp++);
                    ❺ppb_wctr(ppbus, sc->sc_control | LPC_STB);
                      ppb_wctr(ppbus, sc->sc_control);

                        if (--(sc->sc_transfer_count) > 0)
                            ❻return;
                }

            ❼sc->sc_state &= ~LP_BUSY;

                if (!(sc->sc_state & LP_INTERRUPTED))
                    ❽wakeup(lpt_dev);

                return;
        } else {
                if (((status & (LPS_NERR | LPS_OUT)) != LPS_NERR) &&
                    (sc->sc_state & LP_OPEN))
                        sc->sc_state |= LP_ERROR;
        }
}
```

This function first ❶ checks ad nauseam that the printer is online and ready for output. If it is, the ❷ LP_BUSY flag is added to sc->sc_state and the LP_ERROR flag, which denotes a printer error, is removed. Next, sc->sc_ticks is ❸ reset. Then 1 byte from sc->sc_buf is ❹ written to the parallel port's data register and subsequently ❺ sent to the printer (data on the parallel port interface is sent to the printer when the electrical signal at pin 1, dubbed *nSTROBE*, changes from high to low). If there is more data to send (that is, sc->sc_transfer_count is greater than 0), lpt_intr ❻ exits, because it is protocol to wait for an interrupt before sending another byte. If there is no more data to send, LP_BUSY is ❼ cleared from sc->sc_state and lpt_write is ❽ woken up.

lpt_timeout Function

The lpt_timeout function is the callout function for lpt(4). It is designed to deal with missed or unhandled interrupts. Here is its function definition:

```
static void
lpt_timeout(void *arg)
{
        struct lpt_data *sc = arg;
        device_t lpt_dev = sc->sc_dev;

❶      if (sc->sc_state & LP_OPEN) {
                sc->sc_ticks++;
                if (sc->sc_ticks > hz / LP_TOUT_MAX)
                        sc->sc_ticks = hz / LP_TOUT_MAX;
❷              callout_reset(&sc->sc_callout, sc->sc_ticks,
                        lpt_timeout, sc);
        } else
                sc->sc_state &= ~LP_TIMEOUT;

        if (sc->sc_state & LP_ERROR)
❸              sc->sc_state &= ~LP_ERROR;

❹      if (sc->sc_transfer_count)
❺              lpt_intr(sc);
        else {
                sc->sc_state &= ~LP_BUSY;
                wakeup(lpt_dev);
        }
}
```

This function first ❶ checks whether lpt%d is open. If so, lpt_timeout ❷ reschedules itself to execute. Next, LP_ERROR is ❸ removed from sc->sc_state. Now if lpt(4) has ❹ missed an interrupt, ❺ lpt_intr is called to restart transferring data to the printer.

Note that without the if block at ❹, lpt(4) would hang waiting for an interrupt that's been sent and lost.

lpt_push_bytes Function

The lpt_push_bytes function uses polling to transfer data to the printer. This function is called (by lpt_write) only if extended mode is disabled and the printer is not interrupt-driven.

Here is the function definition for lpt_push_bytes:

```
static int
lpt_push_bytes(struct lpt_data *sc)
{
        device_t lpt_dev = sc->sc_dev;
        device_t ppbus = device_get_parent(lpt_dev);
        int error, spin, tick;
        char ch;
```

```
❶while (sc->sc_transfer_count > 0) {
        ch = *sc->sc_cp;
        sc->sc_cp++;
        sc->sc_transfer_count--;

        ❷for (spin = 0; NOT_READY(ppbus) && spin < MAX_SPIN; spin++)
                DELAY(1);

        if (spin >= MAX_SPIN) {
                tick = 0;
                while (NOT_READY(ppbus)) {
                        tick = tick + tick + 1;
                        if (tick > MAX_SLEEP)
                                tick = MAX_SLEEP;

                        error = ❸ppb_sleep(ppbus, lpt_dev, LPT_PRI,
                                "lpt_poll", tick);
                        if (error != EWOULDBLOCK)
                                return (error);
                }
        }

        ❹ppb_wdtr(ppbus, ch);
        ❺ppb_wctr(ppbus, sc->sc_control | LPC_STB);
          ppb_wctr(ppbus, sc->sc_control);
}

return (0);
}
```

This function first ❶ verifies that there is data to transfer. Then it ❷ polls the printer to see if it is online and ready for output. If the printer is not ready, lpt_push_bytes ❸ sleeps for a short period of time and then repolls the printer when it wakes up. This cycle of sleeping and polling is repeated until the printer is ready. If the printer is ready, 1 byte from sc->sc_buf is ❹ written to the parallel port's data register and then ❺ sent to the printer. This entire process is repeated until all of the data in sc->sc_buf is transferred.

lpt_close Function

The lpt_close function is defined in lpt_cdevsw as the d_close operation. Here is its function definition:

```
static int
lpt_close(struct cdev *dev, int fflag, int devtype, struct thread *td)
{
        struct lpt_data *sc = dev->si_drv1;
        device_t lpt_dev = sc->sc_dev;
        device_t ppbus = device_get_parent(lpt_dev);
        int error;

        ppb_lock(ppbus);
```

```
❶if (sc->sc_flags & LP_BYPASS)
        goto end_close;

    error = lpt_request_ppbus(lpt_dev, PPB_WAIT | PPB_INTR);
    if (error) {
        ppb_unlock(ppbus);
        return (error);
    }

❷if (!(sc->sc_state & LP_INTERRUPTED) &&
    ❸(sc->sc_irq_status & LP_USE_IRQ))
        while ((ppb_rstr(ppbus) & LP_READY_MASK) != LP_READY ||
          ❹sc->sc_transfer_count)
            if (ppb_sleep(ppbus, lpt_dev, LPT_PRI | PCATCH,
                "lpt_close", hz) != EWOULDBLOCK)
                    break;

❺sc->sc_state &= ~LP_OPEN;
❻callout_stop(&sc->sc_callout);
❼ppb_wctr(ppbus, LPC_NINIT);

    lpt_release_ppbus(lpt_dev);

❽ end_close:
    ❾sc->sc_state = 0;
    ❿sc->sc_transfer_count = 0;
    ppb_unlock(ppbus);
    return (0);
}
```

Like lpt_read and lpt_write, this function first ❶ checks the value of
sc->sc_flags. If it contains the LP_BYPASS flag, lpt_close jumps to ❽ end_close.
Next, lpt(4) is assigned ownership of the parallel port. The following ❷
if block ensures that if there is ❹ still data to transfer and the printer is ❸
interrupt-driven, the transfer is completed before closing lpt%d. Then,
LP_OPEN is ❺ removed from sc->sc_state, lpt_timeout is ❻ stopped, the printer
is ❼ reset, and ownership of the parallel port is relinquished. Lastly, ❾
sc->sc_state and ❿ sc->sc_transfer_count are zeroed.

lpt_ioctl Function

The lpt_ioctl function is defined in lpt_cdevsw as the d_ioctl operation.
Before I describe this function, an explanation of its ioctl command, LPT_IRQ,
is needed. LPT_IRQ is defined in the <dev/ppbus/lptio.h> header as follows:

```
#define LPT_IRQ          _IOW('p', 1, ❶long)
```

As you can see, LPT_IRQ requires a ❶ long int value.

```
static int
lpt_ioctl(struct cdev *dev, u_long cmd, caddr_t data, int fflag,
```

```
      struct thread *td)
{
      struct lpt_data *sc = dev->si_drv1;
      device_t lpt_dev = sc->sc_dev;
      device_t ppbus = device_get_parent(lpt_dev);
      u_short old_irq_status;
      int error = 0;

      switch (cmd) {
❶case LPT_IRQ:
             ppb_lock(ppbus);
             if (sc->sc_irq_status & LP_HAS_IRQ) {
                    old_irq_status = sc->sc_irq_status;
                    switch (*(int *)❷data) {
                    case 0:
                          ❸sc->sc_irq_status &= ~LP_ENABLE_IRQ;
                             break;
                    case 1:
                             sc->sc_irq_status &= ~LP_ENABLE_EXT;
                          ❹sc->sc_irq_status |= LP_ENABLE_IRQ;
                             break;
                    case 2:
                             sc->sc_irq_status &= ~LP_ENABLE_IRQ;
                          ❺sc->sc_irq_status |= LP_ENABLE_EXT;
                             break;
                    case 3:
                          ❻sc->sc_irq_status &= ~LP_ENABLE_EXT;
                             break;
                    default:
                             break;
                    }

                    if (old_irq_status != sc->sc_irq_status)
                          log(LOG_NOTICE,
                             "%s: switched to %s %s mode\n",
                             device_get_nameunit(lpt_dev),
                             (sc->sc_irq_status & LP_ENABLE_IRQ) ?
                             "interrupt-driven" : "polled",
                             (sc->sc_irq_status & LP_ENABLE_EXT) ?
                             "extended" : "standard");
             } else
                    error = EOPNOTSUPP;

             ppb_unlock(ppbus);
             break;
      default:
             error = ENODEV;
             break;
      }

      return (error);
}
```

Based on the ❷ argument given to ❶ LPT_IRQ, lpt_ioctl either ❸ disables interrupt-driven mode (which enables polled mode), ❹ enables interrupt-driven mode, ❺ enables extended mode, or ❻ disables extended mode (which enables standard mode). Note that interrupt-driven mode and extended mode conflict with each other, so if one is enabled, the other is disabled.

NOTE *To run this function, you'd use the lptcontrol(8) utility, whose source code I suggest you take a quick look at.*

lpt_request_ppbus Function

The lpt_request_ppbus function sets lpt(4) as the owner of the parallel port. Recall that owning the parallel port lets a device (such as lpt%d) transfer data to and from it.

Here is the function definition for lpt_request_ppbus:

```
static int
lpt_request_ppbus(device_t dev, int how)
{
        device_t ppbus = device_get_parent(dev);
        struct lpt_data *sc = device_get_softc(dev);
        int error;

        ppb_assert_locked(ppbus);

      ❶if (sc->sc_state & LP_HAVEBUS)
              ❷return (0);

        error = ❸ppb_request_bus(ppbus, dev, how);
        if (!error)
              ❹sc->sc_state |= LP_HAVEBUS;

        return (error);
}
```

This function begins by ❶ checking the value of sc->sc_state. If it contains LP_HAVEBUS, which indicates that lpt(4) currently owns the parallel port, lpt_request_ppbus ❷ exits. Otherwise, ❸ ppb_request_bus is called to set lpt(4) as the owner of the parallel port and sc->sc_state is ❹ assigned LP_HAVEBUS.

lpt_release_ppbus Function

The lpt_release_ppbus function causes lpt(4) to relinquish ownership of the parallel port. Here is its function definition:

```
static int
lpt_release_ppbus(device_t dev)
{
        device_t ppbus = device_get_parent(dev);
        struct lpt_data *sc = device_get_softc(dev);
        int error = 0;
```

```
        ppb_assert_locked(ppbus);

❶if (sc->sc_state & LP_HAVEBUS) {
            error = ❷ppb_release_bus(ppbus, dev);
            if (!error)
                    ❸sc->sc_state &= ~LP_HAVEBUS;
    }

    return (error);
}
```

This function first ❶ verifies that lpt(4) currently owns the parallel port.
Next, it calls ❷ ppb_release_bus to relinquish ownership of the parallel port.
Then LP_HAVEBUS is ❸ removed from sc->sc_state.

Conclusion

This chapter described the entire code base of lpt(4), the parallel port
printer driver.

10

MANAGING AND USING RESOURCES

In Chapter 7 we discussed how to allocate IRQs, I/O ports, and I/O memory. Chapter 8 focused on using IRQs for interrupt handling. This chapter details how to use I/O ports for port-mapped I/O (PMIO) and I/O memory for memory-mapped I/O (MMIO). Before I describe PMIO and MMIO, some background on I/O ports and I/O memory is needed.

I/O Ports and I/O Memory

Every peripheral device is controlled by reading from and writing to its registers (Corbet et al., 2005), which are mapped to either I/O ports or I/O memory. The use of I/O ports or I/O memory is device and architecture dependent. For example, on the *i386*, most ISA devices will map their registers to I/O ports; however, PCI devices tend to map their registers to I/O memory. As you may have guessed, reading and writing to a device's registers, which are mapped to either I/O ports or I/O memory, is called PMIO or MMIO.

Reading from I/O Ports and I/O Memory

After a driver has called bus_alloc_resource to allocate the range of I/O ports or I/O memory it needs, it can read from those I/O regions using one of the following functions:

```
#include <sys/bus.h>
#include <machine/bus.h>

u_int8_t
bus_read_1(struct resource *r, bus_size_t offset);

u_int16_t
bus_read_2(struct resource *r, bus_size_t offset);

u_int32_t
bus_read_4(struct resource *r, bus_size_t offset);

u_int64_t
bus_read_8(struct resource *r, bus_size_t offset);


void
bus_read_multi_1(struct resource *r, bus_size_t offset,
    u_int8_t *datap, bus_size_t count);

void
bus_read_multi_2(struct resource *r, bus_size_t offset,
    u_int16_t *datap, bus_size_t count);

void
bus_read_multi_4(struct resource *r, bus_size_t offset,
    u_int32_t *datap, bus_size_t count);

void
bus_read_multi_8(struct resource *r, bus_size_t offset,
    u_int64_t *datap, bus_size_t count);


void
bus_read_region_1(struct resource *r, bus_size_t offset,
    u_int8_t *datap, bus_size_t count);

void
bus_read_region_2(struct resource *r, bus_size_t offset,
    u_int16_t *datap, bus_size_t count);

void
bus_read_region_4(struct resource *r, bus_size_t offset,
    u_int32_t *datap, bus_size_t count);
```

```
void
bus_read_region_8(struct resource *r, bus_size_t offset,
    u_int64_t *datap, bus_size_t count);
```

The bus_read_*N* functions (where *N* is 1, 2, 4, or 8) read *N* bytes from an offset in r (where r is the return value from a successful bus_alloc_resource call that allocated an I/O region).

The bus_read_multi_*N* functions read *N* bytes from an offset in r, count times, and store the reads into datap. In short, bus_read_multi_*N* reads from the same location multiple times.

The bus_read_region_*N* functions read count *N*–byte values starting from an offset in r, and store the reads into datap. In other words, bus_read_region_*N* reads consecutive *N*-byte values from an I/O region (that is, an array).

Writing to I/O Ports and I/O Memory

A driver writes to an I/O region using one of the following functions:

```
#include <sys/bus.h>
#include <machine/bus.h>

void
bus_write_1(struct resource *r, bus_size_t offset,
    u_int8_t value);

void
bus_write_2(struct resource *r, bus_size_t offset,
    u_int16_t value);

void
bus_write_4(struct resource *r, bus_size_t offset,
    u_int32_t value);

void
bus_write_8(struct resource *r, bus_size_t offset,
    u_int64_t value);


void
bus_write_multi_1(struct resource *r, bus_size_t offset,
    u_int8_t *datap, bus_size_t count);

void
bus_write_multi_2(struct resource *r, bus_size_t offset,
    u_int16_t *datap, bus_size_t count);

void
bus_write_multi_4(struct resource *r, bus_size_t offset,
    u_int32_t *datap, bus_size_t count);
```

```
void
bus_write_multi_8(struct resource *r, bus_size_t offset,
    u_int64_t *datap, bus_size_t count);


void
bus_write_region_1(struct resource *r, bus_size_t offset,
    u_int8_t *datap, bus_size_t count);

void
bus_write_region_2(struct resource *r, bus_size_t offset,
    u_int16_t *datap, bus_size_t count);

void
bus_write_region_4(struct resource *r, bus_size_t offset,
    u_int32_t *datap, bus_size_t count);

void
bus_write_region_8(struct resource *r, bus_size_t offset,
    u_int64_t *datap, bus_size_t count);


void
bus_set_multi_1(struct resource *r, bus_size_t offset,
    u_int8_t value, bus_size_t count);

void
bus_set_multi_2(struct resource *r, bus_size_t offset,
    u_int16_t value, bus_size_t count);

void
bus_set_multi_4(struct resource *r, bus_size_t offset,
    u_int32_t value, bus_size_t count);

void
bus_set_multi_8(struct resource *r, bus_size_t offset,
    u_int64_t value, bus_size_t count);


void
bus_set_region_1(struct resource *r, bus_size_t offset,
    u_int8_t value, bus_size_t count);

void
bus_set_region_2(struct resource *r, bus_size_t offset,
    u_int16_t value, bus_size_t count);

void
bus_set_region_4(struct resource *r, bus_size_t offset,
    u_int32_t value, bus_size_t count);

void
bus_set_region_8(struct resource *r, bus_size_t offset,
    u_int64_t value, bus_size_t count);
```

The bus_write_N functions (where N is 1, 2, 4, or 8) write an N-byte value to an offset in r (where r is the return value from a bus_alloc_resource call that allocated an I/O region).

The bus_write_multi_N functions take count N–byte values from datap and write them to an offset in r. In short, bus_write_multi_N writes multiple values to the same location.

The bus_write_region_N functions take count N–byte values from datap and write them to a region in r, starting at offset. Each successive value is written at an offset of N bytes after the previous value. In short, bus_write_region_N writes consecutive N-byte values to an I/O region (that is, an array).

The bus_set_multi_N functions write an N-byte value to an offset in r, count times. That is, bus_set_multi_N writes the same value to the same location multiple times.

The bus_set_region_N functions write an N-byte value, count times, throughout a region in r, starting at offset. In other words, bus_set_region_N writes the same value consecutively to an I/O region (that is, an array).

Stream Operations

All of the preceding functions handle converting to and from host byte order and bus byte order. In some cases, however, you may need to avoid this conversion. Fortunately, FreeBSD provides the following functions for such an occasion:

```
#include <sys/bus.h>
#include <machine/bus.h>

u_int8_t
bus_read_stream_1(struct resource *r, bus_size_t offset);

u_int16_t
bus_read_stream_2(struct resource *r, bus_size_t offset);

u_int32_t
bus_read_stream_4(struct resource *r, bus_size_t offset);

u_int64_t
bus_read_stream_8(struct resource *r, bus_size_t offset);


void
bus_read_multi_stream_1(struct resource *r, bus_size_t offset,
    u_int8_t *datap, bus_size_t count);

void
bus_read_multi_stream_2(struct resource *r, bus_size_t offset,
    u_int16_t *datap, bus_size_t count);

void
bus_read_multi_stream_4(struct resource *r, bus_size_t offset,
    u_int32_t *datap, bus_size_t count);
```

```
void
bus_read_multi_stream_8(struct resource *r, bus_size_t offset,
    u_int64_t *datap, bus_size_t count);


void
bus_read_region_stream_1(struct resource *r, bus_size_t offset,
    u_int8_t *datap, bus_size_t count);

void
bus_read_region_stream_2(struct resource *r, bus_size_t offset,
    u_int16_t *datap, bus_size_t count);

void
bus_read_region_stream_4(struct resource *r, bus_size_t offset,
    u_int32_t *datap, bus_size_t count);

void
bus_read_region_stream_8(struct resource *r, bus_size_t offset,
    u_int64_t *datap, bus_size_t count);


void
bus_write_stream_1(struct resource *r, bus_size_t offset,
    u_int8_t value);

void
bus_write_stream_2(struct resource *r, bus_size_t offset,
    u_int16_t value);

void
bus_write_stream_4(struct resource *r, bus_size_t offset,
    u_int32_t value);

void
bus_write_stream_8(struct resource *r, bus_size_t offset,
    u_int64_t value);


void
bus_write_multi_stream_1(struct resource *r, bus_size_t offset,
    u_int8_t *datap, bus_size_t count);

void
bus_write_multi_stream_2(struct resource *r, bus_size_t offset,
    u_int16_t *datap, bus_size_t count);

void
bus_write_multi_stream_4(struct resource *r, bus_size_t offset,
    u_int32_t *datap, bus_size_t count);

void
bus_write_multi_stream_8(struct resource *r, bus_size_t offset,
    u_int64_t *datap, bus_size_t count);
```

```
void
bus_write_region_stream_1(struct resource *r, bus_size_t offset,
    u_int8_t *datap, bus_size_t count);

void
bus_write_region_stream_2(struct resource *r, bus_size_t offset,
    u_int16_t *datap, bus_size_t count);

void
bus_write_region_stream_4(struct resource *r, bus_size_t offset,
    u_int32_t *datap, bus_size_t count);

void
bus_write_region_stream_8(struct resource *r, bus_size_t offset,
    u_int64_t *datap, bus_size_t count);


void
bus_set_multi_stream_1(struct resource *r, bus_size_t offset,
    u_int8_t value, bus_size_t count);

void
bus_set_multi_stream_2(struct resource *r, bus_size_t offset,
    u_int16_t value, bus_size_t count);

void
bus_set_multi_stream_4(struct resource *r, bus_size_t offset,
    u_int32_t value, bus_size_t count);

void
bus_set_multi_stream_8(struct resource *r, bus_size_t offset,
    u_int64_t value, bus_size_t count);


void
bus_set_region_stream_1(struct resource *r, bus_size_t offset,
    u_int8_t value, bus_size_t count);

void
bus_set_region_stream_2(struct resource *r, bus_size_t offset,
    u_int16_t value, bus_size_t count);

void
bus_set_region_stream_4(struct resource *r, bus_size_t offset,
    u_int32_t value, bus_size_t count);

void
bus_set_region_stream_8(struct resource *r, bus_size_t offset,
    u_int64_t value, bus_size_t count);
```

These functions are identical to their nonstream counterparts, except that they don't perform any byte order conversions.

Memory Barriers

Sequences of read and write instructions can often be executed more quickly if run in an order that's different from the program text (Corbet et al., 2005). As a result, modern processors customarily reorder read and write instructions. However, this optimization can foul up drivers performing PMIO and MMIO. To prevent instruction reordering, memory barriers are employed. *Memory barriers* ensure that all instructions before the barrier conclude before any instruction after the barrier. For PMIO and MMIO operations, the bus_barrier function provides this ability:

```
#include <sys/bus.h>
#include <machine/bus.h>

void
bus_barrier(struct resource *r, bus_size_t offset, bus_size_t length,
    int flags);
```

The bus_barrier function inserts a memory barrier that enforces the ordering of read or write operations on a region in r, which is described by the offset and length arguments. The flags argument specifies the type of operation to be ordered. Valid values for this argument are shown in Table 10-1.

Table 10-1: bus_barrier Symbolic Constants

Constant	Description
BUS_SPACE_BARRIER_READ	Synchronizes read operations
BUS_SPACE_BARRIER_WRITE	Synchronizes write operations

Note that these flags can be ORed to enforce ordering on both read and write operations. An exemplary use of bus_barrier looks something like this:

```
bus_write_1(r, 0, data0);
bus_barrier(r, 0, 1, BUS_SPACE_BARRIER_WRITE);
bus_write_1(r, 0, data1);
bus_barrier(r, 0, 2, BUS_SPACE_BARRIER_READ | BUS_SPACE_BARRIER_WRITE);
data2 = bus_read_1(r, 1);
bus_barrier(r, 1, 1, BUS_SPACE_BARRIER_READ);
data3 = bus_read_1(r, 1);
```

Here, the calls to bus_barrier guarantee that the writes and reads conclude in the order written.

Tying Everything Together

Listing 10-1 is a simple driver for an i-Opener's LEDs (based on code written by Warner Losh). An i-Opener includes two LEDs that are controlled by bits 0 and 1 of the register located at 0x404c. Hopefully, this example will clarify any misunderstandings you may have about PMIO (and MMIO).

NOTE *Take a quick look at this code and try to discern some of its structure. If you don't understand all of it, don't worry; an explanation follows.*

```
#include <sys/param.h>
#include <sys/module.h>
#include <sys/kernel.h>
#include <sys/systm.h>

#include <sys/bus.h>
#include <sys/conf.h>
#include <sys/uio.h>
#include <sys/lock.h>
#include <sys/mutex.h>

#include <machine/bus.h>
#include <sys/rman.h>
#include <machine/resource.h>

❶ #define LED_IO_ADDR          0x404c
❷ #define LED_NUM              2

struct led_softc {
        int                    sc_io_rid;
        struct resource        *sc_io_resource;
        struct cdev            *sc_cdev0;
        struct cdev            *sc_cdev1;
        u_int32_t              sc_open_mask;
        u_int32_t              sc_read_mask;
        struct mtx             sc_mutex;
};

static devclass_t led_devclass;

static d_open_t               led_open;
static d_close_t              led_close;
static d_read_t               led_read;
static d_write_t              led_write;

static struct cdevsw led_cdevsw = {
        .d_version =          D_VERSION,
        .d_open =             led_open,
        .d_close =            led_close,
        .d_read =             led_read,
        .d_write =            led_write,
        .d_name =             "led"
};

static int
led_open(struct cdev *dev, int oflags, int devtype, struct thread *td)
{
        int led = dev2unit(dev) & 0xff;
        struct led_softc *sc = dev->si_drv1;
```

```
                if (led >= LED_NUM)
                        return (ENXIO);

                mtx_lock(&sc->sc_mutex);
                if (sc->sc_open_mask & (1 << led)) {
                        mtx_unlock(&sc->sc_mutex);
                        return (EBUSY);
                }
                sc->sc_open_mask |= 1 << led;
                sc->sc_read_mask |= 1 << led;
                mtx_unlock(&sc->sc_mutex);

                return (0);
        }

static int
led_close(struct cdev *dev, int fflag, int devtype, struct thread *td)
{
        int led = dev2unit(dev) & 0xff;
        struct led_softc *sc = dev->si_drv1;

        if (led >= LED_NUM)
                return (ENXIO);

        mtx_lock(&sc->sc_mutex);
        sc->sc_open_mask &= ~(1 << led);
        mtx_unlock(&sc->sc_mutex);

        return (0);
}

static int
led_read(struct cdev *dev, struct uio *uio, int ioflag)
{
        int led = dev2unit(dev) & 0xff;
        struct led_softc *sc = dev->si_drv1;
        u_int8_t ch;
        int error;

        if (led >= LED_NUM)
                return (ENXIO);

        mtx_lock(&sc->sc_mutex);
        /* No error EOF condition. */
        if (!(sc->sc_read_mask & (1 << led))) {
                mtx_unlock(&sc->sc_mutex);
                return (0);
        }
        sc->sc_read_mask &= ~(1 << led);
        mtx_unlock(&sc->sc_mutex);

        ch = bus_read_1(sc->sc_io_resource, 0);
        if (ch & (1 << led))
                ch = '1';
```

```
                else
                        ch = '0';

                error = uiomove(&ch, 1, uio);
                return (error);
        }

static int
led_write(struct cdev *dev, struct uio *uio, int ioflag)
{
        int led = dev2unit(dev) & 0xff;
        struct led_softc *sc = dev->si_drv1;
        u_int8_t ch;
        u_int8_t old;
        int error;

        if (led >= LED_NUM)
                return (ENXIO);

        error = uiomove(&ch, 1, uio);
        if (error)
                return (error);

        old = bus_read_1(sc->sc_io_resource, 0);
        if (ch & 1)
                old |= (1 << led);
        else
                old &= ~(1 << led);

        bus_write_1(sc->sc_io_resource, 0, old);

        return (error);
        }

static void
led_identify(driver_t *driver, device_t parent)
{
        device_t child;

        child = device_find_child(parent, "led", -1);
        if (!child) {
                child = BUS_ADD_CHILD(parent, 0, "led", -1);
                bus_set_resource(child, SYS_RES_IOPORT, 0, LED_IO_ADDR, 1);
        }
}

static int
led_probe(device_t dev)
{
        if (!bus_get_resource_start(dev, SYS_RES_IOPORT, 0))
                return (ENXIO);

        device_set_desc(dev, "I/O Port Example");
        return (BUS_PROBE_SPECIFIC);
}
```

```
static int
led_attach(device_t dev)
{
        struct led_softc *sc = device_get_softc(dev);

        sc->sc_io_rid = 0;
        sc->sc_io_resource = bus_alloc_resource_any(dev, SYS_RES_IOPORT,
            &sc->sc_io_rid, RF_ACTIVE);
        if (!sc->sc_io_resource) {
                device_printf(dev, "unable to allocate resource\n");
                return (ENXIO);
        }

        sc->sc_open_mask = 0;
        sc->sc_read_mask = 0;
        mtx_init(&sc->sc_mutex, "led", NULL, MTX_DEF);

        sc->sc_cdev0 = make_dev(&led_cdevsw, 0, UID_ROOT, GID_WHEEL, 0644,
            "led0");
        sc->sc_cdev1 = make_dev(&led_cdevsw, 1, UID_ROOT, GID_WHEEL, 0644,
            "led1");
        sc->sc_cdev0->si_drv1 = sc;
        sc->sc_cdev1->si_drv1 = sc;

        return (0);
}

static int
led_detach(device_t dev)
{
        struct led_softc *sc = device_get_softc(dev);

        destroy_dev(sc->sc_cdev0);
        destroy_dev(sc->sc_cdev1);

        mtx_destroy(&sc->sc_mutex);

        bus_release_resource(dev, SYS_RES_IOPORT, sc->sc_io_rid,
            sc->sc_io_resource);

        return (0);
}

static device_method_t led_methods[] = {
        /* Device interface. */
        DEVMETHOD(device_identify,      led_identify),
        DEVMETHOD(device_probe,         led_probe),
        DEVMETHOD(device_attach,        led_attach),
        DEVMETHOD(device_detach,        led_detach),
        { 0, 0 }
};

static driver_t led_driver = {
        "led",
```

```
        led_methods,
        sizeof(struct led_softc)
};

DRIVER_MODULE(led, isa, led_driver, led_devclass, 0, 0);
```

Listing 10-1: led.c

Before I describe the functions defined in Listing 10-1, note that the constant ❶ LED_IO_ADDR is defined as 0x404c and that the constant ❷ LED_NUM is defined as 2.

The following sections describe the functions defined in Listing 10-1 in the order they would roughly execute.

led_identify Function

The led_identify function is the device_identify implementation for this driver. This function is required because the ISA bus cannot identify its children unaided. Here is the function definition for led_identify (again):

```
static void
led_identify(driver_t *driver, device_t parent)
{
        device_t child;

        child = ❶device_find_child(parent, ❷"led", -1);
        if (!child) {
                child = ❸BUS_ADD_CHILD(parent, 0, "led", -1);
                ❹bus_set_resource(child, SYS_RES_IOPORT, 0, LED_IO_ADDR, 1);
        }
}
```

This function first ❶ determines if the ISA bus has identified a child device named ❷ "led". If it has not, then "led" is ❸ appended to the ISA bus's catalog of identified children. Afterward, ❹ bus_set_resource is called to specify that I/O port access for "led" starts at LED_IO_ADDR.

led_probe Function

The led_probe function is the device_probe implementation for this driver. Here is its function definition (again):

```
static int
led_probe(device_t dev)
{
        ❶if (!bus_get_resource_start(dev, SYS_RES_IOPORT, 0))
                return (ENXIO);

        ❷device_set_desc(dev, "I/O Port Example");
        ❸return (BUS_PROBE_SPECIFIC);
}
```

This function first ❶ checks if "led" can acquire I/O port access. Afterward, the verbose description of "led" is ❷ set and the success code ❸ BUS_PROBE_SPECIFIC is returned.

led_attach Function

The led_attach function is the device_attach implementation for this driver. Here is its function definition (again):

```
static int
led_attach(device_t dev)
{
        struct led_softc *sc = device_get_softc(dev);

        sc->sc_io_rid = 0;
        sc->sc_io_resource = ❶bus_alloc_resource_any(dev, SYS_RES_IOPORT,
            &sc->sc_io_rid, RF_ACTIVE);
        if (!sc->sc_io_resource) {
                device_printf(dev, "unable to allocate resource\n");
            ❷return (ENXIO);
        }

     ❸sc->sc_open_mask = 0;
     ❹sc->sc_read_mask = 0;
        mtx_init(❺&sc->sc_mutex, "led", NULL, MTX_DEF);

        sc->sc_cdev0 = ❻make_dev(&led_cdevsw, 0, UID_ROOT, GID_WHEEL, 0644,
            "led0");
        sc->sc_cdev1 = ❼make_dev(&led_cdevsw, 1, UID_ROOT, GID_WHEEL, 0644,
            "led1");
        sc->sc_cdev0->si_drv1 = sc;
        sc->sc_cdev1->si_drv1 = sc;

        return (0);
}
```

This function begins by ❶ acquiring an I/O port. If unsuccessful, the error code ❷ ENXIO is returned. Then the member variables ❸ sc_open_mask and ❹ sc_read_mask are zeroed; in the d_foo functions, these variables will be protected by ❺ sc_mutex. Finally, led_attach creates a ❻ ❼ character device node for each LED.

led_detach Function

The led_detach function is the device_detach implementation for this driver. Here is its function definition (again):

```
static int
led_detach(device_t dev)
{
```

```
        struct led_softc *sc = device_get_softc(dev);

❶destroy_dev(sc->sc_cdev0);
❷destroy_dev(sc->sc_cdev1);

❸mtx_destroy(&sc->sc_mutex);

❹bus_release_resource(dev, SYS_RES_IOPORT, sc->sc_io_rid,
        sc->sc_io_resource);

        return (0);
}
```

This function begins by ❶ ❷ destroying its device nodes. Once this is done, it ❸ destroys its mutex and ❹ releases its I/O port.

led_open Function

The led_open function is defined in led_cdevsw (that is, the character device switch table) as the d_open operation. Here is its function definition (again):

```
static int
led_open(struct cdev *dev, int oflags, int devtype, struct thread *td)
{
    ❶int led = dev2unit(dev) & 0xff;
        struct led_softc *sc = dev->si_drv1;

    ❷if (led >= LED_NUM)
            ❸return (ENXIO);

    mtx_lock(&sc->sc_mutex);
    ❹if (sc->sc_open_mask & (1 << led)) {
            mtx_unlock(&sc->sc_mutex);
            ❺return (EBUSY);
    }
    ❻sc->sc_open_mask |= 1 << led;
    ❼sc->sc_read_mask |= 1 << led;
    mtx_unlock(&sc->sc_mutex);

        return (0);
}
```

This function first ❶ stores in led the unit number of the device node being opened. If led is ❷ greater than or equal to LED_NUM, then ENXIO is ❸ returned. Next, the value of sc_open_mask is ❹ examined. If its led bit does not equal 0, which indicates that another process has opened the device, then EBUSY is ❺ returned. Otherwise, sc_open_mask and sc_read_mask are ❻ ❼ set to include 1 << led. That is, their led bit will be changed to 1.

led_close Function

The led_close function is defined in led_cdevsw as the d_close operation. Here is its function definition (again):

```
static int
led_close(struct cdev *dev, int fflag, int devtype, struct thread *td)
{
        int led = dev2unit(dev) & 0xff;
        struct led_softc *sc = dev->si_drv1;

        if (led >= LED_NUM)
                return (ENXIO);

        mtx_lock(&sc->sc_mutex);
    ❶sc->sc_open_mask &= ~(1 << led);
        mtx_unlock(&sc->sc_mutex);

        return (0);
}
```

As you can see, this function simply ❶ clears sc_open_mask's led bit (which allows another process to open this device).

led_read Function

The led_read function is defined in led_cdevsw as the d_read operation. This function returns one character indicating whether the LED is on (1) or off (0). Here is its function definition (again):

```
static int
led_read(struct cdev *dev, struct uio *uio, int ioflag)
{
        int led = dev2unit(dev) & 0xff;
        struct led_softc *sc = dev->si_drv1;
        u_int8_t ch;
        int error;

        if (led >= LED_NUM)
                return (ENXIO);

        mtx_lock(&sc->sc_mutex);
        /* No error EOF condition. */
    ❶if (!(sc->sc_read_mask & (1 << led))) {
                mtx_unlock(&sc->sc_mutex);
            ❷return (0);
        }
        sc->sc_read_mask &= ~(1 << led);
        mtx_unlock(&sc->sc_mutex);
```

```
❸ch = bus_read_1(sc->sc_io_resource, 0);
❹if (ch & (1 << led))
        ch = '1';
    else
        ch = '0';

    error = ❺uiomove(&ch, 1, uio);
    return (error);
}
```

This function first ❶ checks that sc_read_mask's led bit is set; otherwise, it ❷ exits. Next, 1 byte from the LED's control register is ❸ read into ch. Then ch's led bit is ❹ isolated and its value is ❺ returned to user space.

led_write Function

The led_write function is defined in led_cdevsw as the d_write operation. This function takes in one character to turn on (1) or off (0) the LED. Here is its function definition (again):

```
static int
led_write(struct cdev *dev, struct uio *uio, int ioflag)
{
    int led = dev2unit(dev) & 0xff;
    struct led_softc *sc = dev->si_drv1;
    u_int8_t ch;
    u_int8_t old;
    int error;

    if (led >= LED_NUM)
        return (ENXIO);

    error = ❶uiomove(&ch, 1, uio);
    if (error)
        return (error);

❷old = bus_read_1(sc->sc_io_resource, 0);
❸if (ch & 1)
    ❹old |= (1 << led);
    else
    ❺old &= ~(1 << led);

❻bus_write_1(sc->sc_io_resource, 0, old);

    return (error);
}
```

This function first ❶ copies one character from user space to ch. Next, 1 byte from the LED's control register is ❷ read into old. Then, based on the ❸ value from user space, old's led bit is turned ❹ on or ❺ off. Afterward, old is ❻ written back to the LED's control register.

Conclusion

This chapter described all of the functions provided by FreeBSD for performing PMIO and MMIO (that is, for accessing a device's registers). The next chapter discusses using PMIO and MMIO with PCI devices, which are more involved than what's been shown here.

11

CASE STUDY: INTELLIGENT PLATFORM MANAGEMENT INTERFACE DRIVER

This chapter examines parts of ipmi(4), the Intelligent Platform Management Interface (IPMI) driver. The IPMI specification defines a standard for monitoring and managing system hardware.

NOTE *For our purposes, this description of IPMI is sufficient, as the point of this chapter is to demonstrate how PCI drivers such as* ipmi(4) *employ PMIO and MMIO.*

The code base for ipmi(4) is composed of 10 source files and 1 header file. In this chapter, we'll walk through one of these files, *ipmi_pci.c*, which contains code that's related to the PCI bus.

Code Analysis

Listing 11-1 provides a terse, source-level overview of *ipmi_pci.c*.

```
#include <sys/param.h>
#include <sys/module.h>
#include <sys/kernel.h>
```

```
#include <sys/systm.h>

#include <sys/bus.h>
#include <sys/condvar.h>
#include <sys/eventhandler.h>
#include <sys/selinfo.h>

#include <machine/bus.h>
#include <sys/rman.h>
#include <machine/resource.h>

#include <dev/pci/pcireg.h>
#include <dev/pci/pcivar.h>

#include <dev/ipmi/ipmivars.h>

static struct ipmi_ident {
        u_int16_t      vendor;
        u_int16_t      device;
        char           *description;
} ipmi_identifiers[] = {
        { 0x1028, 0x000d, "Dell PE2650 SMIC interface" },
        { 0, 0, 0 }
};

const char *
ipmi_pci_match(uint16_t vendor, uint16_t device)
{
...
}

static int
ipmi_pci_probe(device_t dev)
{
...
}

static int
ipmi_pci_attach(device_t dev)
{
...
}

static device_method_t ipmi_methods[] = {
        /* Device interface. */
        DEVMETHOD(device_probe,         ipmi_pci_probe),
        DEVMETHOD(device_attach,        ipmi_pci_attach),
        DEVMETHOD(device_detach,        ipmi_detach),
        { 0, 0 }
};

static driver_t ipmi_pci_driver = {
        "ipmi",
        ipmi_methods,
        sizeof(struct ipmi_softc)
```

```
};
```

❶ `DRIVER_MODULE(ipmi_pci, pci, ipmi_pci_driver, ipmi_devclass, 0, 0);`

```
static int
ipmi2_pci_probe(device_t dev)
{
...
}

static int
ipmi2_pci_attach(device_t dev)
{
...
}

static device_method_t ipmi2_methods[] = {
        /* Device interface. */
        DEVMETHOD(device_probe,       ipmi2_pci_probe),
        DEVMETHOD(device_attach,      ipmi2_pci_attach),
        DEVMETHOD(device_detach,      ipmi_detach),
        { 0, 0 }
};

static driver_t ipmi2_pci_driver = {
        "ipmi",
        ipmi2_methods,
        sizeof(struct ipmi_softc)
};
```

❷ `DRIVER_MODULE(ipmi2_pci, pci, ipmi2_pci_driver, ipmi_devclass, 0, 0);`

Listing 11-1: ipmi_pci.c

Before I describe the functions in Listing 11-1, note that it contains two
❶ ❷ `DRIVER_MODULE` calls. In other words, Listing 11-1 declares two Newbus drivers; each designed to handle a distinct group of devices (as you'll soon see).
Now let's discuss the functions found in Listing 11-1.

ipmi_pci_probe Function

The `ipmi_pci_probe` function is the `device_probe` implementation for the first
Newbus driver found in Listing 11-1. Here is its function definition:

```
static int
ipmi_pci_probe(device_t ❶dev)
{
        const char *desc;

     ❷if (ipmi_attached)
             ❸return (ENXIO);
```

```
        desc = ❹ipmi_pci_match(pci_get_vendor(dev), pci_get_device(dev));
        if (desc != NULL) {
                device_set_desc(dev, desc);
                return (BUS_PROBE_DEFAULT);
        }

        return (ENXIO);
}
```

This function first ❷ checks the value of the global variable ipmi_attached. If it is nonzero, which signifies that ipmi(4) is currently in use, the error code ❸ ENXIO is returned; otherwise, ❹ ipmi_pci_match is called to determine whether this driver can handle ❶ dev.

ipmi_pci_match Function

The ipmi_pci_match function takes in a PCI Vendor ID/Device ID (VID/DID) pair and verifies whether it recognizes those IDs. Before I define (and subsequently walk through) this function, a description of the ipmi_identifiers array is needed. This array is defined near the beginning of Listing 11-1 like so:

```
static struct ipmi_ident {
        ❶u_int16_t       vendor;
        ❷u_int16_t       device;
        ❸char           *description;
} ipmi_identifiers[] = {
        { 0x1028, 0x000d, "Dell PE2650 SMIC interface" },
        { 0, 0, 0 }
};
```

As you can see, the ipmi_identifiers array is composed of ipmi_ident structures. Each ipmi_ident structure includes a ❶ ❷ VID/DID pair and a ❸ description of the PCI device. As you may have guessed, ipmi_identifiers lists the devices that the first Newbus driver in Listing 11-1 supports.

Now that we've discussed ipmi_identifiers, let's walk through ipmi_pci_match.

```
const char *
ipmi_pci_match(uint16_t vendor, uint16_t device)
{
        struct ipmi_ident *m;

    ❶for (m = ipmi_identifiers; m->vendor != 0; m++)
            ❷if (m->vendor == vendor && m->device == device)
                    ❸return (m->description);

        return (NULL);
}
```

This function determines whether a specific ❷ VID/DID pair is listed in ❶ ipmi_identifiers. If so, its ❸ description is returned.

ipmi_pci_attach Function

The ipmi_pci_attach function is the device_attach implementation for the first Newbus driver found in Listing 11-1. Here is its function definition:

```
static int
ipmi_pci_attach(device_t dev)
{
        struct ipmi_softc *sc = device_get_softc(dev);
        struct ipmi_get_info info;
        const char *mode;
        int error, type;

    ❶if (!ipmi_smbios_identify(&info))
            return (ENXIO);

        sc->ipmi_dev = dev;

    ❷switch (info.iface_type) {
        case KCS_MODE:
                mode = "KCS";
                break;
        case SMIC_MODE:
                mode = "SMIC";
                break;
        case BT_MODE:
                device_printf(dev, "BT mode is unsupported\n");
                return (ENXIO);
        default:
                device_printf(dev, "No IPMI interface found\n");
                return (ENXIO);
        }

        device_printf(dev,
            "%s mode found at %s 0x%jx alignment 0x%x on %s\n",
            mode,
            info.io_mode ? "I/O port" : "I/O memory",
            (uintmax_t)info.address,
            info.offset,
            device_get_name(device_get_parent(dev)));

        if (info.io_mode)
            ❸type = SYS_RES_IOPORT;
        else
            ❹type = SYS_RES_MEMORY;

        sc->ipmi_io_rid = ❺PCIR_BAR(0);
        sc->ipmi_io_res[0] = bus_alloc_resource_any(dev, type,
          ❻&sc->ipmi_io_rid, RF_ACTIVE);
        sc->ipmi_io_type = type;
        sc->ipmi_io_spacing = info.offset;
```

```
        if (sc->ipmi_io_res[0] == NULL) {
                device_printf(dev, "could not configure PCI I/O resource\n");
                return (ENXIO);
        }

        sc->ipmi_irq_rid = 0;
        sc->ipmi_irq_res = ❼bus_alloc_resource_any(dev, SYS_RES_IRQ,
            &sc->ipmi_irq_rid, RF_SHAREABLE | RF_ACTIVE);

        switch (info.iface_type) {
        case KCS_MODE:
                error = ❽ipmi_kcs_attach(sc);
                if (error)
                        goto bad;
                break;
        case SMIC_MODE:
                error = ❾ipmi_smic_attach(sc);
                if (error)
                        goto bad;
                break;
        }

        error = ❿ipmi_attach(dev);
        if (error)
                goto bad;

        return (0);

bad:
        ipmi_release_resources(dev);
        return (error);
}
```

This function begins by ❶ retrieving the IPMI data structure stored in the computer's *System Management BIOS (SMBIOS)*, which is responsible for maintaining hardware configuration information.

Based on the SMBIOS data, `ipmi_pci_attach` determines `ipmi(4)`'s ❷ mode of operation and whether it requires ❸ I/O port or ❹ I/O memory access. Currently, `ipmi(4)` supports only Keyboard Controller Style (KCS) and Server Management Interface Chip (SMIC) modes. These modes dictate how IPMI messages are transferred. For our purposes, you won't need to understand the specifics of either mode.

The next block of code acquires I/O region access for `ipmi(4)`. Before I describe this code, some background on PCI devices is needed. After bootup, PCI devices can remap their device registers to a different location, thus avoiding address conflicts with other devices. Because of this, PCI devices store the size and current location of their I/O-mapped registers in their base address registers (BARs). Thus, this block of code first calls ❺ `PCIR_BAR(0)` to get the address of the first BAR. Then it passes that address as the ❻ rid argument to `bus_alloc_resource_any`, thereby acquiring I/O access to the device's registers.

To be accurate, the `PCIR_BAR(x)` *macro returns the RID of the* x*th BAR.*

The remainder of `ipmi_pci_attach` ❼ acquires an IRQ, starts up ❽ KCS or ❾ SMIC mode, and calls ❿ `ipmi_attach` to finish initializing the device.

ipmi2_pci_probe Function

The `ipmi2_pci_probe` function is the `device_probe` implementation for the second Newbus driver found in Listing 11-1. Here is its function definition:

```
static int
ipmi2_pci_probe(device_t dev)
{
        if (pci_get_class(dev) == PCIC_SERIALBUS &&
            pci_get_subclass(dev) == ❶PCIS_SERIALBUS_IPMI) {
                ❷device_set_desc(dev, "IPMI System Interface");
                ❸return (BUS_PROBE_GENERIC);
        }

        return (ENXIO);
}
```

This function determines if `dev` is a ❶ generic IPMI device on the PCI bus. If so, its verbose description is ❷ set, and the success code ❸ `BUS_PROBE_GENERIC` is returned. In short, this driver handles any standard IPMI device on the PCI bus.

As you may have guessed, the first Newbus driver is a hack (that is to say, a workaround) for the Dell PE2650, because it does not adhere to the IPMI specification.

ipmi2_pci_attach Function

The `ipmi2_pci_attach` function is the `device_attach` implementation for the second Newbus driver found in Listing 11-1. Here is its function definition:

```
static int
ipmi2_pci_attach(device_t dev)
{
        struct ipmi_softc *sc = device_get_softc(dev);
        int error, iface, type;

        sc->ipmi_dev = dev;

      ❶switch (pci_get_progif(dev)) {
        case PCIP_SERIALBUS_IPMI_SMIC:
                iface = SMIC_MODE;
                break;
        case PCIP_SERIALBUS_IPMI_KCS:
                iface = KCS_MODE;
                break;
        case PCIP_SERIALBUS_IPMI_BT:
                device_printf(dev, "BT interface is unsupported\n");
                return (ENXIO);
```

```
        default:
                device_printf(dev, "unsupported interface: %d\n",
                    pci_get_progif(dev));
                return (ENXIO);
        }

        sc->ipmi_io_rid = ❷PCIR_BAR(0);
❸if (PCI_BAR_IO(pci_read_config(dev, PCIR_BAR(0), 4)))
                ❹type = SYS_RES_IOPORT;
        else
                ❺type = SYS_RES_MEMORY;
        sc->ipmi_io_type = type;
        sc->ipmi_io_spacing = 1;
        sc->ipmi_io_res[0] = ❻bus_alloc_resource_any(dev, type,
            &sc->ipmi_io_rid, RF_ACTIVE);
        if (sc->ipmi_io_res[0] == NULL) {
                device_printf(dev, "could not configure PCI I/O resource\n");
                return (ENXIO);
        }

        sc->ipmi_irq_rid = 0;
        sc->ipmi_irq_res = ❼bus_alloc_resource_any(dev, SYS_RES_IRQ,
            &sc->ipmi_irq_rid, RF_SHAREABLE | RF_ACTIVE);

        switch (iface) {
        case KCS_MODE:
                device_printf(dev, "using KCS interface\n");

                if (!ipmi_kcs_probe_align(sc)) {
                        device_printf(dev,
                            "unable to determine alignment\n");
                        error = ENXIO;
                        goto bad;
                }

                error = ❽ipmi_kcs_attach(sc);
                if (error)
                        goto bad;
                break;
        case SMIC_MODE:
                device_printf(dev, "using SMIC interface\n");

                error = ❾ipmi_smic_attach(sc);
                if (error)
                        goto bad;
                break;
        }

        error = ❿ipmi_attach(dev);
        if (error)
                goto bad;

        return (0);
```

```
bad:
        ipmi_release_resources(dev);
        return (error);
}
```

This function begins by ❶ examining dev's programming interface to determine ipmi(4)'s mode of operation (either SMIC or KCS). Then ❷ PCIR_BAR(0) is called to obtain the address of the first BAR. From this BAR, ipmi2_pci_attach ❸ identifies whether ipmi(4) requires ❹ I/O port or ❺ I/O memory access before ❻ acquiring it. Lastly, ipmi2_pci_attach ❼ obtains an IRQ, starts up ❽ KCS or ❾ SMIC mode, and calls ❿ ipmi_attach to finish initializing dev.

Conclusion

This chapter examined the PCI code base for ipmi(4) and introduced two fundamentals. First, a single source file can contain more than one driver. Second, to acquire I/O region access, PCI drivers must first call PCIR_BAR.

12

DIRECT MEMORY ACCESS

Direct Memory Access (DMA) is a feature of modern processors that lets a device transfer data to and from main memory independently of the CPU. With DMA, the CPU merely initiates the data transfer (that is to say, it does not complete it), and then the device (or a separate DMA controller) actually moves the data. Because of this, DMA tends to provide higher system performance as the CPU is free to perform other tasks during the data transfer.

NOTE   *There is some overhead in performing DMA. Accordingly, only devices that move large amounts of data (for example, storage devices) use DMA. You wouldn't use DMA just to transfer one or two bytes of data.*

Implementing DMA

Unlike with previous topics, I'm going to take a holistic approach here. Namely, I'm going to show an example first, and then I'll describe the DMA family of functions.

The following pseudocode is a `device_attach` routine for a fictitious device that uses DMA.

```
static int
foo_attach(device_t dev)
{
        struct foo_softc *sc = device_get_softc(dev);
        int error;

        bzero(sc, sizeof(*sc));

        if (❶bus_dma_tag_create(bus_get_dma_tag(dev),   /* parent       */
                              1,                         /* alignment    */
                              0,                         /* boundary     */
                              BUS_SPACE_MAXADDR,         /* lowaddr      */
                              BUS_SPACE_MAXADDR,         /* highaddr     */
                              NULL,                      /* filter       */
                              NULL,                      /* filterarg    */
                              BUS_SPACE_MAXSIZE_32BIT,   /* maxsize      */
                              BUS_SPACE_UNRESTRICTED,    /* nsegments    */
                              BUS_SPACE_MAXSIZE_32BIT,   /* maxsegsize   */
                              0,                         /* flags        */
                              NULL,                      /* lockfunc     */
                              NULL,                      /* lockfuncarg  */
                       ❷&sc->foo_parent_dma_tag)) {
                device_printf(dev, "Cannot allocate parent DMA tag!\n");
                return (ENOMEM);
        }

        if (bus_dma_tag_create(❸sc->foo_parent_dma_tag,/* parent        */
                              1,                         /* alignment    */
                              0,                         /* boundary     */
                              BUS_SPACE_MAXADDR,         /* lowaddr      */
                              BUS_SPACE_MAXADDR,         /* highaddr     */
                              NULL,                      /* filter       */
                              NULL,                      /* filterarg    */
                              MAX_BAZ_SIZE,              /* maxsize      */
                              MAX_BAZ_SCATTER,           /* nsegments    */
                              BUS_SPACE_MAXSIZE_32BIT,   /* maxsegsize   */
                              0,                         /* flags        */
                              NULL,                      /* lockfunc     */
                              NULL,                      /* lockfuncarg  */
                       ❹&sc->foo_baz_dma_tag)) {
                device_printf(dev, "Cannot allocate baz DMA tag!\n");
                return (ENOMEM);
        }

        if (bus_dmamap_create(sc->foo_baz_dma_tag,       /* DMA tag      */
                              0,                         /* flags        */
```

```
                          ❺&sc->foo_baz_dma_map)) {
                device_printf(dev, "Cannot allocate baz DMA map!\n");
                return (ENOMEM);
        }

        bzero(sc->foo_baz_buf, BAZ_BUF_SIZE);

        error = ❻bus_dmamap_load(sc->foo_baz_dma_tag,   /* DMA tag     */
                            ❼sc->foo_baz_dma_map,       /* DMA map     */
                            ❽sc->foo_baz_buf,           /* buffer      */
                            BAZ_BUF_SIZE,               /* buffersize  */
                            ❾foo_callback,              /* callback    */
                            &sc->foo_baz_busaddr,       /* callbackarg */
                            BUS_DMA_NOWAIT);            /* flags       */
        if (error || sc->foo_baz_busaddr == 0) {
                device_printf(dev, "Cannot map baz DMA memory!\n");
                return (ENOMEM);
        }

        ...
}
```

This pseudocode begins by calling ❶ bus_dma_tag_create to create a DMA tag named ❷ foo_parent_dma_tag. At heart, *DMA tags* describe the characteristics and restrictions of DMA transactions.

Next, bus_dma_tag_create is called again. Notice that foo_parent_dma_tag is this call's ❸ first argument. See, DMA tags can inherit the characteristics and restrictions of other tags. Of course, child tags cannot loosen the restrictions set up by their parents. Consequently, the DMA tag ❹ foo_baz_dma_tag is a "draconian" version of foo_parent_dma_tag.

The next statement, bus_dmamap_create, creates a DMA map named ❺ foo_baz_dma_map. Loosely speaking, *DMA maps* represent memory areas that have been allocated according to the properties of a DMA tag and are within device visible address space.

Finally, ❻ bus_dmamap_load loads the buffer ❽ foo_baz_buf into the device visible address associated with the DMA map ❼ foo_baz_dma_map.

NOTE *Any arbitrary buffer can be used for DMA. However, buffers are inaccessible to devices until they've been loaded (or mapped) into a device visible address (that is, a DMA map).*

Note that bus_dmamap_load requires a ❾ callback function, which typically looks something like this:

```
static void
❶ foo_callback(void ❷*arg, bus_dma_segment_t *segs, int nseg, int error)
{
        if (error)
                ❸return;

        *(bus_addr_t *)❹arg = ❺segs[0].ds_addr;
}
```

Here, ❷ arg dereferences to the sixth argument passed to bus_dmamap_load, which was foo_baz_busaddr.

This callback function executes after the buffer-load operation completes. If successful, the ❺ address where the buffer was loaded is returned in ❹ arg. If unsuccessful, ❶ foo_callback does ❸ nothing.

Initiating a DMA Data Transfer

Assuming the buffer-load operation completed successfully, one can initiate a DMA data transfer with something like this:

NOTE   *Most devices just require the device visible address of a buffer to be written to a specific register to start a DMA data transfer.*

```
❶bus_write_4(sc->foo_io_resource, ❷FOO_BAZ, ❸sc->foo_baz_busaddr);
```

Here, the ❸ device visible address of a buffer is ❶ written to a ❷ device register. Recall that the foo_callback function described in the previous section returns in ❸ foo_baz_busaddr the device visible address of foo_baz_buf.

Dismantling DMA

Now that you know how to implement DMA, I'll demonstrate how to dismantle it.

```
static int
foo_detach(device_t dev)
{
        struct foo_softc *sc = device_get_softc(dev);

        if (sc->foo_baz_busaddr != 0)
                bus_dmamap_unload(sc->foo_baz_dma_tag, sc->foo_baz_dma_map);

        if (sc->foo_baz_dma_map != NULL)
                bus_dmamap_destroy(sc->foo_baz_dma_tag, sc->foo_baz_dma_map);

        if (sc->foo_baz_dma_tag != NULL)
                bus_dma_tag_destroy(sc->foo_baz_dma_tag);

        if (sc->foo_parent_dma_tag != NULL)
                bus_dma_tag_destroy(sc->foo_parent_dma_tag);

...
}
```

As you can see, this pseudocode simply tears down everything in the opposite order that it was built up.

Now, let's discuss in detail the different functions encountered here and in the previous two sections.

Creating DMA Tags

As mentioned earlier, DMA tags describe the characteristics and restrictions of DMA transactions and are created by using the bus_dma_tag_create function.

```
#include <machine/bus.h>

int
bus_dma_tag_create(bus_dma_tag_t parent, bus_size_t alignment,
    bus_size_t boundary, bus_addr_t lowaddr, bus_addr_t highaddr,
    bus_dma_filter_t *filtfunc, void *filtfuncarg, bus_size_t maxsize,
    int nsegments, bus_size_t maxsegsz, int flags,
    bus_dma_lock_t *lockfunc, void *lockfuncarg, bus_dma_tag_t *dmat);
```

Here, the parent argument identifies the parent DMA tag. To create a top-level DMA tag, pass bus_get_dma_tag(device_t dev) as parent.

The alignment argument denotes the physical alignment, in bytes, of each DMA segment. Recall that DMA maps represent memory areas that have been allocated according to the properties of a DMA tag. These memory areas are known as *DMA segments*. If you return to the foo_callback function described in "Implementing DMA" on page 194, you'll see that arg is actually assigned the address of a DMA segment.

The alignment argument must be 1, which denotes no specific alignment, or a power of two. As an example, drivers that require DMA buffers to begin on a multiple of 4KB would pass 4096 as alignment.

The boundary argument specifies the physical address boundaries that cannot be crossed by each DMA segment; that is, they cannot cross any multiple of boundary. This argument must be 0, which indicates no boundary restrictions, or a power of two.

The lowaddr and highaddr arguments outline the address range that cannot be employed for DMA. For example, devices incapable of DMA above 4GB would have 0xFFFFFFFF as lowaddr and BUS_SPACE_MAXADDR as highaddr.

NOTE   *0xFFFFFFFF equals 4GB, and the constant* BUS_SPACE_MAXADDR *signifies the maximum addressable memory for your architecture.*

The filtfunc and filtfuncarg arguments denote an optional callback function and its first argument, respectively. This function is executed for every attempt to load (or map) a DMA buffer between lowaddr and highaddr. If there's a device-accessible region between lowaddr and highaddr, filtfunc is supposed to tell the system. Here is the function prototype for filtfunc:

```
int filtfunc(void *filtfuncarg, bus_addr_t ❶addr)
```

This function must return 0 if the address ❶ addr is device-accessible or a nonzero value if it's inaccessible.

If filtfunc and filtfuncarg are NULL, the entire address range from lowaddr to highaddr is considered inaccessible.

The maxsize argument denotes the maximum amount of memory, in bytes, that may be allocated for a single DMA map.

The nsegments argument specifies the number of scatter/gather segments allowed in a single DMA map. A *scatter/gather segment* is simply a memory page. The name comes from the fact that when you take a set of physically discontinuous pages and virtually assemble them into a single contiguous buffer, you must "scatter" your writes and "gather" your reads. Some devices require blocks of contiguous memory; however sometimes a large enough block is not available. So the kernel "tricks" the device by using a buffer composed of scatter/gather segments. Every DMA segment is a scatter/gather segment.

The nsegments argument may be BUS_SPACE_UNRESTRICTED, which indicates no number restriction. DMA tags made with BUS_SPACE_UNRESTRICTED cannot create DMA maps; they can only be parent tags, because the system cannot support DMA maps composed of an unlimited number of scatter/gather segments.

The maxsegsz argument denotes the maximum size, in bytes, of an individual DMA segment within a single DMA map.

The flags argument modifies bus_dma_tag_create's behavior. Table 12-1 displays its only valid value.

Table 12-1: bus_dma_tag_create Symbolic Constants

Constant	Description
BUS_DMA_ALLOCNOW	Preallocates enough resources to handle at least one buffer-load operation; if sufficient resources are unavailable, ENOMEM is returned.

The lockfunc and lockfuncarg arguments denote an optional callback function and its first argument, respectively. Remember how bus_dmamap_load requires a callback function? Well, lockfunc executes right before and after that function to acquire and release any necessary synchronization primitives. Here is lockfunc's function prototype:

```
void lockfunc(void *lockfuncarg, bus_dma_lock_op_t ❶op)
```

When lockfunc executes, ❶ op contains either BUS_DMA_LOCK or BUS_DMA_UNLOCK. That is, op dictates what lock operation to perform.

The dmat argument expects a pointer to bus_dma_tag_t; assuming bus_dma_tag_create is successful, this pointer will store the resulting DMA tag.

Tearing Down DMA Tags

DMA tags are torn down by the bus_dma_tag_destroy function.

```
#include <machine/bus.h>

int
bus_dma_tag_destroy(bus_dma_tag_t dmat);
```

This function returns EBUSY if there are any DMA maps still associated with dmat.

DMA Map Management Routines, Part 1

As mentioned earlier, DMA maps represent memory areas (that is to say, DMA segments) that have been allocated according to the properties of a DMA tag and are within device visible address space.

DMA maps can be managed with the following functions:

```
#include <machine/bus.h>

int
bus_dmamap_create(bus_dma_tag_t dmat, int flags, bus_dmamap_t *mapp);

int
bus_dmamap_destroy(bus_dma_tag_t dmat, bus_dmamap_t map);
```

The bus_dmamap_create function creates a DMA map based on the DMA tag dmat and stores the result in mapp. The flags argument modifies bus_dmamap_create's behavior. Table 12-2 displays its only valid value.

Table 12-2: bus_dmamap_create Symbolic Constants

Constant	Description
BUS_DMA_COHERENT	Causes cache synchronization operations to be as cheap as possible for your DMA buffers; this flag is implemented only on *sparc64*.

The bus_dmamap_destroy function tears down the DMA map map. The dmat argument is the DMA tag that map was based on.

Loading (DMA) Buffers into DMA Maps

The FreeBSD kernel provides four functions for loading a buffer into the device visible address associated with a DMA map:

- bus_dmamap_load
- bus_dmamap_load_mbuf
- bus_dmamap_load_mbuf_sg
- bus_dmamap_load_uio

Before I describe these functions, an explanation of bus_dma_segment structures is needed.

bus_dma_segment Structures

A bus_dma_segment structure describes a single DMA segment.

```
typedef struct bus_dma_segment {
        bus_addr_t    ❶ds_addr;
        bus_size_t    ❷ds_len;
} bus_dma_segment_t;
```

The ❶ ds_addr field contains its device visible address and ❷ ds_len contains its length.

bus_dmamap_load Function

We first discussed the bus_dmamap_load function in "Implementing DMA" on page 194.

```
#include <machine/bus.h>

int
bus_dmamap_load(bus_dma_tag_t dmat, bus_dmamap_t map, void *buf,
    bus_size_t buflen, bus_dmamap_callback_t *callback,
    void *callbackarg, int flags);
```

This function loads the buffer buf into the device visible address associated with the DMA map map. The dmat argument is the DMA tag that map is based on. The buflen argument is the number of bytes from buf to load. bus_dmamap_load returns immediately and never blocks for any reason.

The callback and callbackarg arguments denote a callback function and its first argument, respectively. callback executes after the buffer-load operation completes. If resources are lacking, the buffer-load operation and callback will be deferred. If bus_dmamap_load returns EINPROGRESS, this has occurred. Here is callback's function prototype:

```
void callback(void *callbackarg, bus_dma_segment_t ❶*segs, int ❷nseg,
              int ❸error)
```

When callback executes, ❸ error discloses the success (0) or failure (EFBIG) of the buffer-load operation (the error code EFBIG stands for *error: file too large*). The ❶ segs argument is the array of DMA segments that buf has been loaded into; ❷ nseg is this array's size.

The following pseudocode is an example callback function:

```
static void
foo_callback(void *callbackarg, bus_dma_segment_t *segs, int nseg, int error)
{
        struct foo_softc *sc = callbackarg;
        int i;

        if (error)
                return;

        sc->sg_num = nseg;
    ❶for (i = 0; i < nseg; i++)
```

```
            sc->sg_addr[i] = ❷segs[i].ds_addr;
}
```

This function ❶ iterates through segs to return the ❷ device visible address of each DMA segment that buf has been loaded into.

NOTE   *If buf can fit into one DMA segment, the foo_callback function described in "Implementing DMA" on page 194 may be used as callback.*

The flags argument modifies bus_dmamap_load's behavior. Valid values for this argument are shown in Table 12-3.

Table 12-3: bus_dmamap_load Symbolic Constants

Constant	Description
BUS_DMA_NOWAIT	If memory resources are lacking, the buffer-load operation and callback will *not* be deferred.
BUS_DMA_NOCACHE	Prevents caching the DMA buffer, thereby causing all DMA transactions to be executed without reordering; this flag is implemented only on *sparc64*.

bus_dmamap_load_mbuf Function

The bus_dmamap_load_mbuf function is a variant of bus_dmamap_load that loads mbuf chains (you'll learn about mbuf chains in Chapter 16).

```
#include <machine/bus.h>

int
bus_dmamap_load_mbuf(bus_dma_tag_t dmat, bus_dmamap_t map,
    struct mbuf *mbuf, bus_dmamap_callback2_t *callback2,
    void *callbackarg, int flags);
```

Most of these arguments are identical to their bus_dmamap_load counterparts except for:

- The mbuf argument, which expects an mbuf chain
- The callback2 argument, which requires a different callback function
- The flags argument, which implicitly sets BUS_DMA_NOWAIT

Here is callback2's function prototype:

```
void callback2(void *callbackarg, bus_dma_segment_t *segs, int nseg,
               bus_size_t ❶mapsize, int error)
```

callback2 is like callback, but it returns the ❶ amount of data loaded.

bus_dmamap_load_mbuf_sg Function

The bus_dmamap_load_mbuf_sg function is an alternative to bus_dmamap_load_mbuf that does not use callback2.

```
#include <machine/bus.h>

int
bus_dmamap_load_mbuf_sg(bus_dma_tag_t dmat, bus_dmamap_t map,
    struct mbuf *mbuf, bus_dma_segment_t ❶*segs, int ❷*nseg, int flags);
```

As you can see, this function directly and immediately returns ❶ segs and
❷ nseg.

bus_dmamap_load_uio Function

The bus_dmamap_load_uio function is identical to bus_dmamap_load_mbuf except
that it loads the buffers from within a uio structure.

```
#include <machine/bus.h>

int
bus_dmamap_load_uio(bus_dma_tag_t dmat, bus_dmamap_t map,
    struct uio *uio, bus_dmamap_callback2_t *callback2,
    void *callbackarg, int flags);
```

bus_dmamap_unload Function

The bus_dmamap_unload function unloads the buffers from a DMA map.

```
#include <machine/bus.h>

void
bus_dmamap_unload(bus_dma_tag_t dmat, bus_dmamap_t map);
```

DMA Map Management Routines, Part 2

This section describes an alternative set of functions used to manage DMA maps.

```
#include <machine/bus.h>

int
bus_dmamem_alloc(bus_dma_tag_t dmat, void **vaddr, int flags,
    bus_dmamap_t *mapp);

void
bus_dmamem_free(bus_dma_tag_t dmat, void *vaddr, bus_dmamap_t map);
```

The bus_dmamem_alloc function creates a DMA map based on the DMA
tag dmat and stores the result in mapp. This function also allocates maxsize bytes
of contiguous memory (where maxsize is defined by dmat). The address of
this memory is returned in vaddr. As you'll soon see, this contiguous memory

```
```

will eventually become your DMA buffer. The flags argument modifies bus_dmamem_alloc's behavior. Valid values for this argument are shown in Table 12-4.

Table 12-4: bus_dmamem_alloc Symbolic Constants

Constant	Description
BUS_DMA_ZERO	Causes the allocated memory to be set to zero
BUS_DMA_NOWAIT	Causes bus_dmamem_alloc to return ENOMEM if the allocation cannot be immediately fulfilled due to resource shortage
BUS_DMA_WAITOK	Indicates that it is okay to wait for resources; if the allocation cannot be immediately fulfilled, the current process is put to sleep to wait for resources to become available.
BUS_DMA_COHERENT	Causes cache synchronization operations to be as cheap as possible for your DMA buffer; this flag is implemented only on *arm* and *sparc64*.
BUS_DMA_NOCACHE	Prevents caching the DMA buffer, thereby causing all DMA transactions to be executed without reordering; this flag is implemented only on *amd64* and *i386*.

NOTE   *bus_dmamem_alloc is used when you require a physically contiguous DMA buffer.*

The bus_dmamem_free function releases the memory at vaddr that was previously allocated by bus_dmamem_alloc. Then it tears down the DMA map map.

A Straightforward Example

The following pseudocode is a device_attach routine for a fictitious device that requires DMA. This pseudocode should demonstrate how to use bus_dmamem_alloc.

```
static int
foo_attach(device_t dev)
{
        struct foo_softc *sc = device_get_softc(dev);
        int size = BAZ_SIZE;
        int error;

        bzero(sc, sizeof(*sc));

        if (bus_dma_tag_create(bus_get_dma_tag(dev),    /* parent        */
                               1,                       /* alignment     */
                               0,                       /* boundary      */
                               BUS_SPACE_MAXADDR,       /* lowaddr       */
                               BUS_SPACE_MAXADDR,       /* highaddr      */
                               NULL,                    /* filter        */
                               NULL,                    /* filterarg     */
                               BUS_SPACE_MAXSIZE_32BIT, /* maxsize       */
                               BUS_SPACE_UNRESTRICTED,  /* nsegments     */
```

```
                              BUS_SPACE_MAXSIZE_32BIT, /* maxsegsize  */
                              0,                       /* flags       */
                              NULL,                    /* lockfunc    */
                              NULL,                    /* lockfuncarg */
                              &sc->foo_parent_dma_tag)) {
        device_printf(dev, "Cannot allocate parent DMA tag!\n");
        return (ENOMEM);
}

if (bus_dma_tag_create(sc->foo_parent_dma_tag, /* parent      */
                       64,                     /* alignment   */
                       0,                      /* boundary    */
                       BUS_SPACE_MAXADDR_32BIT, /* lowaddr     */
                       BUS_SPACE_MAXADDR,      /* highaddr    */
                       NULL,                   /* filter      */
                       NULL,                   /* filterarg   */
                     ❶size,                    /* maxsize     */
                     ❷1,                       /* nsegments   */
                     ❸size,                    /* maxsegsize  */
                       0,                      /* flags       */
                       NULL,                   /* lockfunc    */
                       NULL,                   /* lockfuncarg */
                       &sc->foo_baz_dma_tag)) {
        device_printf(dev, "Cannot allocate baz DMA tag!\n");
        return (ENOMEM);
}

if (❹bus_dmamem_alloc(sc->foo_baz_dma_tag,      /* DMA tag     */
                  ❺(void **)&sc->foo_baz_buf,   /* vaddr       */
                    BUS_DMA_NOWAIT,             /* flags       */
                  ❻&sc->foo_baz_dma_map)) {
        device_printf(dev, "Cannot allocate baz DMA memory!\n");
        return (ENOMEM);
}

bzero(sc->foo_baz_buf, size);

error = ❼bus_dmamap_load(sc->foo_baz_dma_tag,   /* DMA tag     */
                    ❽sc->foo_baz_dma_map,       /* DMA map     */
                    ❾sc->foo_baz_buf,           /* buffer      */
                      size,                     /* buffersize  */
                    ❿foo_callback,              /* callback    */
                      &sc->foo_baz_busaddr,     /* callbackarg */
                      BUS_DMA_NOWAIT);          /* flags       */
if (error || sc->foo_baz_busaddr == 0) {
        device_printf(dev, "Cannot map baz DMA memory!\n");
        return (ENOMEM);
}


...
}
```

Although ❹ bus_dmamem_alloc allocates ❺ memory and creates a ❻ DMA map, ❼ loading that ❾ memory into the ❽ DMA map still needs to occur.

Also, since bus_dmamem_alloc allocates contiguous memory, the nsegments argument must be ❷ 1. Likewise, the ❶ maxsize and ❸ maxsegsz arguments must be identical.

Lastly, since nsegments is 1, ❿ callback can be the foo_callback function shown in "Implementing DMA" on page 194.

Synchronizing DMA Buffers

DMA buffers must be synchronized after each write completed by the CPU/ driver or a device. The exact reason why is beyond the scope of this book. But it's basically done to ensure that the CPU/driver and device have a consistent view of the DMA buffer.

DMA buffers are synchronized with the bus_dmamap_sync function.

```
#include <machine/bus.h>

void
bus_dmamap_sync(bus_dma_tag_t dmat, bus_dmamap_t map, bus_dmasync_op_t op);
```

This function synchronizes the DMA buffer currently loaded in the DMA map map. The dmat argument is the DMA tag that map is based on. The op argument identifies the type of synchronization operation to perform. Valid values for this argument are shown in Table 12-5.

Table 12-5: bus_dmamap_sync Symbolic Constant

Constant	Description
BUS_DMASYNC_PREWRITE	Used to synchronize after the CPU/driver writes to the DMA buffer
BUS_DMASYNC_POSTREAD	Used to synchronize after a device writes to the DMA buffer

Conclusion

This chapter detailed FreeBSD's DMA management routines. These routines are primarily used by storage and network drivers, which are discussed in Chapters 13, 16, and 17.

13

STORAGE DRIVERS

In FreeBSD, *storage drivers* provide access to devices that transfer randomly accessible data in blocks (such as disk drives, flash memory, and so on). A *block* is a fixed-size chunk of data (Corbet et al., 2005). In this chapter I'll discuss how to manage devices that employ block-centric I/O. To that end, some familiarity with disk and bio structures is needed, so that is where we'll start.

disk Structures

A disk structure is the kernel's representation of an individual disk-like storage device. It is defined in the <geom/geom_disk.h> header as follows:

```
struct disk {
        /* GEOM Private Data */
        struct g_geom          *d_geom;
        struct devstat         *d_devstat;
```

```
        int                    d_destroyed;

        /* Shared Objects */
        struct bio_queue_head  *d_queue;
        struct mtx             *d_lock;

        /* Descriptive Fields */
        const char             *d_name;
        u_int                   d_unit;
        u_int                   d_flags;

        /* Storage Device Methods */
        disk_open_t            *d_open;
        disk_close_t           *d_close;
        disk_strategy_t        *d_strategy;
        disk_ioctl_t           *d_ioctl;
        dumper_t               *d_dump;

        /* Mandatory Media Properties */
        u_int                   d_sectorsize;
        off_t                   d_mediasize;
        u_int                   d_maxsize;

        /* Optional Media Properties */
        u_int                   d_fwsectors;
        u_int                   d_fwheads;
        u_int                   d_stripesize;
        u_int                   d_stripeoffset;
        char                    d_ident[DISK_IDENT_SIZE];

        /* Driver Private Data */
        void                   *d_drv1;
};
```

Many of the fields in struct disk must be initialized by a storage driver. These fields are described in the following sections.

Descriptive Fields

The d_name and d_unit fields specify the storage device's name and unit number, respectively. These fields must be defined in every disk structure.

The d_flags field further qualifies the storage device's characteristics. Valid values for this field are shown in Table 13-1.

Table 13-1: disk Structure Symbolic Constants

Constant	Description
DISKFLAG_NEEDSGIANT	Indicates that the storage device needs to be protected by Giant
DISKFLAG_CANDELETE	Indicates that the storage device wants to be notified when a block is no longer required so that it can perform some special handling (for example, drivers for solid-state drives that support the TRIM command employ this flag)
DISKFLAG_CANFLUSHCACHE	Indicates that the storage device can flush its local write cache

The d_flags field is optional and may be undefined.

Storage Device Methods

The d_open field identifies the storage device's open routine. If no function is provided, open will always succeed.

The d_close field identifies the storage device's close routine. If no function is provided, close will always succeed. The d_close routine should always terminate anything set up by the d_open routine.

The d_strategy field identifies the storage device's strategy routine. *Strategy routines* are called to process block-centric reads, writes, and other I/O operations. Accordingly, d_strategy must be defined in every disk structure. I'll discuss block-centric I/O and strategy routines in greater detail later.

The d_ioctl field identifies the storage device's ioctl routine. This field is optional and may be undefined.

The d_dump field identifies the storage device's dump routine. *Dump routines* are called after a kernel panic to record the contents of physical memory to a storage device. Note that d_dump is optional and may be undefined.

Mandatory Media Properties

The d_sectorsize and d_mediasize fields specify the storage device's sector and media size in bytes, respectively. These fields must be defined in every disk structure.

The d_maxsize field denotes the maximum size in bytes that an I/O operation, for the storage device, can be. This field must be defined in every disk structure.

Note that you can safely modify the values for d_sectorsize, d_mediasize, and d_maxsize in the d_open routine.

Optional Media Properties

The d_fwsectors and d_fwheads fields identify the number of sectors and heads on the storage device. These fields are optional and may be undefined; however, certain platforms require these fields for disk partitioning.

The d_stripesize field specifies the width of any natural request boundaries for the storage device (for example, the size of a stripe on a RAID-5 unit), and the d_stripeoffset field represents the location or offset to the first stripe. These fields are optional and may be undefined. For more on d_stripesize and d_stripeoffset, see */sys/geom/notes*.

The d_ident field denotes the storage device's serial number. This field is optional and may be undefined, but it's good practice to define it.

Note that you can safely modify the abovementioned fields in the d_open routine.

Driver Private Data

The d_drv1 field may be used by the storage driver to house data. Typically, d_drv1 will contain a pointer to the storage driver's softc structure.

disk Structure Management Routines

The FreeBSD kernel provides the following functions for working with disk structures:

```
#include <geom/geom_disk.h>

struct disk *
disk_alloc(void);

void
disk_create(struct disk *disk, int version);

void
disk_destroy(struct disk *disk);
```

A disk structure is a dynamically allocated structure that's owned by the kernel. That is, you cannot allocate a struct disk on your own. Instead, you must call disk_alloc.

Allocating a disk structure does not make the storage device available to the system. To do that, you must initialize the structure (by defining the necessary fields) and then call disk_create. The version argument must always be DISK_VERSION.

Note that as soon as disk_create returns, the device is "live" and its routines can be called at any time. Therefore, you should call disk_create only when your driver is completely ready to handle any operation.

When a disk structure is no longer needed, it should be freed with disk_destroy. You can destroy an opened disk structure. Of course, you'll need to free any resources that were allocated during d_open afterward, as d_close can no longer be called.

Block I/O Structures

A bio structure represents a block-centric I/O request. Loosely speaking, when the kernel needs to transfer some data to or from a storage device, it puts together a bio structure to describe that operation; then it passes that structure to the appropriate driver.

struct bio is defined in the <sys/bio.h> header as follows:

```
struct bio {
        uint8_t bio_cmd;         /* I/O operation.             */
        uint8_t bio_flags;       /* General flags.             */
        uint8_t bio_cflags;      /* Private use by the consumer. */
        uint8_t bio_pflags;      /* Private use by the provider. */
```

```
            struct cdev *bio_dev;           /* Device to perform I/O on.   */
            struct disk *bio_disk;          /* Disk structure.             */
            off_t   bio_offset;             /* Requested position in file. */
            long    bio_bcount;             /* Number of (valid) bytes.    */
            caddr_t bio_data;               /* Data.                       */
            int     bio_error;              /* Error number for BIO_ERROR. */
            long    bio_resid;              /* Remaining I/O (in bytes).   */
            void (*bio_done)(struct bio *); /* biodone() handler function. */

            void    *bio_driver1;           /* Private use by the provider. */
            void    *bio_driver2;           /* Private use by the provider. */
            void    *bio_caller1;           /* Private use by the consumer. */
            void    *bio_caller2;           /* Private use by the consumer. */

            TAILQ_ENTRY(bio) bio_queue;     /* bioq linkage.               */
            const char *bio_attribute;      /* For BIO_[GS]ETATTR.         */
            struct g_consumer *bio_from;    /* GEOM linkage.               */
            struct g_provider *bio_to;      /* GEOM linkage.               */

            off_t   bio_length;             /* Like bio_bcount.            */
            off_t   bio_completed;          /* Opposite of bio_resid.      */
            u_int   bio_children;           /* Number of spawned bios.     */
            u_int   bio_inbed;              /* Number of children home.    */
            struct bio *bio_parent;         /* Parent pointer.             */
            struct bintime bio_t0;          /* Time I/O request started.   */

            bio_task_t *bio_task;   /* bio_taskqueue() handler function.   */
            void    *bio_task_arg;          /* bio_task's argument.        */
            void    *bio_classifier1;       /* Classifier tag.             */
            void    *bio_classifier2;       /* Classifier tag.             */

            daddr_t bio_pblkno;             /* Physical block number.      */
};

/* Bits for bio_cmd.  */
#define BIO_READ        0x01
#define BIO_WRITE       0x02
#define BIO_DELETE      0x04
#define BIO_GETATTR     0x08
#define BIO_FLUSH       0x10
#define BIO_CMD0        0x20            /* For local hacks.           */
#define BIO_CMD1        0x40            /* For local hacks.           */
#define BIO_CMD2        0x80            /* For local hacks.           */

/* Bits for bio_flags.  */
#define BIO_ERROR       0x01
#define BIO_DONE        0x02
#define BIO_ONQUEUE     0x04
```

We'll examine struct bio in greater detail later. In the interim, you just need to remember that strategy routines are called to process newly received bio structures.

Block I/O Queues

All storage drivers maintain a *block I/O queue* to house any pending block-centric I/O requests. Generally speaking, these requests are stored in increasing or decreasing device-offset order so that when they are processed, the disk head will move in a single direction (instead of bouncing around) to maximize performance.

The FreeBSD kernel provides the following functions for working with block I/O queues:

```
#include <sys/bio.h>

void
bioq_init(struct bio_queue_head *head);

void
bioq_disksort(struct bio_queue_head *head, struct bio *bp);

struct bio *
bioq_first(struct bio_queue_head *head);

struct bio *
bioq_takefirst(struct bio_queue_head *head);

void
bioq_insert_head(struct bio_queue_head *head, struct bio *bp);

void
bioq_insert_tail(struct bio_queue_head *head, struct bio *bp);

void
bioq_remove(struct bio_queue_head *head, struct bio *bp);

void
bioq_flush(struct bio_queue_head *head, struct devstat *stp, int error);
```

A block I/O queue is a statically allocated structure that's owned by the driver. To initialize a block I/O queue, you must call bioq_init.

To perform an ordered insertion, call bioq_disksort. To return the head of the queue (that is, the next request to process), use bioq_first. Lastly, to return and remove the head of the queue, call bioq_takefirst.

The abovementioned functions are the main methods for managing a block I/O queue. If a queue is manipulated using only these functions, it will contain at most one inversion point (that is, two sorted sequences).

The bioq_insert_head function inserts a request at the head of the queue. Additionally, it creates a "barrier" so that all subsequent insertions performed using bioq_disksort will end up after this request.

The bioq_insert_tail function is similar to bioq_insert_head, but it inserts the request at the end of the queue. Note that bioq_insert_tail also creates a barrier.

Generally speaking, you'd utilize a barrier to ensure that all preceding requests are serviced before continuing.

The `bioq_remove` function removes a request from the queue. If `bioq_remove` is invoked on the head of the queue, its effect is identical to `bioq_takefirst`.

If a block I/O queue is manipulated using `bioq_insert_head`, `bioq_insert_tail`, or `bioq_remove`, it may contain multiple inversion points.

The `bioq_flush` function expunges all of the queued requests and causes them to return the error code `error`.

NOTE *For storage devices that incorporate request scheduling (such as SATA Native Command Queuing, SCSI Tagged Command Queuing, and so on), `bioq_disksort` is essentially pointless, as the devices will (re)sort the requests internally. In those cases, a straightforward FIFO block I/O queue that uses `bioq_insert_tail` will suffice.*

Tying Everything Together

Now that you've gained some familiarity with `disk` and `bio` structures, let's dissect a real-world storage driver.

Listing 13-1 is the storage driver for Atmel's AT45D series of DataFlash chips. DataFlash is Atmel's serial interface for flash memory, employed on the Serial Peripheral Interface (SPI) bus. In short, Listing 13-1 is a storage driver for flash memory on the SPI bus.

NOTE *Take a quick look at this code and try to discern some of its structure. If you don't understand all of it, don't worry; an explanation follows.*

```
#include <sys/param.h>
#include <sys/module.h>
#include <sys/kernel.h>
#include <sys/systm.h>

#include <sys/bus.h>
#include <sys/conf.h>
#include <sys/bio.h>
#include <sys/kthread.h>
#include <sys/lock.h>
#include <sys/mutex.h>
#include <geom/geom_disk.h>

#include <dev/spibus/spi.h>
#include "spibus_if.h"

#define MANUFACTURER_ID             0x9f
#define STATUS_REGISTER_READ        0xd7
#define CONTINUOUS_ARRAY_READ_HF    0x0b
#define PROGRAM_THROUGH_BUFFER      0x82

struct at45d_softc {
        device_t                    at45d_dev;
        struct mtx                  at45d_mtx;
        struct intr_config_hook     at45d_ich;
```

```
                struct disk                    *at45d_disk;
                struct bio_queue_head           at45d_bioq;
                struct proc                    *at45d_proc;
        };

        static devclass_t at45d_devclass;

        static void                    at45d_delayed_attach(void *);
        static void                    at45d_task(void *);
        static void                    at45d_strategy(struct bio *);

        static int
❶ at45d_probe(device_t dev)
        {
                device_set_desc(dev, "AT45 flash family");
                return (BUS_PROBE_SPECIFIC);
        }

        static int
        at45d_attach(device_t dev)
        {
                struct at45d_softc *sc = device_get_softc(dev);
                int error;

                sc->at45d_dev = dev;
                mtx_init(&sc->at45d_mtx, device_get_nameunit(dev), "at45d", MTX_DEF);

                sc->at45d_ich.ich_func = at45d_delayed_attach;
                sc->at45d_ich.ich_arg = sc;
                error = config_intrhook_establish(&sc->at45d_ich);
                if (error)
                        device_printf(dev, "config_intrhook_establish() failed!\n");

                return (0);
        }

        static int
❷ at45d_detach(device_t dev)
        {
                return (EIO);
        }

        static int
        at45d_get_info(device_t dev, uint8_t *r)
        {
                struct spi_command cmd;
                uint8_t tx_buf[8], rx_buf[8];
                int error;

                memset(&cmd, 0, sizeof(cmd));
                memset(tx_buf, 0, sizeof(tx_buf));
                memset(rx_buf, 0, sizeof(rx_buf));

                tx_buf[0] = MANUFACTURER_ID;
                cmd.tx_cmd = &tx_buf[0];
```

```
        cmd.rx_cmd = &rx_buf[0];
        cmd.tx_cmd_sz = 5;
        cmd.rx_cmd_sz = 5;
        error = SPIBUS_TRANSFER(device_get_parent(dev), dev, &cmd);
        if (error)
                return (error);

        memcpy(r, &rx_buf[1], 4);
        return (0);
}

static uint8_t
at45d_get_status(device_t dev)
{
        struct spi_command cmd;
        uint8_t tx_buf[8], rx_buf[8];

        memset(&cmd, 0, sizeof(cmd));
        memset(tx_buf, 0, sizeof(tx_buf));
        memset(rx_buf, 0, sizeof(rx_buf));

        tx_buf[0] = STATUS_REGISTER_READ;
        cmd.tx_cmd = &tx_buf[0];
        cmd.rx_cmd = &rx_buf[0];
        cmd.tx_cmd_sz = 2;
        cmd.rx_cmd_sz = 2;
        SPIBUS_TRANSFER(device_get_parent(dev), dev, &cmd);

        return (rx_buf[1]);
}

static void
at45d_wait_for_device_ready(device_t dev)
{
        while ((at45d_get_status(dev) & 0x80) == 0)
                continue;
}

static void
at45d_delayed_attach(void *arg)
{
        struct at45d_softc *sc = arg;
        uint8_t buf[4];

        at45d_get_info(sc->at45d_dev, buf);
        at45d_wait_for_device_ready(sc->at45d_dev);

        sc->at45d_disk = disk_alloc();
        sc->at45d_disk->d_name = "at45d";
        sc->at45d_disk->d_unit = device_get_unit(sc->at45d_dev);
        sc->at45d_disk->d_strategy = at45d_strategy;
        sc->at45d_disk->d_sectorsize = 1056;
        sc->at45d_disk->d_mediasize = 8192 * 1056;
        sc->at45d_disk->d_maxsize = DFLTPHYS;
        sc->at45d_disk->d_drv1 = sc;
```

```
        bioq_init(&sc->at45d_bioq);
        kproc_create(&at45d_task, sc, &sc->at45d_proc, 0, 0, "at45d");

        disk_create(sc->at45d_disk, DISK_VERSION);
        config_intrhook_disestablish(&sc->at45d_ich);
}

static void
at45d_strategy(struct bio *bp)
{
        struct at45d_softc *sc = bp->bio_disk->d_drv1;

        mtx_lock(&sc->at45d_mtx);
        bioq_disksort(&sc->at45d_bioq, bp);
        wakeup(sc);
        mtx_unlock(&sc->at45d_mtx);
}

static void
at45d_task(void *arg)
{
        struct at45d_softc *sc = arg;
        struct bio *bp;
        struct spi_command cmd;
        uint8_t tx_buf[8], rx_buf[8];
        int ss = sc->at45d_disk->d_sectorsize;
        daddr_t block, end;
        char *vaddr;

        for (;;) {
                mtx_lock(&sc->at45d_mtx);
                do {
                        bp = bioq_first(&sc->at45d_bioq);
                        if (bp == NULL)
                                mtx_sleep(sc, &sc->at45d_mtx, PRIBIO,
                                    "at45d", 0);
                } while (bp == NULL);
                bioq_remove(&sc->at45d_bioq, bp);
                mtx_unlock(&sc->at45d_mtx);

                end = bp->bio_pblkno + (bp->bio_bcount / ss);
                for (block = bp->bio_pblkno; block < end; block++) {
                        vaddr = bp->bio_data + (block - bp->bio_pblkno) * ss;
                        if (bp->bio_cmd == BIO_READ) {
                                tx_buf[0] = CONTINUOUS_ARRAY_READ_HF;
                                cmd.tx_cmd_sz = 5;
                                cmd.rx_cmd_sz = 5;
                        } else {
                                tx_buf[0] = PROGRAM_THROUGH_BUFFER;
                                cmd.tx_cmd_sz = 4;
                                cmd.rx_cmd_sz = 4;
                        }
```

```
                    /* FIXME: This works only on certain devices. */
                    tx_buf[1] = ((block >> 5) & 0xff);
                    tx_buf[2] = ((block << 3) & 0xf8);
                    tx_buf[3] = 0;
                    tx_buf[4] = 0;
                    cmd.tx_cmd = &tx_buf[0];
                    cmd.rx_cmd = &rx_buf[0];
                    cmd.tx_data = vaddr;
                    cmd.rx_data = vaddr;
                    cmd.tx_data_sz = ss;
                    cmd.rx_data_sz = ss;
                    SPIBUS_TRANSFER(device_get_parent(sc->at45d_dev),
                        sc->at45d_dev, &cmd);
            }
            biodone(bp);
        }
}

static device_method_t at45d_methods[] = {
        /* Device interface. */
        DEVMETHOD(device_probe,         at45d_probe),
        DEVMETHOD(device_attach,        at45d_attach),
        DEVMETHOD(device_detach,        at45d_detach),
        { 0, 0 }
};

static driver_t at45d_driver = {
        "at45d",
        at45d_methods,
        sizeof(struct at45d_softc)
};

DRIVER_MODULE(at45d, spibus, at45d_driver, at45d_devclass, 0, 0);
```

Listing 13-1: at45d.c

The following sections describe the functions defined in Listing 13-1 roughly in the order they would execute.

Incidentally, because ❶ at45d_probe and ❷ at45d_detach are extremely rudimentary and because you've seen similar code elsewhere, I'll omit discussing them.

at45d_attach Function

The at45d_attach function is the device_attach implementation for this storage driver. Here is its function definition (again):

```
static int
at45d_attach(device_t dev)
{
        struct at45d_softc *sc = device_get_softc(dev);
        int error;
```

```
        sc->at45d_dev = dev;
❶mtx_init(&sc->at45d_mtx, device_get_nameunit(dev), "at45d",
        MTX_DEF);

        sc->at45d_ich.ich_func = ❷at45d_delayed_attach;
        sc->at45d_ich.ich_arg = sc;
        error = ❸config_intrhook_establish(&sc->at45d_ich);
        if (error)
                device_printf(dev, "config_intrhook_establish() failed!\n");

        return (0);
}
```

This function first ❶ initializes the mutex at45d_mtx, which will protect at45d's block I/O queue. Then it ❸ schedules ❷ at45d_delayed_attach to execute when interrupts are enabled.

NOTE *During the initial autoconfiguration phase (that is, right after the system boots), interrupts are disabled. However, some drivers (such as at45d) require interrupts for device initialization. In those cases, you'd use config_intrhook_establish, which schedules a function to execute as soon as interrupts are enabled but before root is mounted; if the system has already passed this point, the function is called immediately.*

at45d_delayed_attach Function

The at45d_delayed_attach function is, loosely speaking, the second half of at45d_attach. That is, it completes the device's initialization. Here is its function definition (again):

```
static void
at45d_delayed_attach(void *arg)
{
        struct at45d_softc *sc = arg;
        uint8_t buf[4];

    ❶at45d_get_info(sc->at45d_dev, buf);
    ❷at45d_wait_for_device_ready(sc->at45d_dev);

        sc->at45d_disk = ❸disk_alloc();
        sc->at45d_disk->d_name = "at45d";
        sc->at45d_disk->d_unit = device_get_unit(sc->at45d_dev);
        sc->at45d_disk->d_strategy = at45d_strategy;
        sc->at45d_disk->d_sectorsize = 1056;
        sc->at45d_disk->d_mediasize = 8192 * 1056;
        sc->at45d_disk->d_maxsize = DFLTPHYS;
        sc->at45d_disk->d_drv1 = sc;

    ❹bioq_init(&sc->at45d_bioq);
    ❺kproc_create(❻&at45d_task, sc, &sc->at45d_proc, 0, 0, "at45d");
```

```
❼disk_create(sc->at45d_disk, DISK_VERSION);
❽config_intrhook_disestablish(&sc->at45d_ich);
}
```

This function can be split into multiple parts. The first ❶ gets the device's manufacturer ID. Then at45d_delayed_attach ❷ hangs until the device is ready. These two actions require interrupts to be enabled.

The second part ❸ allocates and defines at45d's disk structure, ❹ initializes at45d's block I/O queue, and ❺ creates a new kernel process (to execute the ❻ at45d_task function).

Finally, at45d's device node is ❼ created, and at45d_delayed_attach is ❽ torn down.

NOTE *During the boot process—before root is mounted—the system stalls until every function scheduled via config_intrhook_establish completes and tears itself down. In other words, if at45d_delayed_attach didn't call config_intrhook_disestablish, the system would hang.*

at45d_get_info Function

The at45d_get_info function gets the storage device's manufacturer ID. Here is its function definition (again):

```
static int
at45d_get_info(device_t dev, uint8_t *r)
{
        struct spi_command cmd;
        uint8_t tx_buf[8], rx_buf[8];
        int error;

        memset(&cmd, 0, sizeof(cmd));
❶memset(tx_buf, 0, sizeof(tx_buf));
❷memset(rx_buf, 0, sizeof(rx_buf));

❸tx_buf[0] = MANUFACTURER_ID;
❹cmd.tx_cmd = &tx_buf[0];
❺cmd.rx_cmd = &rx_buf[0];
❻cmd.tx_cmd_sz = 5;
❼cmd.rx_cmd_sz = 5;
        error = ❽SPIBUS_TRANSFER(device_get_parent(dev), dev, &cmd);
        if (error)
                return (error);

❾memcpy(r, &rx_buf[1], 4);
        return (0);
}
```

This function begins by zeroing its ❶ transmit and ❷ receive buffers.

Every SPI data transfer is a full-duplex data transmission. That is, it always requires a transmit and receive buffer, because the master and slave both transmit data—even if the data to be sent is meaningless or garbage, it's still transferred.

The remainder of this function ❸ places `MANUFACTURER_ID` in the transmit buffer, sets up the `spi_command` structure (which denotes the ❹ transmit and ❺ receive buffers and their ❻ ❼ data lengths), ❽ initiates the data transfer, and finally ❾ returns the manufacturer ID to the caller.

at45d_wait_for_device_ready Function

The `at45d_wait_for_device_ready` function "spins" until the storage device is ready. Here is its function definition (again):

```
static void
at45d_wait_for_device_ready(device_t dev)
{
    ❶while ((at45d_get_status(dev) & 0x80) == 0)
            continue;
}
```

This function continually calls ❶ `at45d_get_status` until `0x80`, which designates that the device is not busy and is ready to accept the next command, is returned.

at45d_get_status Function

The `at45d_get_status` function gets the storage device's status. Here is its function definition (again):

```
static uint8_t
at45d_get_status(device_t dev)
{
    struct spi_command cmd;
    uint8_t tx_buf[8], rx_buf[8];

    memset(&cmd, 0, sizeof(cmd));
    memset(tx_buf, 0, sizeof(tx_buf));
    memset(rx_buf, 0, sizeof(rx_buf));

    ❶tx_buf[0] = STATUS_REGISTER_READ;
    cmd.tx_cmd = &tx_buf[0];
    cmd.rx_cmd = &rx_buf[0];
    cmd.tx_cmd_sz = 2;
    cmd.rx_cmd_sz = 2;
    SPIBUS_TRANSFER(device_get_parent(dev), dev, &cmd);

    return (rx_buf[1]);
}
```

As you can see, this function is nearly identical to the `at45d_get_info` function, except that it ❶ employs a different command. As such, I'll omit walking through it.

at45d_strategy Function

The `at45d_strategy` function is defined in `at45d_delayed_attach` as the `d_strategy` routine; it is executed anytime `at45d` receives a `bio` structure. Here is its function definition (again):

```
static void
at45d_strategy(❶struct bio *bp)
{
        struct at45d_softc *sc = bp->bio_disk->d_drv1;

        mtx_lock(&sc->at45d_mtx);
        ❷bioq_disksort(&sc->at45d_bioq, bp);
        ❸wakeup(sc);
        mtx_unlock(&sc->at45d_mtx);
}
```

This function simply takes a ❶ bio structure and ❷ adds it to at45d's block I/O queue. Then it ❸ gets at45d_task to actually process the bio structure(s).

NOTE   *Most strategy routines do something similar. That is to say, they don't actually process the bio structures; they only place them on the block I/O queue, and another function or thread sees to them.*

at45d_task Function

As mentioned in the previous section, the `at45d_task` function processes the bio structures on at45d's block I/O queue. Here is its function definition (again):

```
static void
at45d_task(void *arg)
{
        struct at45d_softc *sc = arg;
        struct bio *bp;
        struct spi_command cmd;
        uint8_t tx_buf[8], rx_buf[8];
        int ss = sc->at45d_disk->d_sectorsize;
        daddr_t block, end;
        char *vaddr;

        for (;;) {
                mtx_lock(&sc->at45d_mtx);
                do {
                        bp = ❶bioq_first(&sc->at45d_bioq);
                        if (bp == NULL)
                                ❷mtx_sleep(sc, &sc->at45d_mtx, PRIBIO,
                                        "at45d", 0);
```

```
          } while (bp == NULL);
  ❸bioq_remove(&sc->at45d_bioq, bp);
    mtx_unlock(&sc->at45d_mtx);

    end = bp->bio_pblkno + (bp->bio_bcount / ss);
    for (block = bp->bio_pblkno; block < end; block++) {
        ❹vaddr = bp->bio_data +
            (block - bp->bio_pblkno) * ss;
        ❺if (bp->bio_cmd == BIO_READ) {
                tx_buf[0] = CONTINUOUS_ARRAY_READ_HF;
                cmd.tx_cmd_sz = 5;
                cmd.rx_cmd_sz = 5;
        ❻} else {
                tx_buf[0] = PROGRAM_THROUGH_BUFFER;
                cmd.tx_cmd_sz = 4;
                cmd.rx_cmd_sz = 4;
        }

        /* FIXME: This works only on certain devices. */
        tx_buf[1] = ((block >> 5) & 0xff);
        tx_buf[2] = ((block << 3) & 0xf8);
        tx_buf[3] = 0;
        tx_buf[4] = 0;
        cmd.tx_cmd = &tx_buf[0];
        cmd.rx_cmd = &rx_buf[0];
        cmd.tx_data = vaddr;
        cmd.rx_data = vaddr;
        cmd.tx_data_sz = ss;
        cmd.rx_data_sz = ss;
        ❼SPIBUS_TRANSFER(device_get_parent(sc->at45d_dev),
            sc->at45d_dev, &cmd);
    }
  ❽biodone(bp);
    }
}
```

This function can be split into four parts. The first ❶ determines whether at45d's block I/O queue is empty. If so, at45d_task ❷ sleeps; otherwise, it ❸ acquires (and removes) the head of the queue. The second part determines whether the block-centric I/O request is a ❺ read or a ❻ write.

NOTE   *Block-centric I/O requests are seen from the driver's point of view. So, BIO_READ means reading from the device.*

The second part also ❹ calculates the offset in bio_data (that is, the location in main memory) to read from or write to. This is crucial because each I/O operation transmits 1 block of data, not 1 byte (that is, the abovementioned offset is a multiple of 1 block).

In case you have trouble following the offset calculation, here is a brief description of each variable involved: The ss variable is the device's sector size. The bio_pblkno variable is the first block of device memory to read from or write to, end is the last block, and block is the current block at45d_task is working with.

The third part sets up the `spi_command` structure and ❼ initiates the data transfer. Finally, the fourth part ❽ tells the kernel that the block-centric I/O request bp has been serviced.

Block I/O Completion Routines

As seen in the previous section, after processing a block-centric I/O request, you must inform the kernel with:

```
#include <sys/bio.h>

void
biodone(struct bio *bp);

void
biofinish(struct bio *bp, struct devstat *stat, int error);
```

The `biodone` function tells the kernel that the block-centric I/O request bp has been serviced successfully.

The `biofinish` function is identical to biodone, except that it sets bp to return the error code error (that is to say, biofinish can tell the kernel that bp was invalid, successful, or unsuccessful).

NOTE *Typically, the* `stat` *argument is set to* `NULL`*. For more on* `struct` `devstat`*, see the* `devstat(9)` *manual page (though it's somewhat antiquated).*

Conclusion

This chapter focused on implementing and understanding storage drivers. You learned how to manage both `disk` and `bio` structures and studied a real-world storage driver.

14

COMMON ACCESS METHOD

Common Access Method (CAM) is an ANSI standard. Although primarily used for SCSI, CAM is a method for separating host bus adapter (HBA) drivers from storage drivers. HBAs are devices (that is, a card or integrated circuit) that connect the host to other devices. For example, USB HBAs allow the host to communicate with USB devices.

By separating HBA drivers from storage drivers, CAM reduces the complexity of individual drivers. Furthermore, this separation enables storage drivers (such as CD-ROM and tape drivers) to control their devices on any I/O bus (such as IDE, SCSI, and so on) as long as an appropriate HBA driver is available. In other words, CAM modularizes HBA and storage drivers.

In CAM vernacular, HBA drivers are known as software interface modules (SIMs), and storage drivers are known as peripheral modules. Incidentally, the storage drivers discussed in Chapter 13 are not under CAM. To avoid confusion, I'll refer to storage drivers under CAM as peripheral modules from now on.

The FreeBSD CAM implementation contains SIMs for SCSI Parallel Interface (SPI), Fibre Channel (FC), USB Mass Storage (UMASS), FireWire (IEEE 1394), and Advanced Technology Attachment Packet Interface (ATAPI). It has peripheral modules for disks (da), CD-ROMs (cd), tapes (sa), tape changers (ch), processor type devices (pt), and enclosure services (ses). Also, it provides a "pass-through" interface that allows user applications to send I/O requests directly to any CAM-controlled device (McKusick and Neville-Neil, 2005). This interface is, fundamentally, a SIM (as you'll soon see).

In this chapter you'll learn how to manage HBAs using CAM. Of course, before you can do that, you'll need to know how CAM interfaces peripheral modules with SIMs. Because peripheral modules are just storage drivers with some CAM-related code, they're only briefly discussed in this chapter.

How CAM Works

CAM is most easily understood by tracing an I/O request through it.

In Figure 14-1,[1] the kernel passes a block-centric I/O request to the da(4) peripheral module. As you would expect, this causes da(4)'s strategy routine (dastrategy) to execute.

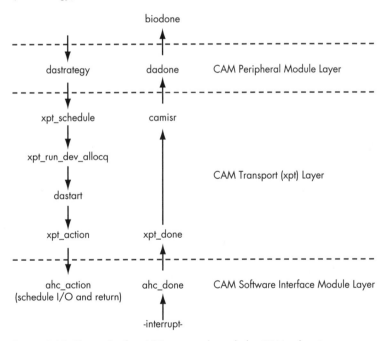

Figure 14-1: The path of an I/O request through the CAM subsystem

The dastrategy function gets the block-centric I/O request and inserts it on the appropriate block I/O queue via bioq_disksort. It concludes by calling the xpt_schedule function. (The da(4) peripheral module supports every SCSI disk. Consequently, it manages multiple block I/O queues.)

1. Figure 14-1 is adapted from *The Design and Implementation of the FreeBSD Operating System* by Marshall Kirk McKusick and George V. Neville-Neil (Addison-Wesley, 2005).

The xpt_schedule function, by and large, schedules a peripheral module to receive a *CAM Control Block (CCB)*. A CCB describes the location (or path) to the target device (that is, the intended recipient of the I/O request). The xpt_schedule function concludes by calling the xpt_run_dev_allocq function. (Note that my definition of CCB isn't complete. I'll expand this definition throughout this chapter.)

The xpt_run_dev_allocq function allocates and constructs a CCB. Afterward, it calls the peripheral module's start routine (dastart in this example).

The dastart function takes the first block-centric I/O request off the appropriate block I/O queue and converts that into a SCSI command. This command is stored in the CCB constructed by xpt_run_dev_allocq. The dastart function ends by calling the xpt_action function.

The xpt_action function uses the path information stored in the CCB to determine the SIM to which the SCSI command should be sent. It then calls that SIM's action routine (ahc_action in this case).

NOTE *A SIM was pseudo-randomly chosen for this example, so the fact that it's ahc(4) is irrelevant.*

The ahc_action function gets the CCB and translates the SCSI command into a hardware-specific command. This hardware-specific command is then passed to the device to be executed. Afterward, ahc_action returns back to the caller of dastrategy.

As soon as the device completes the hardware-specific command (which may involve DMA), it sends an interrupt, which causes ahc(4)'s done routine (ahc_done) to execute.

The ahc_done function appends the completion status (that is, successful or unsuccessful) to the CCB related to the completed hardware-specific command. It then calls the xpt_done function.

The xpt_done function gets the completed CCB and sets it up for processing by camisr, the CAM interrupt service routine. It then schedules camisr to run.

Loosely speaking, the camisr function carries out some "housekeeping" on the CCB. It ends by calling the CCB's specified completion function (dadone in this example).

The dadone function, more or less, tells the kernel that the block-centric I/O request has been serviced by calling biodone.

A (Somewhat) Simple Example

Now that you're familiar with the CAM subsystem, let's work through some code. After that, I'll detail the different CAM-related functions.

Listing 14-1 is a SIM for a pseudo-HBA (taken from the mfi(4) code base).

NOTE *Take a quick look at this code and try to discern some of its structure. If you don't understand all of it, don't worry; an explanation follows.*

```
#include <sys/param.h>
#include <sys/module.h>
```

```
#include <sys/kernel.h>
#include <sys/systm.h>

#include <sys/selinfo.h>
#include <sys/bus.h>
#include <sys/conf.h>
#include <sys/bio.h>
#include <sys/malloc.h>
#include <sys/uio.h>

#include <cam/cam.h>
#include <cam/cam_ccb.h>
#include <cam/cam_debug.h>
#include <cam/cam_sim.h>
#include <cam/cam_xpt_sim.h>
#include <cam/scsi/scsi_all.h>

#include <machine/md_var.h>
#include <machine/bus.h>
#include <sys/rman.h>

#include <dev/mfi/mfireg.h>
#include <dev/mfi/mfi_ioctl.h>
#include <dev/mfi/mfivar.h>

#define ccb_mfip_ptr            sim_priv.entries[0].ptr

struct mfip {
        device_t                dev;
        struct mfi_softc        *mfi;
        struct cam_devq         *devq;
        struct cam_sim          *sim;
        struct cam_path         *path;
};

static devclass_t               mfip_devclass;

static void                     mfip_action(struct cam_sim *, union ccb *);
static void                     mfip_poll(struct cam_sim *);
static struct mfi_command *     mfip_start(void *);
static void                     mfip_done(struct mfi_command *);

static int
mfip_probe(device_t dev)
{
        device_set_desc(dev, "SCSI pass-through bus");
        return (BUS_PROBE_SPECIFIC);
}

static int
mfip_attach(device_t dev)
{
        struct mfip *sc;
        struct mfi_softc *mfi;
```
❶

```
        sc = device_get_softc(dev);
        if (sc == NULL)
                return (EINVAL);

        mfi = device_get_softc(device_get_parent(dev));
        sc->dev = dev;
        sc->mfi = mfi;
        mfi->mfi_cam_start = mfip_start;

        if ((sc->devq = cam_simq_alloc(MFI_SCSI_MAX_CMDS)) == NULL)
                return (ENOMEM);

        sc->sim = cam_sim_alloc(mfip_action, mfip_poll, "mfi", sc,
            device_get_unit(dev), &mfi->mfi_io_lock, 1, MFI_SCSI_MAX_CMDS,
            sc->devq);
        if (sc->sim == NULL) {
                cam_simq_free(sc->devq);
                device_printf(dev, "cannot allocate CAM SIM\n");
                return (EINVAL);
        }

        mtx_lock(&mfi->mfi_io_lock);
        if (xpt_bus_register(sc->sim, dev, 0) != 0) {
                device_printf(dev,
                    "cannot register SCSI pass-through bus\n");
                cam_sim_free(sc->sim, FALSE);
                cam_simq_free(sc->devq);
                mtx_unlock(&mfi->mfi_io_lock);
                return (EINVAL);
        }
        mtx_unlock(&mfi->mfi_io_lock);

        return (0);
}

static int
mfip_detach(device_t dev)
{
        struct mfip *sc;

        sc = device_get_softc(dev);
        if (sc == NULL)
                return (EINVAL);

        if (sc->sim != NULL) {
                mtx_lock(&sc->mfi->mfi_io_lock);
                xpt_bus_deregister(cam_sim_path(sc->sim));
                cam_sim_free(sc->sim, FALSE);
                mtx_unlock(&sc->mfi->mfi_io_lock);
        }

        if (sc->devq != NULL)
                cam_simq_free(sc->devq);

        return (0);
```

```
        }

        static void
        mfip_action(struct cam_sim *sim, union ccb *ccb)
        {
                struct mfip *sc;
                struct mfi_softc *mfi;

                sc = cam_sim_softc(sim);
                mfi = sc->mfi;
                mtx_assert(&mfi->mfi_io_lock, MA_OWNED);

                switch (ccb->ccb_h.func_code) {
                case XPT_PATH_INQ:
                {
                        struct ccb_pathinq *cpi;

                        cpi = &ccb->cpi;
                        cpi->version_num = 1;
                        cpi->hba_inquiry = PI_SDTR_ABLE | PI_TAG_ABLE | PI_WIDE_16;
                        cpi->target_sprt = 0;
                        cpi->hba_misc = PIM_NOBUSRESET | PIM_SEQSCAN;
                        cpi->hba_eng_cnt = 0;
                        cpi->max_target = MFI_SCSI_MAX_TARGETS;
                        cpi->max_lun = MFI_SCSI_MAX_LUNS;
                        cpi->initiator_id = MFI_SCSI_INITIATOR_ID;
                        strncpy(cpi->sim_vid, "FreeBSD", SIM_IDLEN);
                        strncpy(cpi->hba_vid, "LSI", HBA_IDLEN);
                        strncpy(cpi->dev_name, cam_sim_name(sim), DEV_IDLEN);
                        cpi->unit_number = cam_sim_unit(sim);
                        cpi->bus_id = cam_sim_bus(sim);
                        cpi->base_transfer_speed = 150000;
                        cpi->protocol = PROTO_SCSI;
                        cpi->protocol_version = SCSI_REV_2;
                        cpi->transport = XPORT_SAS;
                        cpi->transport_version = 0;

                        cpi->ccb_h.status = CAM_REQ_CMP;
                        break;
                }
                case XPT_RESET_BUS:
                        ccb->ccb_h.status = CAM_REQ_CMP;
                        break;
                case XPT_RESET_DEV:
                        ccb->ccb_h.status = CAM_REQ_CMP;
                        break;
                case XPT_GET_TRAN_SETTINGS:
                {
                        struct ccb_trans_settings_sas *sas;

                        ccb->cts.protocol = PROTO_SCSI;
                        ccb->cts.protocol_version = SCSI_REV_2;
                        ccb->cts.transport = XPORT_SAS;
                        ccb->cts.transport_version = 0;
                        sas = &ccb->cts.xport_specific.sas;
```

```
                    sas->valid &= ~CTS_SAS_VALID_SPEED;
                    sas->bitrate = 150000;

                    ccb->ccb_h.status = CAM_REQ_CMP;
                    break;
            }
        case XPT_SET_TRAN_SETTINGS:
                    ccb->ccb_h.status = CAM_FUNC_NOTAVAIL;
                    break;
        case XPT_SCSI_IO:
            {
                    struct ccb_hdr *ccb_h = &ccb->ccb_h;
                    struct ccb_scsiio *csio = &ccb->csio;

                    ccb_h->status = CAM_REQ_INPROG;
                    if (csio->cdb_len > MFI_SCSI_MAX_CDB_LEN) {
                            ccb_h->status = CAM_REQ_INVALID;
                            break;
                    }
                    if ((ccb_h->flags & CAM_DIR_MASK) != CAM_DIR_NONE) {
                            if (ccb_h->flags & CAM_DATA_PHYS) {
                                    ccb_h->status = CAM_REQ_INVALID;
                                    break;
                            }
                            if (ccb_h->flags & CAM_SCATTER_VALID) {
                                    ccb_h->status = CAM_REQ_INVALID;
                                    break;
                            }
                    }

                    ccb_h->ccb_mfip_ptr = sc;
                    TAILQ_INSERT_TAIL(&mfi->mfi_cam_ccbq, ccb_h, sim_links.tqe);
                    mfi_startio(mfi);

                    return;
            }
        default:
                    ccb->ccb_h.status = CAM_REQ_INVALID;
                    break;
        }

        xpt_done(ccb);
        return;
}

static void
mfip_poll(struct cam_sim *sim)
{
        return;
}

static struct mfi_command *
mfip_start(void *data)
{
```

```
            union ccb *ccb = data;
            struct ccb_hdr *ccb_h = &ccb->ccb_h;
            struct ccb_scsiio *csio = &ccb->csio;
            struct mfip *sc;
            struct mfi_command *cm;
            struct mfi_pass_frame *pt;

            sc = ccb_h->ccb_mfip_ptr;

            if ((cm = mfi_dequeue_free(sc->mfi)) == NULL)
                    return (NULL);

            pt = &cm->cm_frame->pass;
            pt->header.cmd = MFI_CMD_PD_SCSI_IO;
            pt->header.cmd_status = 0;
            pt->header.scsi_status = 0;
            pt->header.target_id = ccb_h->target_id;
            pt->header.lun_id = ccb_h->target_lun;
            pt->header.flags = 0;
            pt->header.timeout = 0;
            pt->header.data_len = csio->dxfer_len;
            pt->header.sense_len = MFI_SENSE_LEN;
            pt->header.cdb_len = csio->cdb_len;
            pt->sense_addr_lo = cm->cm_sense_busaddr;
            pt->sense_addr_hi = 0;
            if (ccb_h->flags & CAM_CDB_POINTER)
                    bcopy(csio->cdb_io.cdb_ptr, &pt->cdb[0], csio->cdb_len);
            else
                    bcopy(csio->cdb_io.cdb_bytes, &pt->cdb[0], csio->cdb_len);

            cm->cm_complete = mfip_done;
            cm->cm_private = ccb;
            cm->cm_sg = &pt->sgl;
            cm->cm_total_frame_size = MFI_PASS_FRAME_SIZE;
            cm->cm_data = csio->data_ptr;
            cm->cm_len = csio->dxfer_len;
            switch (ccb_h->flags & CAM_DIR_MASK) {
            case CAM_DIR_IN:
                    cm->cm_flags = MFI_CMD_DATAIN;
                    break;
            case CAM_DIR_OUT:
                    cm->cm_flags = MFI_CMD_DATAOUT;
                    break;
            case CAM_DIR_NONE:
            default:
                    cm->cm_data = NULL;
                    cm->cm_len = 0;
                    cm->cm_flags = 0;
                    break;
            }

            TAILQ_REMOVE(&sc->mfi->mfi_cam_ccbq, ccb_h, sim_links.tqe);
            return (cm);
    }
```

```c
static void
mfip_done(struct mfi_command *cm)
{
        union ccb *ccb = cm->cm_private;
        struct ccb_hdr *ccb_h = &ccb->ccb_h;
        struct ccb_scsiio *csio = &ccb->csio;
        struct mfip *sc;
        struct mfi_pass_frame *pt;

        sc = ccb_h->ccb_mfip_ptr;
        pt = &cm->cm_frame->pass;

        switch (pt->header.cmd_status) {
        case MFI_STAT_OK:
        {
                uint8_t command, device;

                ccb_h->status = CAM_REQ_CMP;
                csio->scsi_status = pt->header.scsi_status;

                if (ccb_h->flags & CAM_CDB_POINTER)
                        command = ccb->csio.cdb_io.cdb_ptr[0];
                else
                        command = ccb->csio.cdb_io.cdb_bytes[0];

                if (command == INQUIRY) {
                        device = ccb->csio.data_ptr[0] & 0x1f;
                        if ((device == T_DIRECT) || (device == T_PROCESSOR))
                                csio->data_ptr[0] =
                                        (device & 0xe0) | T_NODEVICE;
                }

                break;
        }
        case MFI_STAT_SCSI_DONE_WITH_ERROR:
        {
                int sense_len;

                ccb_h->status = CAM_SCSI_STATUS_ERROR | CAM_AUTOSNS_VALID;
                csio->scsi_status = pt->header.scsi_status;

                sense_len = min(pt->header.sense_len,
                    sizeof(struct scsi_sense_data));
                bzero(&csio->sense_data, sizeof(struct scsi_sense_data));
                bcopy(&cm->cm_sense->data[0], &csio->sense_data, sense_len);
                break;
        }
        case MFI_STAT_DEVICE_NOT_FOUND:
                ccb_h->status = CAM_SEL_TIMEOUT;
                break;
        case MFI_STAT_SCSI_IO_FAILED:
                ccb_h->status = CAM_REQ_CMP_ERR;
                csio->scsi_status = pt->header.scsi_status;
                break;
```

```
                default:
                        ccb_h->status = CAM_REQ_CMP_ERR;
                        csio->scsi_status = pt->header.scsi_status;
                        break;
                }

                mfi_release_command(cm);
                xpt_done(ccb);
}

static device_method_t mfip_methods[] = {
        /* Device interface. */
        DEVMETHOD(device_probe,         mfip_probe),
        DEVMETHOD(device_attach,        mfip_attach),
        DEVMETHOD(device_detach,        mfip_detach),
        { 0, 0 }
};

static driver_t mfip_driver = {
        "mfip",
        mfip_methods,
        sizeof(struct mfip)
};

DRIVER_MODULE(mfip, mfi, mfip_driver, mfip_devclass, 0, 0);
MODULE_DEPEND(mfip, cam, 1, 1, 1);
MODULE_DEPEND(mfip, mfi, 1, 1, 1);
```

Listing 14-1: mfi_cam.c

The following sections describe the functions defined in Listing 14-1 roughly in the order they would execute.

As an aside, because ❶ mfip_probe is extremely rudimentary and because we've examined similar code elsewhere, I'll omit discussing it.

mfip_attach Function

The mfip_attach function is the device_attach implementation for this driver. Here is its function definition (again):

```
static int
mfip_attach(device_t dev)
{
        struct mfip *sc;
        struct mfi_softc *mfi;

        sc = device_get_softc(dev);
        if (sc == NULL)
                return (EINVAL);

        mfi = device_get_softc(device_get_parent(dev));
        sc->dev = dev;
        sc->mfi = mfi;
        mfi->mfi_cam_start = mfip_start;
```

```
if ((sc->devq = ❶cam_simq_alloc(MFI_SCSI_MAX_CMDS)) == NULL)
        return (ENOMEM);

sc->sim = ❷cam_sim_alloc(mfip_action, mfip_poll, "mfi", sc,
    device_get_unit(dev), &mfi->mfi_io_lock, 1, MFI_SCSI_MAX_CMDS,
    sc->devq);
if (sc->sim == NULL) {
        cam_simq_free(sc->devq);
        device_printf(dev, "cannot allocate CAM SIM\n");
        return (EINVAL);
}

mtx_lock(&mfi->mfi_io_lock);
if (❸xpt_bus_register(sc->sim, dev, 0) != 0) {
        device_printf(dev,
            "cannot register SCSI pass-through bus\n");
        cam_sim_free(sc->sim, FALSE);
        cam_simq_free(sc->devq);
        mtx_unlock(&mfi->mfi_io_lock);
        return (EINVAL);
}
mtx_unlock(&mfi->mfi_io_lock);

return (0);
}
```

This function first calls ❶ cam_simq_alloc to allocate a SIM queue. Loosely speaking, *SIM queues* ensure that HBAs cannot be swamped by I/O requests. See, I/O requests from peripheral modules are housed on SIM queues to await service. When a queue becomes full, any additional requests are rejected.

Next, ❷ cam_sim_alloc is called to allocate a SIM (or bus) descriptor. Note that if an HBA implements multiple buses (or channels), each bus requires its own descriptor.

Finally, ❸ xpt_bus_register takes the descriptor returned by cam_sim_alloc and registers it with the CAM subsystem.

mfip_detach Function

The mfip_detach function is the device_detach implementation for this driver. Here is its function definition (again):

```
static int
mfip_detach(device_t dev)
{
        struct mfip *sc;

        sc = device_get_softc(dev);
        if (sc == NULL)
                return (EINVAL);

        if (sc->sim != NULL) {
                mtx_lock(&sc->mfi->mfi_io_lock);
```

```
        ❶xpt_bus_deregister(cam_sim_path(sc->sim));
        ❷cam_sim_free(sc->sim, FALSE);
          mtx_unlock(&sc->mfi->mfi_io_lock);
    }

    if (sc->devq != NULL)
          ❸cam_simq_free(sc->devq);

    return (0);
}
```

This function starts by ❶ deregistering and ❷ freeing its SIM descriptor. Afterward, its SIM queue is ❸ freed.

mfip_action Function

The mfip_action function is defined in mfip_attach as the action routine (for verification, see the first argument to cam_sim_alloc). *Action routines* are executed every time a SIM receives a CCB.

NOTE *Recall that a CCB houses an I/O request (or command) to perform along with the identity of the target device (that is, the intended recipient of the I/O request).*

Fundamentally, mfip_action is akin to the ahc_action function shown in Figure 14-1. Here is its function definition (again):

```
static void
mfip_action(struct cam_sim *sim, ❶union ccb *ccb)
{
        struct mfip *sc;
        struct mfi_softc *mfi;

        sc = cam_sim_softc(sim);
        mfi = sc->mfi;
        mtx_assert(&mfi->mfi_io_lock, MA_OWNED);

    ❷switch (ccb->ccb_h.func_code) {
    ❸case XPT_PATH_INQ:
      {
            struct ccb_pathinq *cpi;

            cpi = &ccb->cpi;
            cpi->version_num = 1;
            cpi->hba_inquiry = PI_SDTR_ABLE | PI_TAG_ABLE | PI_WIDE_16;
            cpi->target_sprt = 0;
            cpi->hba_misc = PIM_NOBUSRESET | PIM_SEQSCAN;
            cpi->hba_eng_cnt = 0;
            cpi->max_target = MFI_SCSI_MAX_TARGETS;
            cpi->max_lun = MFI_SCSI_MAX_LUNS;
            cpi->initiator_id = MFI_SCSI_INITIATOR_ID;
            strncpy(cpi->sim_vid, "FreeBSD", SIM_IDLEN);
            strncpy(cpi->hba_vid, "LSI", HBA_IDLEN);
            strncpy(cpi->dev_name, cam_sim_name(sim), DEV_IDLEN);
```

```
                cpi->unit_number = cam_sim_unit(sim);
                cpi->bus_id = cam_sim_bus(sim);
                cpi->base_transfer_speed = 150000;
                cpi->protocol = PROTO_SCSI;
                cpi->protocol_version = SCSI_REV_2;
                cpi->transport = XPORT_SAS;
                cpi->transport_version = 0;

                cpi->ccb_h.status = CAM_REQ_CMP;
                break;
        }
❹case XPT_RESET_BUS:
                ccb->ccb_h.status = CAM_REQ_CMP;
                break;
❺case XPT_RESET_DEV:
                ccb->ccb_h.status = CAM_REQ_CMP;
                break;
❻case XPT_GET_TRAN_SETTINGS:
        {
                struct ccb_trans_settings_sas *sas;

                ccb->cts.protocol = PROTO_SCSI;
                ccb->cts.protocol_version = SCSI_REV_2;
                ccb->cts.transport = XPORT_SAS;
                ccb->cts.transport_version = 0;
                sas = &ccb->cts.xport_specific.sas;
                sas->valid &= ~CTS_SAS_VALID_SPEED;
                sas->bitrate = 150000;

                ccb->ccb_h.status = CAM_REQ_CMP;
                break;
        }
❼case XPT_SET_TRAN_SETTINGS:
                ccb->ccb_h.status = CAM_FUNC_NOTAVAIL;
                break;
❽case XPT_SCSI_IO:
        {
                struct ccb_hdr *ccb_h = &ccb->ccb_h;
                struct ccb_scsiio *csio = &ccb->csio;

                ccb_h->status = CAM_REQ_INPROG;
                if (csio->cdb_len > MFI_SCSI_MAX_CDB_LEN) {
                        ccb_h->status = CAM_REQ_INVALID;
                        break;
                }
                if ((ccb_h->flags & CAM_DIR_MASK) != CAM_DIR_NONE) {
                        if (ccb_h->flags & CAM_DATA_PHYS) {
                                ccb_h->status = CAM_REQ_INVALID;
                                break;
                        }
                        if (ccb_h->flags & CAM_SCATTER_VALID) {
                                ccb_h->status = CAM_REQ_INVALID;
                                break;
                        }
                }
```

```
                ccb_h->ccb_mfip_ptr = sc;
                TAILQ_INSERT_TAIL(&mfi->mfi_cam_ccbq, ccb_h, sim_links.tqe);
                mfi_startio(mfi);

                return;
        }
        default:
                ccb->ccb_h.status = CAM_REQ_INVALID;
                break;
        }

        xpt_done(ccb);
        return;
}
```

Most action routines simply take a ❶ CCB and ❷ branch according to the ccb_h.func_code variable, which denotes the I/O operation to perform.

For now, I'm going to focus on the structure of mfip_action and avoid its specifics. An in-depth explanation of mfip_action appears in "Action Routines" on page 243.

As you can see, this function can perform one of six I/O operations: it can ❸ return the SIM and HBA properties, reset a ❹ bus or ❺ device, ❻ get or ❼ set the transfer settings, or ❽ issue a SCSI command to a device.

mfip_poll Function

The mfip_poll function is defined in mfip_attach as the poll routine (for verification, see the second argument to cam_sim_alloc). Customarily, *poll routines* wrap a SIM's interrupt handler. See, when interrupts are unavailable (for example, after a kernel panic) the CAM subsystem will use poll routines to run its interrupt handlers.

The following is the function definition for mfip_poll (again):

```
static void
mfip_poll(struct cam_sim *sim)
{
        ❶return;
}
```

Because this SIM does not implement an interrupt handler, mfip_poll just ❶ returns.

mfip_start Function

The mfip_start function transforms a SCSI command into a hardware-specific command. This function is called exclusively by mfi_startio.

NOTE *The* mfi_startio *function is defined in* mfi.c *(which is not described in this book).* mfi_startio *is called by* mfip_action *(described in "mfip_action Function" on page 236) to issue a SCSI command to a device.*

Here is the function definition for mfip_start (again):

```
static struct mfi_command *
mfip_start(void *data)
{
        union ccb *ccb = data;
        struct ccb_hdr *ccb_h = &ccb->ccb_h;
        struct ccb_scsiio *csio = &ccb->csio;
        struct mfip *sc;
        struct mfi_command *cm;
        struct mfi_pass_frame *pt;

        sc = ccb_h->ccb_mfip_ptr;

        if ((cm = mfi_dequeue_free(sc->mfi)) == NULL)
                return (NULL);

        pt = &cm->cm_frame->pass;
        pt->header.cmd = MFI_CMD_PD_SCSI_IO;
        pt->header.cmd_status = 0;
        pt->header.scsi_status = 0;
        pt->header.target_id = ccb_h->target_id;
        pt->header.lun_id = ccb_h->target_lun;
        pt->header.flags = 0;
        pt->header.timeout = 0;
        pt->header.data_len = csio->dxfer_len;
        pt->header.sense_len = MFI_SENSE_LEN;
        pt->header.cdb_len = csio->cdb_len;
        pt->sense_addr_lo = cm->cm_sense_busaddr;
        pt->sense_addr_hi = 0;
        if (ccb_h->flags & CAM_CDB_POINTER)
                bcopy(csio->cdb_io.cdb_ptr, &pt->cdb[0], csio->cdb_len);
        else
                bcopy(csio->cdb_io.cdb_bytes, &pt->cdb[0], csio->cdb_len);

        cm->cm_complete = ❶mfip_done;
        cm->cm_private = ccb;
        cm->cm_sg = &pt->sgl;
        cm->cm_total_frame_size = MFI_PASS_FRAME_SIZE;
        cm->cm_data = csio->data_ptr;
        cm->cm_len = csio->dxfer_len;
        switch (ccb_h->flags & CAM_DIR_MASK) {
        case CAM_DIR_IN:
                cm->cm_flags = MFI_CMD_DATAIN;
                break;
        case CAM_DIR_OUT:
                cm->cm_flags = MFI_CMD_DATAOUT;
                break;
```

```
        case CAM_DIR_NONE:
        default:
                cm->cm_data = NULL;
                cm->cm_len = 0;
                cm->cm_flags = 0;
                break;
        }

        TAILQ_REMOVE(&sc->mfi->mfi_cam_ccbq, ccb_h, sim_links.tqe);
        return (cm);
}
```

As you can see, this function is fairly straightforward—it's just a bunch of assignments. Until we've examined struct `ccb_scsiio` and struct `ccb_hdr`, which occurs in "XPT_SCSI_IO" on page 250, I'm going to postpone walking through this function.

Note that ❶ `mfip_done` is set as the done routine for the hardware-specific command.

mfip_done Function

As implied previously, the `mfip_done` function is the done routine for this SIM. It is executed by `mfi_intr` immediately after a device completes a hardware-specific command.

NOTE *The* `mfi_intr` *function is* `mfi(4)`*'s interrupt handler. It is defined in* mfi.c.

Fundamentally, `mfip_done` is akin to the `ahc_done` function shown in Figure 14-1. Here is its function definition (again):

```
static void
mfip_done(❶struct mfi_command *cm)
{
        union ccb *ccb = cm->cm_private;
        struct ccb_hdr *ccb_h = &ccb->ccb_h;
        struct ccb_scsiio *csio = &ccb->csio;
        struct mfip *sc;
        struct mfi_pass_frame *pt;

        sc = ccb_h->ccb_mfip_ptr;
        pt = &cm->cm_frame->pass;

        switch (pt->header.cmd_status) {
        case MFI_STAT_OK:
        {
                uint8_t command, device;

                ❷ccb_h->status = CAM_REQ_CMP;
                csio->scsi_status = pt->header.scsi_status;

                if (ccb_h->flags & CAM_CDB_POINTER)
                        command = ccb->csio.cdb_io.cdb_ptr[0];
```

```
                        else
                                command = ccb->csio.cdb_io.cdb_bytes[0];

                        if (command == INQUIRY) {
                                device = ccb->csio.data_ptr[0] & 0x1f;
                                if ((device == T_DIRECT) || (device == T_PROCESSOR))
                                        csio->data_ptr[0] =
                                                (device & 0xe0) | T_NODEVICE;
                        }

                        break;
                }
                case MFI_STAT_SCSI_DONE_WITH_ERROR:
                {
                        int sense_len;

                    ❸ccb_h->status = CAM_SCSI_STATUS_ERROR | CAM_AUTOSNS_VALID;
                        csio->scsi_status = pt->header.scsi_status;

                        sense_len = min(pt->header.sense_len,
                            sizeof(struct scsi_sense_data));
                        bzero(&csio->sense_data, sizeof(struct scsi_sense_data));
                        bcopy(&cm->cm_sense->data[0], &csio->sense_data, sense_len);
                        break;
                }
                case MFI_STAT_DEVICE_NOT_FOUND:
                    ❹ccb_h->status = CAM_SEL_TIMEOUT;
                        break;
                case MFI_STAT_SCSI_IO_FAILED:
                    ❺ccb_h->status = CAM_REQ_CMP_ERR;
                        csio->scsi_status = pt->header.scsi_status;
                        break;
                default:
                    ❻ccb_h->status = CAM_REQ_CMP_ERR;
                        csio->scsi_status = pt->header.scsi_status;
                        break;
                }

                mfi_release_command(cm);
            ❼xpt_done(ccb);
        }
```

Commonly, done routines take a ❶ hardware-specific command and append the completion status (that is, successful or unsuccessful) to its associated ❷ ❸ ❹ ❺ ❻ CCB. Once this is done, ❼ xpt_done is called to process the completed CCB.

NOTE   *The mfi(4) code base uses DMA to acquire the completion status from a device.*

Now that you're familiar with Listing 14-1, I'll expound on the different functions, structures, and constructs it employs.

SIM Registration Routines

As alluded to previously, registering a SIM with the CAM subsystem involves three functions:

- cam_simq_alloc
- cam_sim_alloc
- xpt_bus_register

cam_simq_alloc Function

The cam_simq_alloc function allocates a SIM queue.

```
#include <cam/cam_sim.h>
#include <cam/cam_queue.h>

struct cam_devq *
cam_simq_alloc(u_int32_t max_sim_transactions);
```

Here, max_sim_transactions denotes the size of the SIM queue. Normally, it is calculated like so:

```
max_sim_transactions = number_of_supported_devices *
    number_of_commands_that_can_be_concurrently_processed_per_device;
```

cam_sim_alloc Function

The cam_sim_alloc function allocates a SIM (or bus) descriptor.

NOTE   *If an HBA implements multiple buses (or channels), each bus requires its own descriptor.*

```
#include <sys/param.h>
#include <sys/lock.h>
#include <sys/mutex.h>

#include <cam/cam_sim.h>
#include <cam/cam_queue.h>

struct cam_sim *
cam_sim_alloc(sim_action_func sim_action, sim_poll_func sim_poll,
    const char *sim_name, void *softc, u_int32_t unit, struct mtx *mtx,
    int max_dev_transactions, int max_tagged_dev_transactions,
    struct cam_devq *queue);
```

Because the first six arguments to cam_sim_alloc are fairly obvious—they're exactly what their name implies—I'll omit discussing them.

The max_dev_transactions argument specifies the maximum number of concurrent transactions per device. This argument applies only to devices that do not support SCSI Tagged Command Queuing (SCSI TCQ). Generally, max_dev_transactions is always set to 1.

The `max_tagged_dev_transactions` argument is identical to `max_dev_transactions`, but it applies only to devices that support SCSI TCQ.

The `queue` argument expects a pointer to a SIM queue (that is, `cam_simq_alloc`'s return value).

xpt_bus_register Function

The `xpt_bus_register` function registers a SIM with the CAM subsystem.

```
#include <cam/cam_sim.h>
#include <cam/cam_xpt_sim.h>

int32_t
xpt_bus_register(struct cam_sim *sim, device_t parent, u_int32_t bus)
```

Here, `sim` specifies the SIM to register (that is, `cam_sim_alloc`'s return value) and `bus` denotes its bus number. The `parent` argument is currently unused.

NOTE *If an HBA implements multiple buses (or channels), each bus needs its own unique bus number.*

Action Routines

As mentioned previously, action routines are executed every time a SIM receives a CCB. You can think of action routines like the "main function" for a SIM.

Here is the function prototype for an action routine (taken from the `<cam/cam_sim.h>` header):

```
typedef void (*sim_action_func)(struct cam_sim *sim, union ccb *ccb);
```

Recall that action routines `switch` according to the `ccb->ccb_h.func_code` variable, which contains a constant that symbolizes the I/O operation to perform. For the rest of this chapter, I'll detail the most common constants/operations.

NOTE *For the complete list of constants/operations, see the `xpt_opcode` enumeration defined in the `<cam/cam_ccb.h>` header.*

XPT_PATH_INQ

The `XPT_PATH_INQ` constant specifies a path inquiry operation, which returns the SIM and HBA properties. Action routines that are passed `XPT_PATH_INQ` simply fill in a `ccb_pathinq` structure and then return.

`struct ccb_pathinq` is defined in the `<cam/cam_ccb.h>` header as follows:

```
struct ccb_pathinq {
        struct ccb_hdr ccb_h;      /* Header information fields.  */
        u_int8_t    version_num;   /* Version number.             */
        u_int8_t    hba_inquiry;   /* Imitate INQ byte 7.         */
```

```
u_int8_t    target_sprt;      /* Target mode support flags.      */
u_int8_t    hba_misc;         /* Miscellaneous HBA features.     */
u_int16_t   hba_eng_cnt;      /* HBA engine count.               */

u_int8_t vuhba_flags[VUHBALEN]; /* Vendor unique capabilities.   */
u_int32_t   max_target;       /* Maximum supported targets.      */
u_int32_t   max_lun;          /* Maximum supported LUN.          */
u_int32_t   async_flags;      /* Asynchronous handler flags.     */
path_id_t   hpath_id;       /* Highest path ID in the subsystem. */
target_id_t initiator_id;     /* HBA ID on the bus.              */

char sim_vid[SIM_IDLEN];      /* SIM vendor ID.                  */
char hba_vid[HBA_IDLEN];      /* HBA vendor ID.                  */
char dev_name[DEV_IDLEN];     /* SIM device name.                */

u_int32_t   unit_number;      /* SIM unit number.                */
u_int32_t   bus_id;           /* SIM bus ID.                     */
u_int32_t base_transfer_speed; /* Base bus speed in KB/sec.      */

cam_proto   protocol;         /* CAM protocol.                   */
u_int       protocol_version; /* CAM protocol version.           */
cam_xport   transport;        /* Transport (e.g., FC, USB).      */
u_int       transport_version; /* Transport version.             */
union {
        struct ccb_pathinq_settings_spi spi;
        struct ccb_pathinq_settings_fc fc;
        struct ccb_pathinq_settings_sas sas;
        char ccb_pathinq_settings_opaque[PATHINQ_SETTINGS_SIZE];
} xport_specific;

u_int maxio;    /* Maximum supported I/O size (in bytes).        */
};
```

Here is an example XPT_PATH_INQ operation (taken from Listing 14-1):

```
static void
mfip_action(struct cam_sim *sim, union ccb *ccb)
{
        struct mfip *sc;
        struct mfi_softc *mfi;

        sc = cam_sim_softc(sim);
        mfi = sc->mfi;
        mtx_assert(&mfi->mfi_io_lock, MA_OWNED);

        switch (ccb->ccb_h.func_code) {
        case XPT_PATH_INQ:
        {
                struct ccb_pathinq *cpi;

                cpi = ❶&ccb->cpi;
                cpi->version_num = 1;
                cpi->hba_inquiry = PI_SDTR_ABLE | PI_TAG_ABLE | PI_WIDE_16;
                cpi->target_sprt = 0;
```

```
                cpi->hba_misc = PIM_NOBUSRESET | PIM_SEQSCAN;
                cpi->hba_eng_cnt = 0;
                cpi->max_target = MFI_SCSI_MAX_TARGETS;
                cpi->max_lun = MFI_SCSI_MAX_LUNS;
                cpi->initiator_id = MFI_SCSI_INITIATOR_ID;
                strncpy(cpi->sim_vid, "FreeBSD", SIM_IDLEN);
                strncpy(cpi->hba_vid, "LSI", HBA_IDLEN);
                strncpy(cpi->dev_name, cam_sim_name(sim), DEV_IDLEN);
                cpi->unit_number = cam_sim_unit(sim);
                cpi->bus_id = cam_sim_bus(sim);
                cpi->base_transfer_speed = 150000;
                cpi->protocol = PROTO_SCSI;
                cpi->protocol_version = SCSI_REV_2;
                cpi->transport = XPORT_SAS;
                cpi->transport_version = 0;

            ❷cpi->ccb_h.status = ❸CAM_REQ_CMP;
                break;
        }
...
        default:
            ❹ccb->ccb_h.status = ❺CAM_REQ_INVALID;
                break;
        }

        xpt_done(ccb);
        return;
}
```

Notice that the ccb_pathinq structure is provided by the ❶ CCB. More-over, notice that the ❸ success or ❺ failure of any operation is returned in ❷ ❹ ccb_h.status.

XPT_RESET_BUS

The XPT_RESET_BUS constant specifies a bus reset operation. As you'd expect, XPT_RESET_BUS is horrifically hardware specific. Here is a minimalist implementation (taken from Listing 14-1):

```
static void
mfip_action(struct cam_sim ❶*sim, union ccb *ccb)
{
        struct mfip *sc;
        struct mfi_softc *mfi;

        sc = cam_sim_softc(sim);
        mfi = sc->mfi;
        mtx_assert(&mfi->mfi_io_lock, MA_OWNED);

        switch (ccb->ccb_h.func_code) {
...
        case XPT_RESET_BUS:
                ccb->ccb_h.status = ❷CAM_REQ_CMP;
```

```
                        break;
...
        default:
                ccb->ccb_h.status = CAM_REQ_INVALID;
                break;
        }

        xpt_done(ccb);
        return;
}
```

Here, ❶ sim is the bus to reset. Unsurprisingly, minimalist implementations forgo any "real" work and simply return ❷ success.

Many SIMs use a minimalist implementation. A "proper" implementation is out of the scope of this book.

XPT_GET_TRAN_SETTINGS

The XPT_GET_TRAN_SETTINGS constant denotes an I/O operation that returns the current transfer settings or the user-defined upper limits. Action routines that are passed XPT_GET_TRAN_SETTINGS simply fill in a ccb_trans_settings structure and then return.

struct ccb_trans_settings is defined in <cam/cam_ccb.h> like so:

```
typedef enum {
        CTS_TYPE_CURRENT_SETTINGS,        /* Current transfer settings.   */
        CTS_TYPE_USER_SETTINGS            /* User-defined upper limits.    */
} cts_type;

struct ccb_trans_settings {
        struct ccb_hdr ccb_h;             /* Header information fields.    */
        cts_type  type;                   /* Current or user settings?     */
        cam_proto protocol;               /* CAM protocol.                 */
        u_int     protocol_version;       /* CAM protocol version.         */
        cam_xport transport;              /* Transport (e.g., FC, USB).    */
        u_int     transport_version;      /* Transport version.            */

      ❶union {
                u_int valid;              /* Which field(s) to honor.      */
                struct ccb_trans_settings_scsi scsi;
        } proto_specific;

      ❷union {
                u_int valid;              /* Which field(s) to honor.      */
                struct ccb_trans_settings_spi spi;
                struct ccb_trans_settings_fc fc;
                struct ccb_trans_settings_sas sas;
                struct ccb_trans_settings_ata ata;
                struct ccb_trans_settings_sata sata;
        } xport_specific;
};
```

As you can see, `ccb_trans_settings` marshals a ❶ protocol structure and five ❷ transport-specific structures. These structures are defined in <cam/cam_ccb.h> like so:

```
struct ccb_trans_settings_scsi {
        u_int           valid;          /* Which field(s) to honor.    */
#define CTS_SCSI_VALID_TQ               0x01
        u_int           flags;
#define CTS_SCSI_FLAGS_TAG_ENB          0x01
};


struct ccb_trans_settings_spi {
        u_int           valid;          /* Which field(s) to honor.    */
#define CTS_SPI_VALID_SYNC_RATE         0x01
#define CTS_SPI_VALID_SYNC_OFFSET       0x02
#define CTS_SPI_VALID_BUS_WIDTH         0x04
#define CTS_SPI_VALID_DISC              0x08
#define CTS_SPI_VALID_PPR_OPTIONS       0x10
        u_int           flags;
#define CTS_SPI_FLAGS_DISC_ENB          0x01
        u_int           sync_period;    /* Sync period.                */
        u_int           sync_offset;    /* Sync offset.                */
        u_int           bus_width;      /* Bus width.                  */
        u_int           ppr_options;    /* Parallel protocol request.  */
};


struct ccb_trans_settings_fc {
        u_int           valid;          /* Which field(s) to honor.    */
#define CTS_FC_VALID_WWNN               0x8000
#define CTS_FC_VALID_WWPN               0x4000
#define CTS_FC_VALID_PORT               0x2000
#define CTS_FC_VALID_SPEED              0x1000
        u_int64_t       wwnn;           /* World wide node name.       */
        u_int64_t       wwpn;           /* World wide port name.       */
        u_int32_t       port;           /* 24-bit port ID (if known).  */
        u_int32_t       bitrate;        /* Mbps.                       */
};


struct ccb_trans_settings_sas {
        u_int           valid;          /* Which field(s) to honor.    */
#define CTS_SAS_VALID_SPEED             0x1000
        u_int32_t       bitrate;        /* Mbps.                       */
};


struct ccb_trans_settings_ata {
        u_int           valid;          /* Which field(s) to honor.    */
#define CTS_ATA_VALID_MODE              0x01
#define CTS_ATA_VALID_BYTECOUNT         0x02
#define CTS_ATA_VALID_ATAPI             0x20
        int             mode;           /* Mode.                       */
        u_int           bytecount;      /* PIO transaction length.     */
        u_int           atapi;          /* ATAPI CDB length.           */
};
```

```c
struct ccb_trans_settings_sata {
        u_int           valid;          /* Which field(s) to honor.     */
#define CTS_SATA_VALID_MODE             0x01
#define CTS_SATA_VALID_BYTECOUNT        0x02
#define CTS_SATA_VALID_REVISION         0x04
#define CTS_SATA_VALID_PM               0x08
#define CTS_SATA_VALID_TAGS             0x10
#define CTS_SATA_VALID_ATAPI            0x20
#define CTS_SATA_VALID_CAPS             0x40
        int             mode;           /* Legacy PATA mode.            */
        u_int           bytecount;      /* PIO transaction length.      */
        int             revision;       /* SATA revision.               */
        u_int           pm_present;     /* PM is present (XPT->SIM).     */
        u_int           tags;           /* Number of allowed tags.      */
        u_int           atapi;          /* ATAPI CDB length.            */
        u_int           caps;           /* Host and device SATA caps.   */
#define CTS_SATA_CAPS_H                 0x0000ffff
#define CTS_SATA_CAPS_H_PMREQ           0x00000001
#define CTS_SATA_CAPS_H_APST            0x00000002
#define CTS_SATA_CAPS_H_DMAAA           0x00000010
#define CTS_SATA_CAPS_D                 0xffff0000
#define CTS_SATA_CAPS_D_PMREQ           0x00010000
#define CTS_SATA_CAPS_D_APST            0x00020000
};
```

Here is an example XPT_GET_TRAN_SETTINGS operation (taken from Listing 14-1):

```c
static void
mfip_action(struct cam_sim *sim, union ccb *ccb)
{
        struct mfip *sc;
        struct mfi_softc *mfi;

        sc = cam_sim_softc(sim);
        mfi = sc->mfi;
        mtx_assert(&mfi->mfi_io_lock, MA_OWNED);

        switch (ccb->ccb_h.func_code) {
...
        case XPT_GET_TRAN_SETTINGS:
        {
                struct ccb_trans_settings_sas *sas;

        ❶ccb->❷cts.protocol = PROTO_SCSI;
                ccb->cts.protocol_version = SCSI_REV_2;
                ccb->cts.transport = XPORT_SAS;
                ccb->cts.transport_version = 0;
                sas = &ccb->cts.xport_specific.sas;
                sas->valid &= ~CTS_SAS_VALID_SPEED;
                sas->bitrate = 150000;
```

```
                ccb->ccb_h.status = CAM_REQ_CMP;
                break;
        }
...
        default:
                ccb->ccb_h.status = CAM_REQ_INVALID;
                break;
        }

        xpt_done(ccb);
        return;
}
```

Notice that the ❷ ccb_trans_settings structure is provided by the ❶ CCB. Naturally, only the fields applicable to the HBA are filled in.

XPT_SET_TRAN_SETTINGS

As you'd expect, XPT_SET_TRAN_SETTINGS is the opposite of XPT_GET_TRAN_SETTINGS. That is, XPT_SET_TRAN_SETTINGS changes the current transfer settings based on a ccb_trans_settings structure. Unsurprisingly, not all SIMs support this operation. For example:

```
static void
mfip_action(struct cam_sim *sim, union ccb *ccb)
{
        struct mfip *sc;
        struct mfi_softc *mfi;

        sc = cam_sim_softc(sim);
        mfi = sc->mfi;
        mtx_assert(&mfi->mfi_io_lock, MA_OWNED);

        switch (ccb->ccb_h.func_code) {
...
        case XPT_SET_TRAN_SETTINGS:
                ccb->ccb_h.status = ❶CAM_FUNC_NOTAVAIL;
                break;
...
        default:
                ccb->ccb_h.status = CAM_REQ_INVALID;
                break;
        }

        xpt_done(ccb);
        return;
}
```

This function states that XPT_SET_TRAN_SETTINGS is ❶ not available. Note that a "proper" implementation is hardware specific and not covered in this book.

XPT_SCSI_IO

The XPT_SCSI_IO constant denotes an I/O operation that issues a SCSI command to a device. The particulars of this SCSI command are stored in two structures: ccb_scsiio and ccb_hdr.

struct ccb_scsiio is defined in <cam/cam_ccb.h> like so:

```
struct ccb_scsiio {
        struct ccb_hdr ccb_h;           /* Header information fields.  */
        union ccb *next_ccb;            /* Next CCB to process.        */
        u_int8_t  *req_map;             /* Mapping information.        */
        u_int8_t  *data_ptr;            /* Data buffer or S/G list.    */
        u_int32_t dxfer_len;            /* Length of data to transfer. */

        /* Sense information (used if the command returns an error).   */
        struct scsi_sense_data sense_data;

        u_int8_t   sense_len;           /* Sense information length.   */
        u_int8_t   cdb_len;             /* SCSI command length.        */
        u_int16_t sglist_cnt;           /* Number of S/G segments.     */
        u_int8_t   scsi_status; /* SCSI status (returned by device).   */
        u_int8_t   sense_resid; /* Residual sense information length.  */
        u_int32_t resid;                /* Residual data length.       */
        cdb_t      cdb_io;              /* SCSI command.               */
        u_int8_t  *msg_ptr;             /* Message.                    */
        u_int16_t msg_len;              /* Message length.             */
        u_int8_t   tag_action;          /* Tag action?                 */
        /*
         * tag_action should be the constant below to send a non-tagged
         * transaction or one of the constants in scsi_message.h.
         */
#define CAM_TAG_ACTION_NONE             0x00
        u_int      tag_id;              /* Tag ID (from initiator).    */
        u_int      init_id;             /* Initiator ID.               */
};
```

struct ccb_hdr is also defined in <cam/cam_ccb.h>, like so:

```
struct ccb_hdr {
        cam_pinfo       pinfo;          /* Priority scheduling.        */
        camq_entry      xpt_links;      /* Transport layer links.      */
        camq_entry      sim_links;      /* SIM layer links.            */
        camq_entry      periph_links;   /* Peripheral layer links.     */
        u_int32_t       retry_count;    /* Retry count.                */

        /* Pointer to peripheral module done routine.                  */
        void (*cbfcnp)(struct cam_periph *, union ccb *);

        xpt_opcode      func_code;      /* I/O operation to perform.   */
        u_int32_t       ❶status;        /* Completion status.          */
        struct cam_path *path;          /* Path for this CCB.          */
        path_id_t       path_id;        /* Path ID for the request.    */
        target_id_t     target_id;      /* Target device ID.           */
        lun_id_t        target_lun;     /* Target logical unit number. */
```

```
        u_int32_t       flags;          /* CCB flags.                  */
        ccb_ppriv_area  periph_priv;    /* Private use by peripheral.  */
        ccb_spriv_area  sim_priv;       /* Private use by SIM.         */
        u_int32_t       timeout;        /* Timeout value.              */

        /* Deprecated. Don't use!                                      */
        struct callout_handle timeout_ch;
};
```

struct ccb_hdr should seem familiar—it's used to return the ❶ completion status in every I/O operation.

The following is an example XPT_SCSI_IO operation (taken from Listing 14-1):

```
#define ccb_mfip_ptr            sim_priv.entries[0].ptr
...
static void
mfip_action(struct cam_sim *sim, union ccb *ccb)
{
        struct mfip *sc;
        struct mfi_softc *mfi;

        sc = cam_sim_softc(sim);
        mfi = sc->mfi;
        mtx_assert(&mfi->mfi_io_lock, MA_OWNED);

        switch (ccb->ccb_h.func_code) {
...
        case XPT_SCSI_IO:
        {
                struct ccb_hdr *ccb_h = &ccb->ccb_h;
                struct ccb_scsiio *csio = &ccb->csio;

                ccb_h->status = CAM_REQ_INPROG;
        ❶if (csio->cdb_len > MFI_SCSI_MAX_CDB_LEN) {
                        ccb_h->status = CAM_REQ_INVALID;
                        break;
                }
        ❷if ((ccb_h->flags & CAM_DIR_MASK) != CAM_DIR_NONE) {
                ❸if (ccb_h->flags & CAM_DATA_PHYS) {
                                ccb_h->status = CAM_REQ_INVALID;
                        ❹break;
                        }
                ❺if (ccb_h->flags & CAM_SCATTER_VALID) {
                                ccb_h->status = CAM_REQ_INVALID;
                        ❻break;
                        }
                }

        ❼ccb_h->ccb_mfip_ptr = sc;
                TAILQ_INSERT_TAIL(&mfi->mfi_cam_ccbq, ccb_h, sim_links.tqe);
        ❽mfi_startio(mfi);

                return;
```

```
        }
        default:
                ccb->ccb_h.status = CAM_REQ_INVALID;
                break;
        }

        xpt_done(ccb);
        return;
}
```

This operation begins by ❶ checking that the SCSI command length is acceptable. Then it determines whether the SCSI command uses ❸ physical addresses or ❺ scatter/gather segments to ❷ transfer data. If either is used, this operation ❹ ❻ exits (as it's received invalid arguments). Then ccb_h->ccb_mfip_ptr is ❼ set to the software context and mfi_startio is ❽ called.

NOTE *The mfi_startio function is what actually issues the SCSI command.*

Recall from "mfip_start Function" on page 238 that mfi_startio calls mfip_start to transform the SCSI command into a hardware-specific command.

```
static struct mfi_command *
mfip_start(void *data)
{
        union ccb *ccb = data;
        struct ccb_hdr *ccb_h = &ccb->ccb_h;
        struct ccb_scsiio *csio = &ccb->csio;
        struct mfip *sc;
        struct mfi_command *cm;
        struct mfi_pass_frame *pt;

        sc = ccb_h->ccb_mfip_ptr;

        if ((cm = mfi_dequeue_free(sc->mfi)) == NULL)
                return (NULL);

        pt = &cm->cm_frame->pass;
        pt->header.cmd = MFI_CMD_PD_SCSI_IO;
        pt->header.cmd_status = 0;
        pt->header.scsi_status = 0;
        pt->header.target_id = ❶ccb_h->target_id;
        pt->header.lun_id = ❷ccb_h->target_lun;
        pt->header.flags = 0;
        pt->header.timeout = 0;
        pt->header.data_len = csio->dxfer_len;
        pt->header.sense_len = MFI_SENSE_LEN;
        pt->header.cdb_len = csio->cdb_len;
        pt->sense_addr_lo = cm->cm_sense_busaddr;
        pt->sense_addr_hi = 0;
        if (ccb_h->flags & CAM_CDB_POINTER)
                bcopy(❸csio->cdb_io.cdb_ptr, &pt->cdb[0], ❹csio->cdb_len);
```

```
            else
                    bcopy(❺csio->cdb_io.cdb_bytes, &pt->cdb[0], csio->cdb_len);

            cm->cm_complete = mfip_done;
            cm->cm_private = ccb;
            cm->cm_sg = &pt->sgl;
            cm->cm_total_frame_size = MFI_PASS_FRAME_SIZE;
            cm->cm_data = ❻csio->data_ptr;
            cm->cm_len = ❼csio->dxfer_len;
            switch (ccb_h->flags & CAM_DIR_MASK) {
    ❽case CAM_DIR_IN:
                    cm->cm_flags = MFI_CMD_DATAIN;
                    break;
    ❾case CAM_DIR_OUT:
                    cm->cm_flags = MFI_CMD_DATAOUT;
                    break;
    ❿case CAM_DIR_NONE:
            default:
                    cm->cm_data = NULL;
                    cm->cm_len = 0;
                    cm->cm_flags = 0;
                    break;
            }

            TAILQ_REMOVE(&sc->mfi->mfi_cam_ccbq, ccb_h, sim_links.tqe);
            return (cm);
    }
```

Notice that struct ccb_hdr lists the target's ❶ device ID and ❷ logical unit number. It also lists whether the SCSI command transfers data ❽ in, ❾ out, or ❿ nothing. Note that XPT_SCSI_IO operations are seen from the SIM's point of view. Therefore, "in" means from the device, and "out" means to the device.

The ccb_scsiio structure maintains the ❻ data to transfer and its ❼ length. It also maintains the SCSI command (through a ❸ pointer or a ❺ buffer) and the command's ❹ length.

NOTE *Once more, the hardware-specific command constructed above is issued to the target device via mfi_startio.*

Recall that as soon as a device completes a hardware-specific command, it sends an interrupt, which causes the done routine (mfip_done in this case) to execute.

```
static void
mfip_done(struct mfi_command *cm)
{
        union ccb *ccb = cm->cm_private;
        struct ccb_hdr *ccb_h = &ccb->ccb_h;
        struct ccb_scsiio *csio = &ccb->csio;
        struct mfip *sc;
        struct mfi_pass_frame *pt;

        sc = ccb_h->ccb_mfip_ptr;
```

```
                pt = &cm->cm_frame->pass;

                switch (pt->header.cmd_status) {
                case MFI_STAT_OK:
                {
                        uint8_t command, device;

                        ccb_h->status = CAM_REQ_CMP;
                        csio->scsi_status = pt->header.scsi_status;

                        if (ccb_h->flags & CAM_CDB_POINTER)
                                command = ccb->csio.cdb_io.cdb_ptr[0];
                        else
                                command = ccb->csio.cdb_io.cdb_bytes[0];

                        if (command == INQUIRY) {
                                device = ccb->csio.data_ptr[0] & 0x1f;
                                if ((device == T_DIRECT) || (device == T_PROCESSOR))
                                        csio->data_ptr[0] =
                                                (device & 0xe0) | T_NODEVICE;
                        }

                        break;
                }
❶case MFI_STAT_SCSI_DONE_WITH_ERROR:
                {
                        int sense_len;

                        ccb_h->status = CAM_SCSI_STATUS_ERROR | CAM_AUTOSNS_VALID;
                        csio->scsi_status = pt->header.scsi_status;

                        sense_len = min(pt->header.sense_len,
                            sizeof(struct scsi_sense_data));
                        bzero(&csio->sense_data, sizeof(struct scsi_sense_data));
                        ❷bcopy(❸&cm->cm_sense->data[0], ❹&csio->sense_data,
                            sense_len);
                        break;
                }
                case MFI_STAT_DEVICE_NOT_FOUND:
                        ccb_h->status = CAM_SEL_TIMEOUT;
                        break;
                case MFI_STAT_SCSI_IO_FAILED:
                        ccb_h->status = CAM_REQ_CMP_ERR;
                        csio->scsi_status = pt->header.scsi_status;
                        break;
                default:
                        ccb_h->status = CAM_REQ_CMP_ERR;
                        csio->scsi_status = pt->header.scsi_status;
                        break;
                }

                mfi_release_command(cm);
                xpt_done(ccb);
        }
```

Notice that if the hardware-specific command ❶ returns an error, the ❸ error information (or sense data) is ❷ copied to the ccb_scsiio structure's ❹ sense_data field.

At this point in the game, the unexplained parts of this function should be obvious.

XPT_RESET_DEV

The XPT_RESET_DEV constant specifies a device reset operation. Unsurprisingly, XPT_RESET_DEV is fairly hardware specific. Here is a simple XPT_RESET_DEV operation (taken from *bt.c*):

NOTE *The* bt.c *source file is part of the* bt(4) *code base.*

```
static void
btaction(struct cam_sim *sim, union ccb *ccb)
{
        struct bt_softc *bt;

        bt = (struct bt_softc *)cam_sim_softc(sim);

        switch (ccb->ccb_h.func_code) {
        case XPT_RESET_DEV:
                ❶/* FALLTHROUGH */
        case XPT_SCSI_IO:
                {
...
```

Given that a hardware-specific command must be issued to reset this device, XPT_RESET_DEV simply ❶ cascades into XPT_SCSI_IO.

While not shown here, it should be stressed that all operations conclude by appending their completion status to their CCB and then calling xpt_done(ccb).

Conclusion

This chapter concentrated heavily on HBA drivers, or SIMs, because they're the most commonly written CAM-related driver. Of course, there's more to CAM than what's been shown here. You could conceivably write an entire book on CAM!

15

USB DRIVERS

Universal Serial Bus (USB) is a connection protocol between a host controller (such as a personal computer) and a peripheral device. It was designed to replace a wide range of slow buses—the parallel port, serial port, and PS/2 connector—with a single bus that all devices could connect to (Corbet et al., 2005).

As described in the official USB documentation, available at *http://www.usb.org/developers/*, USB devices are hideously complex. Fortunately, FreeBSD provides a *USB module* to handle most of the complexity. This chapter describes the interactions between the USB module and drivers. But first, some background on USB devices is needed.

About USB Devices

Communication between a USB host controller and a USB device occurs through a pipe (Orwick and Smith, 2007). A *pipe* connects the host controller to an endpoint on a device. USB devices can have up to 32 endpoints.

Each *endpoint* performs a specific communication-related operation for a device, such as receiving commands or transferring data. An endpoint can be one of four types:

- Control
- Interrupt
- Bulk
- Isochronous

Control endpoints are used to send and receive information of a control nature (Oney, 2003). They are commonly used for configuring the device, issuing device commands, retrieving device information, and so on. Control transactions are guaranteed to succeed by the USB protocol. All USB devices have a control endpoint named endpoint 0.

Interrupt endpoints transfer small amounts of data at a fixed rate. See, USB devices cannot interrupt their host in the traditional sense—they don't have an asynchronous interrupt. Instead, USB devices provide interrupt endpoints, which are polled periodically. These endpoints are the main transport method for USB keyboards and mice (Corbet et al., 2005). Interrupt transactions are guaranteed to succeed by the USB protocol.

Bulk endpoints transfer large amounts of data. Bulk transactions are lossless. However, they are not guaranteed by the USB protocol to complete in a specific amount of time. Bulk endpoints are common on printers, mass storage devices, and network devices.

Isochronous endpoints periodically transfer large amounts of data. Isochronous transactions can be lossy. As such, these endpoints are used in devices that can handle data loss but rely on keeping a constant stream of data flowing, such as audio and video devices (Corbet et al., 2005).

More About USB Devices

The endpoints on a USB device are grouped into *interfaces*. For example, a USB speaker might define one group of endpoints as the interface for the buttons and another group of endpoints as the interface for the audio stream.

All interfaces have one or more alternate settings. An *alternate setting* defines the parameters of the interface. For example, a lossy audio stream interface may have several alternate settings that provide increasing levels of audio quality at the cost of additional bandwidth. Naturally, only one alternate setting can be active at a time.

NOTE *The term "alternate setting" is kind of a misnomer, as the default interface setting is the first alternate setting.*

Figure 15-1 depicts the relationship between endpoints, interfaces, and alternate settings.[1]

---

1. Figure 15-1 is adapted from *Developing Drivers with the Windows Driver Foundation* by Penny Orwick and Guy Smith (Microsoft Press, 2007).

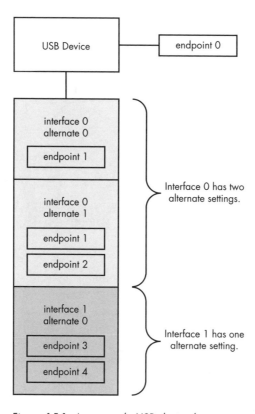

Figure 15-1: An example USB device layout

As you can see, an endpoint cannot be shared among interfaces, but it can be used in multiple alternate settings within one interface. Also, each alternate setting can have a different number of endpoints. Note that endpoint 0, the default control endpoint, is not part of any interface.

A group of interfaces is known as a *device configuration*, or simply a *configuration*.

USB Configuration Structures

In FreeBSD, usb_config structures are used to find and communicate with individual endpoints. struct usb_config is defined in the <dev/usb/usbdi.h> header as follows:

```
struct usb_config {
        /* USB Module Private Data */
        enum usb_hc_mode        usb_mode;

        /* Mandatory Fields */
        uint8_t                 type;
        uint8_t                 endpoint;
        uint8_t                 direction;
        usb_callback_t          *callback;
```

```
        usb_frlength_t            bufsize;

        /* Optional Fields */
        usb_timeout_t             timeout;
        usb_timeout_t             interval;
        usb_frcount_t             frames;
        uint8_t                   ep_index;
        uint8_t                   if_index;

        /* USB Transfer Flags */
        struct usb_xfer_flags   flags;
};
```

Many of the fields in struct usb_config must be initialized by a USB driver. These fields are described in the following sections.

Mandatory Fields

The type field specifies the endpoint type. Valid values for this field are UE_CONTROL, UE_BULK, UE_INTERRUPT, and UE_ISOCHRONOUS.

The endpoint field specifies the endpoint number. A value of UE_ADDR_ANY suggests that the endpoint number is unimportant—the other fields are used to find the correct endpoint.

The direction field specifies the endpoint direction. Valid values for this field are shown in Table 15-1.

Table 15-1: USB Endpoint Direction Symbolic Constants

Constant	Description
UE_DIR_IN	Stipulates that the endpoint be an IN endpoint; that is, the endpoint transfers data to the host from the device
UE_DIR_OUT	Stipulates that the endpoint be an OUT endpoint; that is, the endpoint transfers data to the device from the host
UE_DIR_ANY	Stipulates that the endpoint support bidirectional transfers

NOTE   *The direction of an endpoint is from the host's perspective.*

The callback field denotes a mandatory callback function. This function is executed before and after the endpoint specified by type, endpoint, and direction transfers data. We'll discuss this function further in "USB Transfers (in FreeBSD)" on page 262.

The bufsize field denotes the buffer size for the endpoint specified by type, endpoint, and direction. As you would expect, bufsize is used for type transactions.

As this section's heading implies, the preceding fields must be defined in every usb_config structure.

Optional Fields

The timeout field sets the transaction timeout in milliseconds. If timeout is 0 or undefined and type is UE_ISOCHRONOUS, then a timeout of 250 ms will be used.

The interval field's meaning is based on the value of type. Table 15-2 details interval's purpose (based on type).

Table 15-2: interval's Purpose (Based on Endpoint Type)

Endpoint Type	What interval Does
UE_CONTROL	interval sets the transaction delay in milliseconds; in other words, interval milliseconds must pass before a control transaction can occur
UE_INTERRUPT	interval sets the polling rate in milliseconds; in other words, the host controller will poll the interrupt endpoint every interval milliseconds; if interval is 0 or undefined, then the endpoint's default polling rate will be used
UE_BULK	interval does nothing for bulk endpoints
UE_ISOCHRONOUS	interval does nothing for isochronous endpoints

The frames field denotes the maximum number of USB frames that the endpoint specified by type, endpoint, and direction supports. In FreeBSD, *USB frames* are simply "data packets" that travel to or from an endpoint. USB frames are composed of one or more *USB packets*, which actually contain the data.

The ep_index field demands a non-negative integer. If multiple endpoints are identified by type, endpoint, and direction—which can occur when endpoint is UE_ADDR_ANY—the value of ep_index will be used to select one.

The if_index field specifies the interface number (based on the ifaces argument passed to usbd_transfer_setup, which is described in "USB Configuration Structure Management Routines" on page 264).

USB Transfer Flags

The flags field sets the transactional properties for the endpoint specified by type, endpoint, and direction. This field expects a usb_xfer_flags structure.

struct usb_xfer_flags is defined in the <dev/usb/usbdi.h> header as follows:

```
struct usb_xfer_flags {
        uint8_t force_short_xfer : 1;
        uint8_t short_xfer_ok    : 1;
        uint8_t short_frames_ok  : 1;
        uint8_t pipe_bof         : 1;
        uint8_t proxy_buffer     : 1;
        uint8_t ext_buffer       : 1;
        uint8_t manual_status    : 1;
        uint8_t no_pipe_ok       : 1;
        uint8_t stall_pipe       : 1;
};
```

All of the fields in struct usb_xfer_flags are optional. These fields are 1-bit and function as flags. They are detailed in Table 15-3.

Table 15-3: USB Transfer Flags

Flag	Description
force_short_xfer	Causes a short transfer; *short transfers* basically dispatch a short USB packet, which tends to indicate "end of transaction;" this flag can be set anytime
short_xfer_ok	Indicates that it is okay to receive short transfers; this flag can be set anytime
short_frames_ok	Indicates that it is okay to receive gobs of short USB frames; this flag can only affect UE_INTERRUPT and UE_BULK endpoints; it can be set anytime
pipe_bof	Causes any failed USB transactions to remain first in their queue; this guarantees that all transactions complete in FIFO order; this flag can be set anytime
proxy_buffer	Rounds bufsize up to the maximum USB frame size; this flag cannot be set after driver initialization
ext_buffer	Indicates that an external DMA buffer will be used for all transactions; this flag cannot be set after driver initialization
manual_status	Stops the handshake/status stage from occurring in control transactions; this flag can be set anytime
no_pipe_ok	Causes USB_ERR_NO_PIPE errors to be ignored; this flag cannot be set after driver initialization
stall_pipe	Causes the endpoint specified by type, endpoint, and direction to "stall" before each transaction; this flag can be set anytime

NOTE *If you don't understand some of these descriptions, don't worry; I'll expand on them later.*

USB Transfers (in FreeBSD)

Recall that callback is executed before and after the endpoint specified by type, endpoint, and direction transfers data. Below is its function prototype:

```
typedef void (usb_callback_t)(❶struct usb_xfer *, usb_error_t);
```

Here, ❶ struct usb_xfer * contains the transfer state:

```
struct usb_xfer {
...
        uint8_t         usb_state;
/* Set when callback is executed before a data transfer. */
#define USB_ST_SETUP          0
/* Set when callback is executed after a data transfer. */
#define USB_ST_TRANSFERRED    1
/* Set when a transfer error occurs. */
#define USB_ST_ERROR          2
...
};
```

Generally, you'd use struct usb_xfer * in a switch statement to provide a code block for each transfer state. Some example code should help clarify what I mean.

NOTE *Just concentrate on the structure of this code and ignore what it does.*

```
static void
ulpt_status_callback(❶struct usb_xfer *transfer, usb_error_t error)
{
        struct ulpt_softc *sc = usbd_xfer_softc(transfer);
        struct usb_device_request req;
        struct usb_page_cache *pc;
        uint8_t current_status, new_status;

        switch (❷USB_GET_STATE(transfer)) {
❸case USB_ST_SETUP:
                req.bmRequestType = UT_READ_CLASS_INTERFACE;
                req.bRequest = UREQ_GET_PORT_STATUS;
                USETW(req.wValue, 0);
                req.wIndex[0] = sc->sc_iface_num;
                req.wIndex[1] = 0;
                USETW(req.wLength, 1);

                pc = usbd_xfer_get_frame(transfer, 0);
                usbd_copy_in(pc, 0, &req, sizeof(req));
                usbd_xfer_set_frame_len(transfer, 0, sizeof(req));
                usbd_xfer_set_frame_len(transfer, 1, 1);
                usbd_xfer_set_frames(transfer, 2);
❹usbd_transfer_submit(transfer);

                break;
❺case USB_ST_TRANSFERRED:
                pc = usbd_xfer_get_frame(transfer, 1);
                usbd_copy_out(pc, 0, &current_status, 1);

                current_status = (current_status ^ LPS_INVERT) & LPS_MASK;
                new_status = current_status & ~sc->sc_previous_status;
                sc->sc_previous_status = current_status;

                if (new_status & LPS_NERR)
                        ❻log(LOG_NOTICE, "%s: output error\n",
                                device_get_nameunit(sc->sc_dev));
                else if (new_status & LPS_SELECT)
                        ❼log(LOG_NOTICE, "%s: offline\n",
                                device_get_nameunit(sc->sc_dev));
                else if (new_status & LPS_NOPAPER)
                        ❽log(LOG_NOTICE, "%s: out of paper\n",
                                device_get_nameunit(sc->sc_dev));

                break;
```

```
        default:
                break;
        }
}
```

Notice how ❶ struct usb_xfer * is used as the ❷ expression for the switch statement (as you would expect, the macro USB_GET_STATE returns the transfer state).

The constant ❸ USB_ST_SETUP is set when callback is executed before a data transfer. This case handles any pre-transfer operations. It always ends with ❹ usbd_transfer_submit, which starts the data transfer.

The constant ❺ USB_ST_TRANSFERRED is set when callback is executed after a data transfer. This case performs any post-transfer actions, such as ❻ ❼ ❽ printing log messages.

USB Configuration Structure Management Routines

The FreeBSD kernel provides the following functions for working with usb_config structures:

```
#include <dev/usb/usb.h>
#include <dev/usb/usbdi.h>
#include <dev/usb/usbdi_util.h>

usb_error_t
usbd_transfer_setup(struct usb_device *udev, const uint8_t *ifaces,
    ❶struct usb_xfer **pxfer, ❷const struct usb_config *setup_start,
    ❸uint16_t n_setup, void *priv_sc, struct mtx *priv_mtx);

void
usbd_transfer_unsetup(❹struct usb_xfer **pxfer, ❺uint16_t n_setup);

void
usbd_transfer_start(❻struct usb_xfer *xfer);

void
usbd_transfer_stop(❼struct usb_xfer *xfer);

void
usbd_transfer_drain(struct usb_xfer *xfer);
```

The usbd_transfer_setup function takes an ❷ array of usb_config structures and sets up an ❶ array of usb_xfer structures. The ❸ n_setup argument denotes the number of elements in the arrays.

NOTE   *As you'll see, a usb_xfer structure is required to initiate a USB data transfer.*

The usbd_transfer_unsetup function destroys an ❹ array of usb_xfer structures. The ❺ n_setup argument denotes the number of elements in the array.

The usbd_transfer_start function takes a ❻ usb_xfer structure and starts a USB transfer (that is, it executes callback with USB_ST_SETUP set).

The usbd_transfer_stop function stops any transfers associated with the ❼ xfer argument (that is, it executes callback with USB_ST_ERROR set).

The usbd_transfer_drain function is like usbd_transfer_stop, but it waits for callback to complete before returning.

USB Methods Structure

A usb_fifo_methods structure defines a USB driver's entry points. You can think of struct usb_fifo_methods as struct cdevsw, but for USB drivers.

struct usb_fifo_methods is defined in the <dev/usb/usbdi.h> header as follows:

```
struct usb_fifo_methods {
        /* Executed Unlocked */
        usb_fifo_open_t         *f_open;
        usb_fifo_close_t        *f_close;
        usb_fifo_ioctl_t        *f_ioctl;
        usb_fifo_ioctl_t        *f_ioctl_post;

        /* Executed With Mutex Locked */
        usb_fifo_cmd_t          *f_start_read;
        usb_fifo_cmd_t          *f_stop_read;
        usb_fifo_cmd_t          *f_start_write;
        usb_fifo_cmd_t          *f_stop_write;
        usb_fifo_filter_t       *f_filter_read;
        usb_fifo_filter_t       *f_filter_write;

        const char              *basename[4];
        const char              *postfix[4];
};
```

The FreeBSD kernel provides the following functions for working with usb_fifo_methods structures:

```
#include <dev/usb/usb.h>
#include <dev/usb/usbdi.h>
#include <dev/usb/usbdi_util.h>

int
usb_fifo_attach(struct usb_device *udev, void *priv_sc,
    struct mtx *priv_mtx, struct usb_fifo_methods *pm,
  ❶struct usb_fifo_sc *f_sc, uint16_t unit, uint16_t subunit,
    uint8_t iface_index, uid_t uid, gid_t gid, int mode);

void
usb_fifo_detach(❷struct usb_fifo_sc *f_sc);
```

The usb_fifo_attach function creates a USB device node under /dev. If successful, a magic cookie is saved in ❶ f_sc.

The usb_fifo_detach function takes a ❷ cookie created by usb_fifo_attach and destroys its associated USB device node.

Tying Everything Together

Now that you're familiar with the usb_* structures and their management routines, let's dissect a real-world USB driver.

Listing 15-1 provides a terse, source-level overview of ulpt(4), the USB printer driver.

NOTE *To improve readability, some of the variables and functions presented in this section have been renamed and restructured from their counterparts in the FreeBSD source.*

```
#include <sys/param.h>
#include <sys/module.h>
#include <sys/kernel.h>
#include <sys/systm.h>

#include <sys/conf.h>
#include <sys/bus.h>
#include <sys/lock.h>
#include <sys/mutex.h>
#include <sys/syslog.h>
#include <sys/fcntl.h>

#include <dev/usb/usb.h>
#include <dev/usb/usbdi.h>
#include <dev/usb/usbdi_util.h>

#define ULPT_BUF_SIZE           (1 << 15)
#define ULPT_IFQ_MAX_LEN        2

#define UREQ_GET_PORT_STATUS    0x01
#define UREQ_SOFT_RESET         0x02

#define LPS_NERR                0x08
#define LPS_SELECT              0x10
#define LPS_NOPAPER             0x20
#define LPS_INVERT              (LPS_NERR | LPS_SELECT)
#define LPS_MASK                (LPS_NERR | LPS_SELECT | LPS_NOPAPER)

enum {
        ULPT_BULK_DT_WR,
        ULPT_BULK_DT_RD,
        ULPT_INTR_DT_RD,
        ULPT_N_TRANSFER
};

struct ulpt_softc {
        device_t                sc_dev;
        struct usb_device       *sc_usb_device;
        struct mtx              sc_mutex;
        struct usb_callout      sc_watchdog;
        uint8_t                 sc_iface_num;
        struct usb_xfer         *sc_transfer[ULPT_N_TRANSFER];
        struct usb_fifo_sc      sc_fifo;
```

```
          struct usb_fifo_sc        sc_fifo_no_reset;
          int                       sc_fflags;
          struct usb_fifo           *sc_fifo_open[2];
          uint8_t                   sc_zero_length_packets;
          uint8_t                   sc_previous_status;
};

static device_probe_t             ulpt_probe;
static device_attach_t            ulpt_attach;
static device_detach_t            ulpt_detach;

static usb_fifo_open_t            ulpt_open;
static usb_fifo_open_t            unlpt_open;
static usb_fifo_close_t           ulpt_close;
static usb_fifo_ioctl_t           ulpt_ioctl;
static usb_fifo_cmd_t             ulpt_start_read;
static usb_fifo_cmd_t             ulpt_stop_read;
static usb_fifo_cmd_t             ulpt_start_write;
static usb_fifo_cmd_t             ulpt_stop_write;

static void                       ulpt_reset(struct ulpt_softc *);
static void                       ulpt_watchdog(void *);

static usb_callback_t             ulpt_write_callback;
static usb_callback_t             ulpt_read_callback;
static usb_callback_t             ulpt_status_callback;

❶ static struct usb_fifo_methods ulpt_fifo_methods = {
          .f_open =                &ulpt_open,
          .f_close =               &ulpt_close,
          .f_ioctl =               &ulpt_ioctl,
          .f_start_read =          &ulpt_start_read,
          .f_stop_read =           &ulpt_stop_read,
          .f_start_write =         &ulpt_start_write,
          .f_stop_write =          &ulpt_stop_write,
          .basename[0] =         ❷"ulpt"
};

❸ static struct usb_fifo_methods unlpt_fifo_methods = {
          .f_open =                &unlpt_open,
          .f_close =               &ulpt_close,
          .f_ioctl =               &ulpt_ioctl,
          .f_start_read =          &ulpt_start_read,
          .f_stop_read =           &ulpt_stop_read,
          .f_start_write =         &ulpt_start_write,
          .f_stop_write =          &ulpt_stop_write,
          .basename[0] =         ❹"unlpt"
};

static const struct usb_config ulpt_config[ULPT_N_TRANSFER] = {
     ❺[ULPT_BULK_DT_WR] = {
              .callback =          &ulpt_write_callback,
              .bufsize =           ULPT_BUF_SIZE,
              .flags =             {.pipe_bof = 1, .proxy_buffer = 1},
```

```
                      .type =         UE_BULK,
                      .endpoint =     UE_ADDR_ANY,
                      .direction =    UE_DIR_OUT
            },

      ❻[ULPT_BULK_DT_RD] = {
                      .callback =     &ulpt_read_callback,
                      .bufsize =      ULPT_BUF_SIZE,
                      .flags =        {.short_xfer_ok = 1, .pipe_bof = 1,
                                          .proxy_buffer = 1},
                      .type =         UE_BULK,
                      .endpoint =     UE_ADDR_ANY,
                      .direction =    UE_DIR_IN
            },

      ❼[ULPT_INTR_DT_RD] = {
                      .callback =     &ulpt_status_callback,
                      .bufsize =      sizeof(struct usb_device_request) + 1,
                      .timeout =      1000,            /* 1 second. */
                      .type =         UE_CONTROL,
                      .endpoint =     0x00,
                      .direction =    UE_DIR_ANY
            }
};

static int
ulpt_open(struct usb_fifo *fifo, int fflags)
{
...
}

static void
ulpt_reset(struct ulpt_softc *sc)
{
...
}

static int
unlpt_open(struct usb_fifo *fifo, int fflags)
{
...
}

static void
ulpt_close(struct usb_fifo *fifo, int fflags)
{
...
}

static int
ulpt_ioctl(struct usb_fifo *fifo, u_long cmd, void *data, int fflags)
{
...
}
```

```
static void
ulpt_watchdog(void *arg)
{
...
}

static void
ulpt_start_read(struct usb_fifo *fifo)
{
...
}

static void
ulpt_stop_read(struct usb_fifo *fifo)
{
...
}

static void
ulpt_start_write(struct usb_fifo *fifo)
{
...
}

static void
ulpt_stop_write(struct usb_fifo *fifo)
{
...
}

static void
ulpt_write_callback(struct usb_xfer *transfer, usb_error_t error)
{
...
}

static void
ulpt_read_callback(struct usb_xfer *transfer, usb_error_t error)
{
...
}

static void
ulpt_status_callback(struct usb_xfer *transfer, usb_error_t error)
{
...
}

static int
ulpt_probe(device_t dev)
{
...
}
```

```
static int
ulpt_attach(device_t dev)
{
...
}

static int
ulpt_detach(device_t dev)
{
...
}

static device_method_t ulpt_methods[] = {
        /* Device interface. */
        DEVMETHOD(device_probe,         ulpt_probe),
        DEVMETHOD(device_attach,        ulpt_attach),
        DEVMETHOD(device_detach,        ulpt_detach),
        { 0, 0 }
};

static driver_t ulpt_driver = {
        "ulpt",
        ulpt_methods,
        sizeof(struct ulpt_softc)
};

static devclass_t ulpt_devclass;

DRIVER_MODULE(ulpt, uhub, ulpt_driver, ulpt_devclass, 0, 0);
MODULE_DEPEND(ulpt, usb, 1, 1, 1);
MODULE_DEPEND(ulpt, ucom, 1, 1, 1);
```

Listing 15-1: ulpt.c

Note that Listing 15-1 defines three usb_config structures. Therefore, ulpt(4) communicates with three endpoints: a ❺ bulk OUT, a ❻ bulk IN, and the ❼ default control endpoint.

Also, note that Listing 15-1 defines two ❶ ❸ usb_fifo_methods structures. So, ulpt(4) provides two device nodes: ❷ ulpt%d and ❹ unlpt%d (where %d is the unit number). As you'll see, the ulpt%d device node resets the printer when opened, whereas unlpt%d does not.

Now, let's discuss the functions found in Listing 15-1.

ulpt_probe Function

The ulpt_probe function is the device_probe implementation for ulpt(4). Here is its function definition:

```
static int
ulpt_probe(device_t dev)
{
        ❶struct usb_attach_arg *uaa = device_get_ivars(dev);
```

```
❷if (uaa->usb_mode != USB_MODE_HOST)
        return (ENXIO);

❸if ((uaa->info.bInterfaceClass == UICLASS_PRINTER) &&
    (uaa->info.bInterfaceSubClass == UISUBCLASS_PRINTER) &&
    ((uaa->info.bInterfaceProtocol == UIPROTO_PRINTER_UNI) ||
     (uaa->info.bInterfaceProtocol == UIPROTO_PRINTER_BI) ||
     (uaa->info.bInterfaceProtocol == UIPROTO_PRINTER_1284)))
        return (BUS_PROBE_SPECIFIC);

    return (ENXIO);
}
```

This function first ❷ ensures that the USB host controller is in host mode, which is needed to initiate data transfers. Then ulpt_probe ❸ determines whether dev is a USB printer.

Incidentally, ❶ struct usb_attach_arg contains the printer's instance variables.

ulpt_attach Function

The ulpt_attach function is the device_attach implementation for ulpt(4). Here is its function definition:

```
static int
ulpt_attach(device_t dev)
{
        struct usb_attach_arg *uaa = device_get_ivars(dev);
        struct ulpt_softc *sc = device_get_softc(dev);
        struct usb_interface_descriptor *idesc;
        struct usb_config_descriptor *cdesc;
        uint8_t alt_index, iface_index = uaa->info.bIfaceIndex;
        int error, unit = device_get_unit(dev);

        sc->sc_dev = dev;
        sc->sc_usb_device = uaa->device;
    ❶device_set_usb_desc(dev);
        mtx_init(&sc->sc_mutex, "ulpt", NULL, MTX_DEF | MTX_RECURSE);
    ❷usb_callout_init_mtx(&sc->sc_watchdog, &sc->sc_mutex, 0);

        idesc = usbd_get_interface_descriptor(uaa->iface);
        alt_index = -1;
        for (;;) {
                if (idesc == NULL)
                        break;

                if ((idesc->bDescriptorType == UDESC_INTERFACE) &&
                    (idesc->bLength >= sizeof(*idesc))) {
                        if (idesc->bInterfaceNumber != ❸uaa->info.bIfaceNum)
                                break;
                        else {
                                alt_index++;
```

```
                                 if ((idesc->bInterfaceClass ==
                                        UICLASS_PRINTER) &&
                                     (idesc->bInterfaceSubClass ==
                                        UISUBCLASS_PRINTER) &&
                                     (idesc->bInterfaceProtocol ==
                                     ❹UIPROTO_PRINTER_BI))
                                     goto found;
                        }
                }

                cdesc = usbd_get_config_descriptor(uaa->device);
                idesc = (void *)❺usb_desc_foreach(cdesc, (void *)idesc);
        }
        goto detach;

found:

        if (alt_index) {
                error = ❻usbd_set_alt_interface_index(uaa->device,
                    iface_index, alt_index);
                if (error)
                        goto detach;
        }

        sc->sc_iface_num = idesc->bInterfaceNumber;

        error = ❼usbd_transfer_setup(uaa->device, &iface_index,
            sc->sc_transfer, ulpt_config, ULPT_N_TRANSFER, sc,
            &sc->sc_mutex);
        if (error)
                goto detach;

        device_printf(dev, "using bi-directional mode\n");

        error = ❽usb_fifo_attach(uaa->device, sc, &sc->sc_mutex,
            &ulpt_fifo_methods, &sc->sc_fifo, unit, -1,
            iface_index, UID_ROOT, GID_OPERATOR, 0644);
        if (error)
                goto detach;

        error = ❾usb_fifo_attach(uaa->device, sc, &sc->sc_mutex,
            &unlpt_fifo_methods, &sc->sc_fifo_no_reset, unit, -1,
            iface_index, UID_ROOT, GID_OPERATOR, 0644);
        if (error)
                goto detach;

        mtx_lock(&sc->sc_mutex);
    ❿ulpt_watchdog(sc);
        mtx_unlock(&sc->sc_mutex);
        return (0);

detach:
        ulpt_detach(dev);
        return (ENOMEM);
}
```

This function can be split into three parts. The first ❶ sets the verbose description of dev by calling device_set_usb_desc(dev). Then it ❷ initializes ulpt(4)'s callout structure.

NOTE *All USB devices contain a textual description of themselves, which is why device_set_usb_desc just takes a device_t argument.*

The second part essentially ❺ iterates through the alternate settings for interface number ❸ uaa->info.bIfaceNum, until the alternate setting that supports ❹ bidirectional mode is found. If the alternate setting that supports bidirectional mode is not alternate setting 0, then ❻ usbd_set_alt_interface_index is called to instate this alternate setting. Alternate setting 0 does not need to be instated, because it's used by default.

Finally, the third part ❼ initializes the USB transfers, ❽ ❾ creates ulpt(4)'s device nodes, and calls ❿ ulpt_watchdog (which we'll walk through in "ulpt_watchdog Function" on page 277).

ulpt_detach Function

The ulpt_detach function is the device_detach implementation for ulpt(4). Here is its function definition:

```
static int
ulpt_detach(device_t dev)
{
        struct ulpt_softc *sc = device_get_softc(dev);

    ❶usb_fifo_detach(&sc->sc_fifo);
    ❷usb_fifo_detach(&sc->sc_fifo_no_reset);

        mtx_lock(&sc->sc_mutex);
    ❸usb_callout_stop(&sc->sc_watchdog);
        mtx_unlock(&sc->sc_mutex);

    ❹usbd_transfer_unsetup(sc->sc_transfer, ULPT_N_TRANSFER);
    ❺usb_callout_drain(&sc->sc_watchdog);
    ❻mtx_destroy(&sc->sc_mutex);

        return (0);
}
```

This function starts by ❶ ❷ destroying its device nodes. Then it ❸ stops the callout function, ❹ tears down the USB transfers, ❺ drains the callout function, and ❻ destroys its mutex.

ulpt_open Function

The ulpt_open function is the ulpt%d device node's open routine. Here is its function definition:

```
static int
ulpt_open(struct usb_fifo *fifo, int fflags)
```

```
{
        struct ulpt_softc *sc = usb_fifo_softc(fifo);

        if (sc->sc_fflags == 0)
                ❶ulpt_reset(sc);

        return (❷unlpt_open(fifo, fflags));
}
```

This function first calls ❶ ulpt_reset to reset the printer. Then ❷ unlpt_open is called to (actually) open the printer.

ulpt_reset Function

As mentioned in the previous section, the ulpt_reset function resets the printer. Here is its function definition:

```
static void
ulpt_reset(struct ulpt_softc *sc)
{
        ❶struct usb_device_request req;
        int error;

        req.bRequest = ❷UREQ_SOFT_RESET;
        USETW(req.wValue, 0);
        USETW(req.wIndex, sc->sc_iface_num);
        USETW(req.wLength, 0);

        mtx_lock(&sc->sc_mutex);

        req.bmRequestType = ❸UT_WRITE_CLASS_OTHER;
        error = ❹usbd_do_request_flags(sc->sc_usb_device, &sc->sc_mutex,
            &req, NULL, 0, NULL, 2 * USB_MS_HZ);
        ❺if (error) {
                req.bmRequestType = ❻UT_WRITE_CLASS_INTERFACE;
                ❼usbd_do_request_flags(sc->sc_usb_device, &sc->sc_mutex,
                    &req, NULL, 0, NULL, 2 * USB_MS_HZ);
        }

        mtx_unlock(&sc->sc_mutex);
}
```

This function starts by defining a ❶ usb_device_request structure to ❷ reset the printer. It then ❹ transmits the reset request to the printer.

Note that some printers typify a reset request as ❸ UT_WRITE_CLASS_OTHER and some typify it as ❻ UT_WRITE_CLASS_INTERFACE. Thus, ulpt_reset transmits the reset request a ❼ second time if the first request ❺ fails.

unlpt_open Function

The unlpt_open function is the unlpt%d device node's open routine. Here is its function definition:

NOTE *You'll recall that this function is also called at the end of ulpt_open.*

```
static int
unlpt_open(struct usb_fifo *fifo, int fflags)
{
        struct ulpt_softc *sc = usb_fifo_softc(fifo);
        int error;

    ❶if (sc->sc_fflags & fflags)
                return (EBUSY);

    ❷if (fflags & FREAD) {
                mtx_lock(&sc->sc_mutex);
            ❸usbd_xfer_set_stall(sc->sc_transfer[ULPT_BULK_DT_RD]);
                mtx_unlock(&sc->sc_mutex);

                error = ❹usb_fifo_alloc_buffer(fifo,
                    usbd_xfer_max_len(sc->sc_transfer[ULPT_BULK_DT_RD]),
                    ULPT_IFQ_MAX_LEN);
                if (error)
                        return (ENOMEM);

            ❺sc->sc_fifo_open[USB_FIFO_RX] = fifo;
        }

    ❻if (fflags & FWRITE) {
                mtx_lock(&sc->sc_mutex);
            ❼usbd_xfer_set_stall(sc->sc_transfer[ULPT_BULK_DT_WR]);
                mtx_unlock(&sc->sc_mutex);

                error = ❽usb_fifo_alloc_buffer(fifo,
                    usbd_xfer_max_len(sc->sc_transfer[ULPT_BULK_DT_WR]),
                    ULPT_IFQ_MAX_LEN);
                if (error)
                        return (ENOMEM);

            ❾sc->sc_fifo_open[USB_FIFO_TX] = fifo;
        }

    ❿sc->sc_fflags |= fflags & (FREAD | FWRITE);
        return (0);
}
```

This function first ❶ tests the value of sc->sc_fflags. If it does not equal 0, which implies that another process has opened the printer, the error code EBUSY is returned. Next, unlpt_open determines whether we're opening the printer to ❷ read from or ❻ write to it—the answer is ❿ stored in sc->sc_fflags. Then, a clear-stall request is ❸ ❼ issued to the appropriate endpoint.

NOTE *Any errors that a USB device detects in its own functionality, not counting transmission errors, cause the device to "stall" the endpoint for its current transaction (Oney, 2003). Control endpoints clear their stalls automatically, but other endpoint types require a clear-stall request. Naturally, stalled endpoints cannot perform any transactions.*

Next, memory for the read or write is ❹ ❽ allocated. Afterward, the fifo argument is ❺ ❾ stored in sc->sc_fifo_open.

ulpt_close Function

The ulpt_close function is the close routine for ulpt%d and unlpt%d. Here is its function definition:

```
static void
ulpt_close(struct usb_fifo *fifo, int fflags)
{
        struct ulpt_softc *sc = usb_fifo_softc(fifo);

    ❶sc->sc_fflags &= ~(fflags & (FREAD | FWRITE));

        if (fflags & (FREAD | FWRITE))
            ❷usb_fifo_free_buffer(fifo);
}
```

This function starts by ❶ clearing sc->sc_fflags. Then it ❷ releases the memory allocated in unlpt_open.

ulpt_ioctl Function

The ulpt_ioctl function is the ioctl routine for ulpt%d and unlpt%d. Here is its function definition:

```
static int
ulpt_ioctl(struct usb_fifo *fifo, u_long cmd, void *data, int fflags)
{
    ❶return (ENODEV);
}
```

As you can see, ulpt(4) does ❶ not support ioctl.

ulpt_watchdog Function

The ulpt_watchdog function periodically checks the printer's status. Here is its function definition:

NOTE *You'll recall that this function is called at the end of ulpt_attach.*

```
static void
ulpt_watchdog(void *arg)
{
        struct ulpt_softc *sc = arg;

        mtx_assert(&sc->sc_mutex, MA_OWNED);

    ❶if (sc->sc_fflags == 0)
            ❷usbd_transfer_start(sc->sc_transfer[❸ULPT_INTR_DT_RD]);

    ❹usb_callout_reset(&sc->sc_watchdog, ❺hz, ❻&ulpt_watchdog, sc);
}
```

This function first ❶ ensures that the printer is not open. Then it ❷ starts a transaction with the ❸ default control endpoint (to retrieve the printer's status). Recall that ❷ usbd_transfer_start just executes a callback. In this case, that callback is ulpt_status_callback (for confirmation, see the third usb_config structure in Listing 15-1). Finally, ❻ ulpt_watchdog is ❹ rescheduled to execute after ❺ 1 second.

ulpt_start_read Function

The ulpt_start_read function is executed when a process reads from ulpt%d or unlpt%d (for verification, see their usb_fifo_methods structures). Here is its function definition:

```
static void
ulpt_start_read(struct usb_fifo *fifo)
{
        struct ulpt_softc *sc = usb_fifo_softc(fifo);

    ❶usbd_transfer_start(sc->sc_transfer[❷ULPT_BULK_DT_RD]);
}
```

This function simply ❶ starts a transaction with the printer's ❷ bulk IN endpoint. Note that the callback for a bulk IN endpoint is ulpt_read_callback (for confirmation, see the second usb_config structure in Listing 15-1).

ulpt_stop_read Function

The ulpt_stop_read function is called when a process stops reading from ulpt%d or unlpt%d. Here is its function definition:

```
static void
ulpt_stop_read(struct usb_fifo *fifo)
{
        struct ulpt_softc *sc = usb_fifo_softc(fifo);

        ❶usbd_transfer_stop(sc->sc_transfer[❷ULPT_BULK_DT_RD]);
}
```

This function ❶ stops any transactions associated with the printer's ❷ bulk IN endpoint.

ulpt_start_write Function

The ulpt_start_write function is executed when a process writes to ulpt%d or unlpt%d. Here is its function definition:

```
static void
ulpt_start_write(struct usb_fifo *fifo)
{
        struct ulpt_softc *sc = usb_fifo_softc(fifo);

        ❶usbd_transfer_start(sc->sc_transfer[❷ULPT_BULK_DT_WR]);
}
```

This function simply ❶ starts a transaction with the printer's ❷ bulk OUT endpoint. Note that the callback for a bulk OUT endpoint is ulpt_write_callback (for confirmation, see the first usb_config structure in Listing 15-1).

ulpt_stop_write Function

The ulpt_stop_write function is executed when a process stops writing to ulpt%d or unlpt%d. Here is its function definition:

```
static void
ulpt_stop_write(struct usb_fifo *fifo)
{
        struct ulpt_softc *sc = usb_fifo_softc(fifo);

        ❶usbd_transfer_stop(sc->sc_transfer[❷ULPT_BULK_DT_WR]);
}
```

This function ❶ stops any transactions associated with the printer's ❷ bulk OUT endpoint.

ulpt_write_callback Function

The ulpt_write_callback function transfers data from user space to the printer (to be printed). Recall that this function is the callback for a bulk OUT endpoint, so it's executed before and after a bulk OUT transfers data.

The following is the function definition for ulpt_write_callback:

```
static void
ulpt_write_callback(struct usb_xfer *transfer, usb_error_t error)
{
        struct ulpt_softc *sc = usbd_xfer_softc(transfer);
        struct usb_fifo *fifo = sc->sc_fifo_open[USB_FIFO_TX];
        struct usb_page_cache *pc;
        int actual, max;

        usbd_xfer_status(transfer, &actual, NULL, NULL, NULL);

        if (fifo == NULL)
                return;

        switch (USB_GET_STATE(transfer)) {
        ❶case USB_ST_SETUP:
        ❷case USB_ST_TRANSFERRED:
setup:
                pc = usbd_xfer_get_frame(transfer, 0);
                max = usbd_xfer_max_len(transfer);
                if (❸usb_fifo_get_data(❹fifo, ❺pc, 0, ❻max,
                    ❼&actual, 0)) {
                        ❽usbd_xfer_set_frame_len(transfer, 0, ❾actual);
                        ❿usbd_transfer_submit(transfer);
                }
                break;
        default:
                if (error != USB_ERR_CANCELLED) {
                        /* Issue a clear-stall request. */
                        usbd_xfer_set_stall(transfer);
                        goto setup;
                }
                break;
        }
}
```

This function first ❸ copies *foo* bytes from ❹ user space to ❺ kernel space. At most, ❻ max bytes of data are copied. The number of bytes actually copied is returned in ❼ actual. Next, the ❾ transfer length is ❽ set. Then, the data copied from user space is ❿ sent to the printer.

NOTE *In the preceding paragraph,* foo *is a placeholder, because I don't know how many bytes are copied until* usb_fifo_get_data *returns.*

Note that the ❶ USB_ST_SETUP case and the ❷ USB_ST_TRANSFERRED case are identical. This is because you can print more data than the maximum transfer length. Thus, this function "loops" until all the data is sent.

ulpt_read_callback Function

The ulpt_read_callback function gets data from the printer. Recall that this function is the callback for a bulk IN endpoint, so it's executed before and after a bulk IN transfers data.

The following is the function definition for ulpt_read_callback:

```
static void
ulpt_read_callback(struct usb_xfer *transfer, usb_error_t error)
{
        struct ulpt_softc *sc = usbd_xfer_softc(transfer);
        struct usb_fifo *fifo = sc->sc_fifo_open[USB_FIFO_RX];
        struct usb_page_cache *pc;
        int actual, max;

        usbd_xfer_status(transfer, &actual, NULL, NULL, NULL);

        if (fifo == NULL)
                return;

        switch (USB_GET_STATE(transfer)) {
❶case USB_ST_TRANSFERRED:
        ❷if (actual == 0) {
                ❸if (sc->sc_zero_length_packets == 4)
                        /* Throttle transfers. */
                        ❹usbd_xfer_set_interval(transfer, 500);
                else
                        sc->sc_zero_length_packets++;
        } else {
                /* Disable throttling. */
                usbd_xfer_set_interval(transfer, 0);
                sc->sc_zero_length_packets = 0;
        }

        pc = usbd_xfer_get_frame(transfer, 0);
        ❺usb_fifo_put_data(❻fifo, ❼pc, 0, actual, 1);
        /* FALLTHROUGH */
        case USB_ST_SETUP:
setup:
                if (❽usb_fifo_put_bytes_max(fifo) != 0) {
                        max = usbd_xfer_max_len(transfer);
                        ❾usbd_xfer_set_frame_len(transfer, 0, max);
                        ❿usbd_transfer_submit(transfer);
                }
                break;
        default:
                /* Disable throttling. */
                usbd_xfer_set_interval(transfer, 0);
                sc->sc_zero_length_packets = 0;
```

```
        if (error != USB_ERR_CANCELLED) {
                /* Issue a clear-stall request. */
                usbd_xfer_set_stall(transfer);
                goto setup;
        }
        break;
    }
}
```

This function first ❽ ensures that there's room in user space for the
printer's data. Next, the maximum transfer length is ❾ specified. Then data
from the printer is ❿ retrieved.

After a transfer is ❶ complete, the printer's data is ❺ copied from ❼ kernel space to ❻ user space. Note that if ❷ nothing is returned ❸ four times in
a row, transfer throttling is ❹ enabled.

NOTE   *Some USB devices cannot handle multiple rapid transfer requests, so staggering or
throttling of transfers is required.*

ulpt_status_callback Function

The ulpt_status_callback function returns the printer's current status. Recall
that this function is the callback for the default control endpoint, so it's executed before and after any transactions with endpoint 0.

The following is the function definition for ulpt_status_callback:

```
static void
ulpt_status_callback(struct usb_xfer *transfer, usb_error_t error)
{
        struct ulpt_softc *sc = usbd_xfer_softc(transfer);
        struct usb_device_request req;
        struct usb_page_cache *pc;
        uint8_t current_status, new_status;

        switch (USB_GET_STATE(transfer)) {
        case USB_ST_SETUP:
                req.bmRequestType = UT_READ_CLASS_INTERFACE;
                req.bRequest = ❶UREQ_GET_PORT_STATUS;
                USETW(req.wValue, 0);
                req.wIndex[0] = sc->sc_iface_num;
                req.wIndex[1] = 0;
                USETW(req.wLength, 1);

                pc = usbd_xfer_get_frame(transfer, 0);
        ❷usbd_copy_in(❸pc, 0, ❹&req, sizeof(req));
        ❺usbd_xfer_set_frame_len(transfer, 0, sizeof(req));
        ❻usbd_xfer_set_frame_len(transfer, 1, 1);
                usbd_xfer_set_frames(transfer, ❼2);
        ❽usbd_transfer_submit(transfer);

                break;
```

```
❾case USB_ST_TRANSFERRED:
        pc = usbd_xfer_get_frame(transfer, 1);
      ❿usbd_copy_out(pc, 0, &current_status, 1);

        current_status = (current_status ^ LPS_INVERT) & LPS_MASK;
        new_status = current_status & ~sc->sc_previous_status;
        sc->sc_previous_status = current_status;

        if (new_status & LPS_NERR)
                log(LOG_NOTICE, "%s: output error\n",
                    device_get_nameunit(sc->sc_dev));
        else if (new_status & LPS_SELECT)
                log(LOG_NOTICE, "%s: offline\n",
                    device_get_nameunit(sc->sc_dev));
        else if (new_status & LPS_NOPAPER)
                log(LOG_NOTICE, "%s: out of paper\n",
                    device_get_nameunit(sc->sc_dev));

        break;
default:
        break;
}
}
```

This function first constructs a ❶ get status request. It then ❷ plunks the ❹ request into a ❸ DMA buffer. Shortly afterward, the request is ❽ sent to the printer. Interestingly, this transaction involves ❼ two USB frames. The ❺ first contains the get status request. The ❻ second will hold the printer's status.

After a transaction is ❾ complete, the printer's status is ❿ plucked from the DMA buffer.

The remainder of this function should be self-explanatory.

Conclusion

This chapter was basically a primer on USB devices and drivers. For more information, see the official documentation, available at *http://www.usb.org/developers/*.

16

NETWORK DRIVERS, PART 1: DATA STRUCTURES

Network devices, or *interfaces,* transmit and receive data packets that are driven by the network subsystem (Corbet et al., 2005). In this chapter, we'll examine the data structures used to manage these devices: ifnet, ifmedia, and mbuf. You'll then learn about Message Signaled Interrupts, which are an alternative to traditional interrupts and are commonly used by network devices.

NOTE *To keep things simple, we'll examine only Ethernet drivers. Also, I won't provide a discussion on general networking concepts.*

Network Interface Structures

An ifnet structure is the kernel's representation of an individual network interface. It is defined in the <net/if_var.h> header as follows:

```
struct ifnet {
        void    *if_softc;              /* Driver private data.      */
```

```
void    *if_l2com;              /* Protocol bits.              */
struct  vnet *if_vnet;          /* Network stack instance.     */
TAILQ_ENTRY(ifnet) if_link;     /* ifnet linkage.              */
char    if_xname[IFNAMSIZ];     /* External name.              */
const char *if_dname;           /* Driver name.                */
int     if_dunit;       /* Unit number or IF_DUNIT_NONE.       */
u_int   if_refcount;            /* Reference count.            */

/*
 * Linked list containing every address associated with
 * this interface.
 */
struct  ifaddrhead if_addrhead;

int     if_pcount;      /* Number of promiscuous listeners.    */
struct  carp_if *if_carp;       /* CARP interface.             */
struct  bpf_if *if_bpf;         /* Packet filter.              */
u_short if_index;       /* Numeric abbreviation for interface. */
short   if_timer;       /* Time until if_watchdog is called.   */
struct  ifvlantrunk *if_vlantrunk; /* 802.1Q data.             */
int     if_flags;       /* Flags (e.g., up, down, broadcast).  */
int     if_capabilities;/* Interface features and capabilities. */
int     if_capenable;   /* Enabled features and capabilities.  */
void    *if_linkmib;            /* Link specific MIB data.     */
size_t  if_linkmiblen;          /* Length of above.            */
struct  if_data if_data;        /* Interface information.      */
struct  ifmultihead if_multiaddrs; /* Multicast addresses.     */
int     if_amcount;     /* Number of multicast requests.       */

/* Interface methods.                                          */
int     (❶*if_output)
        (struct ifnet *, struct mbuf *, struct sockaddr *,
            struct route *);
void    (❷*if_input)
        (struct ifnet *, struct mbuf *);
void    (❸*if_start)
        (struct ifnet *);
int     (❹*if_ioctl)
        (struct ifnet *, u_long, caddr_t);
void    (*if_watchdog)
        (struct ifnet *);
void    (❺*if_init)
        (void *);
int     (❻*if_resolvemulti)
        (struct ifnet *, struct sockaddr **, struct sockaddr *);
void    (❼*if_qflush)
        (struct ifnet *);
int     (❽*if_transmit)
        (struct ifnet *, struct mbuf *);
void    (❾*if_reassign)
        (struct ifnet *, struct vnet *, char *);

struct  vnet *if_home_vnet;     /* Where we originate from.    */
struct  ifaddr *if_addr;        /* Link level address.         */
void    *if_llsoftc;            /* Link level softc.           */
```

```
int     if_drv_flags;              /* Driver managed status flags. */
struct  ifaltq ❿if_snd;            /* Output queue, includes altq. */
const u_int8_t *if_broadcastaddr; /* Link level broadcast addr. */
void    *if_bridge;                /* Bridge glue.                 */
struct  label *if_label;           /* Interface MAC label.         */

/* Only used by IPv6.                                              */
struct  ifprefixhead if_prefixhead;
void    *if_afdata[AF_MAX];
int     if_afdata_initialized;
struct  rwlock if_afdata_lock;
struct  task if_linktask;
struct  mtx if_addr_mtx;

LIST_ENTRY(ifnet) if_clones;       /* Clone interfaces.           */
TAILQ_HEAD(, ifg_list) if_groups;  /* Linked list of groups.      */
void    *if_pf_kif;                /* pf(4) glue.                  */
void    *if_lagg;                  /* lagg(4) glue.                */
u_char  if_alloctype;              /* Type (e.g., Ethernet).       */

/* Spare fields.                                                  */
char    if_cspare[3];              /* Spare characters.            */
char    *if_description;           /* Interface description.       */
void    *if_pspare[7];             /* Spare pointers.              */
int     if_ispare[4];              /* Spare integers.              */
};
```

I'll demonstrate how struct ifnet is used in "Hello, world!" on page 291. For now, let's look at its method fields.

The ❺ if_init field identifies the interface's init routine. *Init routines* are called to initialize their interface.

The ❹ if_ioctl field identifies the interface's ioctl routine. Characteristically, *ioctl routines* are used to configure their interface (for example, for setting the maximum transmission unit).

The ❷ if_input field identifies the interface's input routine. An interface sends an interrupt whenever it receives a packet. Its driver-defined interrupt handler then calls its *input routine* to process the packet. Note that this is a departure from the norm. Input routines are called by a driver, while the other routines are called by the network stack. The if_input field generally points to a link layer routine (for example, ether_input) rather than a driver-defined routine.

NOTE *Obviously, link layer routines are kernel defined. Method fields that expect a link layer routine should be defined by an *ifattach function (such as ether_ifattach), not directly by a driver. *ifattach functions are described in "Network Interface Structure Management Routines" on page 286.*

The ❶ if_output field identifies the interface's output routine. *Output routines* are called by the network stack to prepare an upper-layer packet for transmission. Every output routine ends by calling its interface's ❽ transmit routine. If an interface lacks a transmit routine, its ❸ start routine is called instead. Typically, when a network driver defines a transmit routine, its start routine is undefined, and vice versa. The if_output field generally points to a link layer routine (for example, ether_output) rather than a driver-defined routine.

The ❸ if_start field identifies the interface's start routine. Before I describe start routines, it's important to discuss ❿ send queues. Send queues are filled by output routines. *Start routines* remove one packet from their send queue and deposit it in their interface's transmit ring. They repeat this process until the send queue is empty or the transmit ring is full. Transmit rings are simply ring buffers used for transmission. Network interfaces use ring buffers for transmission and reception.

The ❽ if_transmit field identifies the interface's transmit routine. *Transmit routines* are an alternative to start routines. Transmit routines maintain their own send queues. That is, they forego the ❿ predefined send queue, and output routines push packets directly to them. Transmit routines can maintain multiple send queues, which makes them ideal for interfaces with multiple transmit rings.

The ❼ if_qflush field identifies the interface's qflush routine. *Qflush routines* are called to flush the send queues of transmit routines. Every transmit routine must have a corresponding qflush routine.

The ❻ if_resolvemulti field identifies the interface's resolvemulti routine. *Resolvemulti routines* are called to resolve a network layer address into a link layer address when registering a multicast address with their interface. The if_resolvemulti field generally points to a link layer routine (for example, ether_resolvemulti) rather than a driver-defined routine.

The ❾ if_reassign field identifies the interface's reassign routine. *Reassign routines* are called before their interface is moved to another virtual network stack (vnet). They perform any tasks necessary before the move. The if_reassign field generally points to a link layer routine (for example, ether_reassign) rather than a driver-defined routine.

The if_watchdog field is deprecated and must *not* be defined. In FreeBSD version 9, if_watchdog will be removed.

Network Interface Structure Management Routines

The FreeBSD kernel provides the following functions for working with ifnet structures:

```
#include <net/if.h>
#include <net/if_types.h>
#include <net/if_var.h>

struct ifnet *
if_alloc(u_char ❶type);

void
if_initname(struct ifnet ❷*ifp, const char ❸*name, int ❹unit);
```

```
void
if_attach(struct ifnet *ifp);

void
if_detach(struct ifnet *ifp);

void
if_free(struct ifnet *ifp);
```

An ifnet structure is a dynamically allocated structure that's owned by the kernel. That is, you cannot allocate a struct ifnet on your own. Instead, you must call if_alloc. The ❶ type argument is the interface type (for example, Ethernet devices are IFT_ETHER). Symbolic constants for every interface type can be found in the <net/if_types.h> header.

Allocating an ifnet structure does not make the interface available to the system. To do that, you must initialize the structure (by defining the necessary fields) and then call if_attach.

The if_initname function is a convenient function for setting an ❷ interface's ❸ name and ❹ unit number. (Needless to say, this function is used before if_attach.)

When an ifnet structure is no longer needed, it should be deactivated with if_detach, after which it can be freed with if_free.

ether_ifattach Function

The ether_ifattach function is a variant of if_attach that's used for Ethernet devices.

```
#include <net/if.h>
#include <net/if_types.h>
#include <net/if_var.h>
#include <net/ethernet.h>

void
ether_ifattach(struct ifnet *ifp, const u_int8_t *lla);
```

This function is defined in the */sys/net/if_ethersubr.c* source file as follows:

```
void
ether_ifattach(struct ifnet ❶*ifp, const u_int8_t ❷*lla)
{
        struct ifaddr *ifa;
        struct sockaddr_dl *sdl;
        int i;

        ifp->if_addrlen = ETHER_ADDR_LEN;
        ifp->if_hdrlen = ETHER_HDR_LEN;
        if_attach(ifp);
        ifp->if_mtu = ETHERMTU;
      ❸ifp->if_output = ether_output;
      ❹ifp->if_input = ether_input;
      ❺ifp->if_resolvemulti = ether_resolvemulti;
```

```
#ifdef VIMAGE
    ❻ifp->if_reassign = ether_reassign;
#endif
        if (ifp->if_baudrate == 0)
                ifp->if_baudrate = IF_Mbps(10);
        ifp->if_broadcastaddr = etherbroadcastaddr;

        ifa = ifp->if_addr;
        KASSERT(ifa != NULL, ("%s: no lladdr!\n", __func__));
        sdl = (struct sockaddr_dl *)ifa->ifa_addr;
        sdl->sdl_type = IFT_ETHER;
        sdl->sdl_alen = ifp->if_addrlen;
        bcopy(lla, LLADDR(sdl), ifp->if_addrlen);

        bpfattach(ifp, DLT_EN10MB, ETHER_HDR_LEN);
        if (ng_ether_attach_p != NULL)
                (*ng_ether_attach_p)(ifp);

        /* Print Ethernet MAC address (if lla is nonzero). */
        for (i = 0; i < ifp->if_addrlen; i++)
                if (lla[i] != 0)
                        break;
        if (i != ifp->if_addrlen)
                if_printf(ifp, "Ethernet address: %6D\n", lla, ":");
}
```

This function takes an ifnet structure, ❶ ifp, and a link layer address,
❷ lla, and sets up ifp for an Ethernet device.

As you can see, it assigns certain values to ifp, including assigning the
appropriate link layer routine to ❸ if_output, ❹ if_input, ❺ if_resolvemulti,
and ❻ if_reassign.

ether_ifdetach Function

The ether_ifdetach function is a variant of if_detach that's used for Ethernet
devices.

```
#include <net/if.h>
#include <net/if_types.h>
#include <net/if_var.h>
#include <net/ethernet.h>

void
ether_ifdetach(struct ifnet *ifp);
```

This function is used to deactivate an ifnet structure set up by ether_ifattach.

Network Interface Media Structures

An ifmedia structure catalogs every media type that is supported by a network interface (for example, 100BASE-TX, 1000BASE-SX, and so on). It is defined in the <net/if_media.h> header as follows:

```
struct ifmedia {
        int     ifm_mask;               /* Mask of bits to ignore.    */
        int     ifm_media;              /* User-set media word.        */
        struct ifmedia_entry *ifm_cur;  /* Currently selected media.   */

        /*
         * Linked list containing every media type supported by
         * an interface.
         */
        LIST_HEAD(, ifmedia_entry) ifm_list;

        ifm_change_cb_t ifm_change;     /* Media change callback.      */
        ifm_stat_cb_t   ifm_status;     /* Media status callback.      */
};
```

Network Interface Media Structure Management Routines

The FreeBSD kernel provides the following functions for working with ifmedia structures:

```
#include <net/if.h>
#include <net/if_media.h>

void
ifmedia_init(struct ifmedia *ifm, int ❶dontcare_mask,
    ifm_change_cb_t ❷change_callback, ifm_stat_cb_t ❸status_callback);

void
ifmedia_add(struct ifmedia ❹*ifm, int ❺mword, int ❻data, void ❼*aux);

void
ifmedia_set(struct ifmedia ❽*ifm, int ❾mword);

void
ifmedia_removeall(struct ifmedia ❿*ifm);
```

An ifmedia structure is a statically allocated structure that's owned by a network driver. To initialize an ifmedia structure, you must call ifmedia_init. The ❶ dontcare_mask argument marks the bits in ❺ ❾ mword that can be ignored. Usually, dontcare_mask is set to 0.

The ❷ change_callback argument denotes a callback function. This function is executed to change the media type or media options. Here is its function prototype:

```
typedef int (*ifm_change_cb_t)(struct ifnet *ifp);
```

NOTE   *Users can change an interface's media type or media options with ifconfig(8).*

The ❸ status_callback argument denotes a callback function. This function is executed to return the media status. Here is its function prototype:

```
typedef void (*ifm_stat_cb_t)(struct ifnet *ifp, struct ifmediareq *req);
```

NOTE   *Users can query an interface's media status with ifconfig(8).*

The ifmedia_add function adds a media type to ❹ ifm. The ❺ mword argument is a 32-bit "word" that identifies the media type. Valid values for mword are defined in <net/if_media.h>.

Here are the mword values for Ethernet devices:

```
#define IFM_ETHER           0x00000020
#define IFM_10_T            3              /* 10BASE-T, RJ45.                    */
#define IFM_10_2            4              /* 10BASE2, thin Ethernet.           */
#define IFM_10_5            5              /* 10BASE5, thick Ethernet.          */
#define IFM_100_TX          6              /* 100BASE-TX, RJ45.                 */
#define IFM_100_FX          7              /* 100BASE-FX, fiber.                */
#define IFM_100_T4          8              /* 100BASE-T4.                       */
#define IFM_100_VG          9              /* 100VG-AnyLAN.                     */
#define IFM_100_T2          10             /* 100BASE-T2.                       */
#define IFM_1000_SX         11         /* 1000BASE-SX, multimode fiber.         */
#define IFM_10_STP          12         /* 10BASE-T, shielded twisted-pair.      */
#define IFM_10_FL           13             /* 10BASE-FL, fiber.                 */
#define IFM_1000_LX         14         /* 1000BASE-LX, single-mode fiber.       */
#define IFM_1000_CX         15         /* 1000BASE-CX, shielded twisted-pair.   */
#define IFM_1000_T          16             /* 1000BASE-T.                       */
#define IFM_HPNA_1          17             /* HomePNA 1.0 (1Mb/s).              */
#define IFM_10G_LR          18         /* 10GBASE-LR, single-mode fiber.        */
#define IFM_10G_SR          19         /* 10GBASE-SR, multimode fiber.          */
#define IFM_10G_CX4         20             /* 10GBASE-CX4.                      */
#define IFM_2500_SX         21         /* 2500BASE-SX, multimode fiber.         */
#define IFM_10G_TWINAX      22             /* 10GBASE, Twinax.                  */
#define IFM_10G_TWINAX_LONG 23         /* 10GBASE, Twinax long.                 */
#define IFM_10G_LRM         24         /* 10GBASE-LRM, multimode fiber.         */
#define IFM_UNKNOWN         25             /* Undefined.                        */
#define IFM_10G_T           26             /* 10GBASE-T, RJ45.                  */

#define IFM_AUTO            0              /* Automatically select media.       */
#define IFM_MANUAL          1              /* Manually select media.            */
#define IFM_NONE            2              /* Unselect all media.               */

/* Shared options.                                                             */
#define IFM_FDX             0x00100000     /* Force full-duplex.                */
```

```
#define IFM_HDX      0x00200000   /* Force half-duplex.           */
#define IFM_FLOW     0x00400000   /* Enable hardware flow control.*/
#define IFM_FLAG0    0x01000000   /* Driver-defined flag.         */
#define IFM_FLAG1    0x02000000   /* Driver-defined flag.         */
#define IFM_FLAG2    0x04000000   /* Driver-defined flag.         */
#define IFM_LOOP     0x08000000   /* Put hardware in loopback.    */
```

As an example, the `mword` value for 100BASE-TX is the following:

```
IFM_ETHER | IFM_100_TX
```

Table 16-1 describes how each bit in `mword` is used. It also displays the bit-masks that can be passed to `dontcare_mask` to ignore those bits.

Table 16-1: Bit-by-Bit Breakdown of `mword`

Bits	Purpose of Bits	Mask to Ignore Bits
00–04	Denotes the media type variant (for example, 100BASE-TX)	IFM_TMASK
05–07	Denotes the media type (for example, Ethernet)	IFM_NMASK
08–15	Denotes the media type specific options	IFM_OMASK
16–18	Denotes the media type mode (for multimode media only)	IFM_MMASK
19	Reserved for future use	n/a
20–27	Denotes the shared options (for example, force full-duplex)	IFM_GMASK
28–31	Denotes the `mword` instance	IFM_IMASK

The ❻ data and ❼ aux arguments allow drivers to provide metadata about `mword`. Because drivers typically have no metadata to provide, data and aux are frequently set to 0 and NULL, respectively.

The `ifmedia_set` function sets the default ❾ media type for ❽ ifm. This function is used only during device initialization.

The `ifmedia_removeall` function takes an ❿ ifmedia structure and removes every media type from it.

Hello, world!

Now that you're familiar with the if* structures and their management routines, let's go through an example. The following function, named `em_setup_interface` and defined in */sys/dev/e1000/if_em.c*, sets up em(4)'s ifnet and ifmedia structures. (The em(4) driver is for Intel's PCI Gigabit Ethernet adapters.)

```
static int
em_setup_interface(device_t dev, struct adapter *adapter)
{
        struct ifnet *ifp;

        ifp = ❶adapter->ifp = ❷if_alloc(❸IFT_ETHER);
        if (ifp == NULL) {
                device_printf(dev, "cannot allocate ifnet structure\n");
```

```
                    return (-1);
            }

            if_initname(ifp, device_get_name(dev), device_get_unit(dev));
            ifp->if_mtu = ETHERMTU;
            ifp->if_init = em_init;
            ifp->if_softc = adapter;
            ifp->if_flags = IFF_BROADCAST | IFF_SIMPLEX | IFF_MULTICAST;
            ifp->if_ioctl = em_ioctl;
            ifp->if_start = em_start;
            IFQ_SET_MAXLEN(&ifp->if_snd, adapter->num_tx_desc - 1);
            ifp->if_snd.ifq_drv_maxlen = adapter->num_tx_desc - 1;
            IFQ_SET_READY(&ifp->if_snd);

    ❹ether_ifattach(ifp, adapter->hw.mac.addr);

            ifp->if_capabilities = ifp->if_capenable = 0;

            /* Enable checksum offload. */
    ❺ifp->if_capabilities |= IFCAP_HWCSUM | IFCAP_VLAN_HWCSUM;
    ❻ifp->if_capenable |= IFCAP_HWCSUM | IFCAP_VLAN_HWCSUM;

            /* Enable TCP segmentation offload. */
            ifp->if_capabilities |= IFCAP_TSO4;
            ifp->if_capenable |= IFCAP_TSO4;

            /* Enable VLAN support. */
            ifp->if_data.ifi_hdrlen = sizeof(struct ether_vlan_header);
            ifp->if_capabilities |= IFCAP_VLAN_HWTAGGING | IFCAP_VLAN_MTU;
            ifp->if_capenable |= IFCAP_VLAN_HWTAGGING | IFCAP_VLAN_MTU;

            /* Interface can filter VLAN tags. */
            ifp->if_capabilities |= IFCAP_VLAN_HWFILTER;

#ifdef DEVICE_POLLING
            ifp->if_capabilities |= IFCAP_POLLING;
#endif

            /* Enable Wake-on-LAN (WOL) via magic packet? */
    ❼if (adapter->wol) {
                    ifp->if_capabilities |= IFCAP_WOL;
                    ifp->if_capenable |= IFCAP_WOL_MAGIC;
            }

    ❽ifmedia_init(&adapter->media, IFM_IMASK, em_media_change,
                em_media_status);

    ❾if ((adapter->hw.phy.media_type == e1000_media_type_fiber) ||
                (adapter->hw.phy.media_type == e1000_media_type_internal_serdes))
            {
                    u_char fiber_type = IFM_1000_SX;
```

```
                    ifmedia_add(&adapter->media,
                        IFM_ETHER | fiber_type, 0, NULL);
                    ifmedia_add(&adapter->media,
                        IFM_ETHER | fiber_type | IFM_FDX, 0, NULL);
        } else {
                    ifmedia_add(&adapter->media,
                        IFM_ETHER | IFM_10_T, 0, NULL);
                    ifmedia_add(&adapter->media,
                        IFM_ETHER | IFM_10_T | IFM_FDX, 0, NULL);
                    ifmedia_add(&adapter->media,
                        IFM_ETHER | IFM_100_TX, 0, NULL);
                    ifmedia_add(&adapter->media,
                        IFM_ETHER | IFM_100_TX | IFM_FDX, 0, NULL);

                    if (adapter->hw.phy.type != e1000_phy_ife) {
                        ifmedia_add(&adapter->media,
                            IFM_ETHER | IFM_1000_T, 0, NULL);
                        ifmedia_add(&adapter->media,
                            IFM_ETHER | IFM_1000_T | IFM_FDX, 0, NULL);
                    }
        }

        ifmedia_add(&adapter->media, IFM_ETHER | IFM_AUTO, 0, NULL);
    ❿ifmedia_set(&adapter->media, IFM_ETHER | IFM_AUTO);

        return (0);
}
```

This function can be split into three parts. The first ❷ allocates an ❸ Ethernet-specific ifnet structure and stores it in ❶ adapter->ifp. Then adapter->ifp is defined and ❹ activated. (Here, adapter is the name for em(4)'s softc structure.)

The second part ❺ outlines and ❻ enables the interface's features, such as ❼ Wake-on-LAN (WOL). (*WOL* is an Ethernet standard that allows a computer to be turned on, or woken up, by a network message.)

The third part ❽ initializes an ifmedia structure, ❾ adds the interface's supported media to it, and ❿ defines the default media type as *automatically select the best media.*

NOTE   *Of course, em_setup_interface is called during em(4)'s device_attach routine.*

mbuf Structures

An mbuf structure is a memory buffer for network data. Commonly, this data spans multiple mbuf structures, which are arranged into a linked list known as an *mbuf chain.*

struct mbuf is defined in the <sys/mbuf.h> header as follows:

```
struct mbuf {
    ❶struct m_hdr m_hdr;
    ❷union {
```

```
                        struct {
                                struct pkthdr MH_pkthdr;
                                union {
                                        struct m_ext MH_ext;
                                        char MH_databuf[MHLEN];
                                } MH_dat;
                        } MH;
                        char M_databuf[MLEN];
                } M_dat;
};
```

Every mbuf structure contains a ❷ buffer for data and a ❶ header, which looks like this:

```
struct m_hdr {
        struct mbuf     *mh_next;       /* Next mbuf in chain.       */
        struct mbuf     *mh_nextpkt;    /* Next chain in queue/record. */
        caddr_t         mh_data;        /* Location of data.         */
        int             mh_len;         /* Data length.              */
        int             mh_flags;       /* Flags.                    */
        short           mh_type;        /* Data type.                */
        uint8_t         pad[M_HDR_PAD]; /* Padding for word alignment. */
};
```

We'll walk through an example that uses mbufs in Chapter 17. For more on mbufs, see the mbuf(9) manual page.

Message Signaled Interrupts

Message Signaled Interrupts (MSI) and *Extended Message Signaled Interrupts (MSI-X)* are alternative ways to send interrupts. Traditionally, devices include an interrupt pin that they assert in order to generate an interrupt, but MSI- and MSI-X– enabled devices send some data, known as an *MSI message* or *MSI-X message*, to a particular memory address in order to generate an interrupt. MSI- and MSI-X–enabled devices can define multiple unique messages. Subsequently, drivers can define multiple unique interrupt handlers. In other words, MSI- and MSI-X–enabled devices can issue different interrupts, with each interrupt specifying a different condition or task. MSI- and MSI-X–enabled devices can define up to 32 and 2,048 unique messages, respectively. (MSI and MSI-X are not exclusive to network devices. They are, however, exclusive to PCI and PCIe devices.)

Implementing MSI

Unlike with previous topics, I'm going to take a holistic approach here. Namely, I'm going to show an example first, and then I'll describe the MSI family of functions.

The following function, named ciss_setup_msix and defined in */sys/dev/ciss/ciss.c*, sets up MSI for the ciss(4) driver.

NOTE *This function was chosen solely because it's simple. The fact that it's from* ciss(4) *is irrelevant.*

```
static int
ciss_setup_msix(struct ciss_softc *sc)
{
        int i, count, error;

        i = ciss_lookup(sc->ciss_dev);
    ❶if (ciss_vendor_data[i].flags & CISS_BOARD_NOMSI)
                return (EINVAL);

        count = ❷pci_msix_count(sc->ciss_dev);
        if (count < CISS_MSI_COUNT) {
                count = ❸pci_msi_count(sc->ciss_dev);
                if (count < CISS_MSI_COUNT)
                        return (EINVAL);
        }

        count = MIN(count, CISS_MSI_COUNT);
        error = ❹pci_alloc_msix(sc->ciss_dev, &count);
        if (error) {
                error = ❺pci_alloc_msi(sc->ciss_dev, &count);
                if (error)
                        return (EINVAL);
        }

        sc->ciss_msi = count;
        for (i = 0; i < count; i++)
            ❻sc->ciss_irq_rid[i] = i + 1;

        return (0);
}
```

This function is composed of four parts. The first ❶ ensures that the device actually supports MSI.

The second part determines the number of unique ❷ MSI-X or ❸ MSI messages the device maintains, and stores the answer in count.

The third part allocates count ❹ *MSI-X* or ❺ *MSI vectors*, which connect each message to a SYS_RES_IRQ resource with a rid of 1 through count. Thus, in order to assign an interrupt handler to the eighth message, you'd call bus_alloc_resource_any (to allocate a SYS_RES_IRQ resource) and pass 8 as the rid argument. Then you'd call bus_setup_intr as usual.

Lastly, the fourth part ❻ saves the rid of each MSI-X or MSI message in the ciss_irq_rid array.

Naturally, this function is called during ciss(4)'s device_attach routine, like so:

```
...
        /*
         * Use MSI/MSI-X?
         */
```

```
sc->ciss_irq_rid[0] = 0;
if (method == CISS_TRANSPORT_METHOD_PERF) {
        ciss_printf(sc, "Performant Transport\n");

        if (ciss_force_interrupt != 1 && ❶ciss_setup_msix(sc) == 0)
                intr = ciss_perf_msi_intr;
        else
                intr = ciss_perf_intr;

        sc->ciss_interrupt_mask =
            CISS_TL_PERF_INTR_OPQ | CISS_TL_PERF_INTR_MSI;
} else {
        ciss_printf(sc, "Simple Transport\n");

        if (ciss_force_interrupt == 2)
            ❷ciss_setup_msix(sc);

        sc->ciss_perf = NULL;
        intr = ciss_intr;
        sc->ciss_interrupt_mask = sqmask;
}

/*
 * Disable interrupts.
 */
CISS_TL_SIMPLE_DISABLE_INTERRUPTS(sc);

/*
 * Set up the interrupt handler.
 */
sc->ciss_irq_resource = ❸bus_alloc_resource_any(sc->ciss_dev,
    SYS_RES_IRQ, ❹&sc->ciss_irq_rid[0], RF_ACTIVE | RF_SHAREABLE);
if (sc->ciss_irq_resource == NULL) {
        ciss_printf(sc, "cannot allocate interrupt resource\n");
        return (ENXIO);
}

error = bus_setup_intr(sc->ciss_dev, sc->ciss_irq_resource,
    INTR_TYPE_CAM | INTR_MPSAFE, NULL, intr, sc, &sc->ciss_intr);
if (error) {
        ciss_printf(sc, "cannot set up interrupt\n");
        return (ENXIO);
}
```
...

Notice how MSI is ❶ ❷ set up before ❸ acquiring an IRQ. Additionally, notice how the ❹ rid argument is ciss_irq_rid.

NOTE   *As of this writing, ciss(4) supports only the first MSI-X or MSI message.*

MSI Management Routines

The FreeBSD kernel provides the following functions for working with MSI:

```
#include <dev/pci/pcivar.h>

int
pci_msix_count(device_t dev);

int
pci_msi_count(device_t dev);

int
pci_alloc_msix(device_t dev, int *count);

int
pci_alloc_msi(device_t dev, int *count);

int
pci_release_msi(device_t dev);
```

The `pci_msix_count` and `pci_msi_count` functions return the number of unique MSI-X or MSI messages maintained by the device `dev`.

The `pci_alloc_msix` and `pci_alloc_msi` functions allocate `count` MSI-X or MSI vectors based on `dev`. If there are not enough free vectors, fewer than `count` vectors will be allocated. Upon a successful return, `count` will contain the number of vectors allocated. (MSI-X and MSI vectors were described in "Implementing MSI" on page 294.)

The `pci_release_msi` function releases the MSI-X or MSI vectors that were allocated by `pci_alloc_msix` or `pci_alloc_msi`.

Conclusion

This chapter examined `ifnet`, `ifmedia`, and `mbuf` structures, as well as MSI and MSI-X. In Chapter 17, you'll use this information to analyze a network driver.

17

NETWORK DRIVERS, PART 2: PACKET RECEPTION AND TRANSMISSION

This chapter examines the packet reception and transmission components of em(4). Predictably, em(4) uses both mbufs and MSI for packet reception and transmission.

Packet Reception

When an interface receives a packet, it sends an interrupt. Naturally, this causes its interrupt handler to execute. For example, here is what executes in em(4):

```
static void
em_msix_rx(void ❶*arg)
{
        struct rx_ring *rxr = arg;
        struct adapter *adapter = rxr->adapter;
        bool more;

        ++rxr->rx_irq;

        more = ❷em_rxeof(rxr, ❸adapter->rx_process_limit, NULL);
```

```
        if (more)
                ❹taskqueue_enqueue(rxr->tq, &rxr->rx_task);
        else
                ❺E1000_WRITE_REG(&adapter->hw, E1000_IMS, rxr->ims);
}
```

This function takes a ❶ pointer to a ring buffer that contains one or more
received packets, and calls ❷ em_rxeof to process those packets. If there are
more than ❸ rx_process_limit packets, a task structure is ❹ queued; otherwise,
this interrupt is ❺ reenabled. I'll discuss the task structure and its associated
function in "em_handle_rx Function" on page 303.

em_rxeof Function

As mentioned previously, em_rxeof processes received packets. Its function
definition is listed below, but because this function is fairly long and involved,
I'll introduce it in parts. Here is the first part:

```
static bool
em_rxeof(struct rx_ring *rxr, int count, int *done)
{
        struct adapter *adapter = rxr->adapter;
        struct ifnet *ifp = adapter->ifp;
        struct e1000_rx_desc *cur;
        struct mbuf *mp, *sendmp;
        u8 status = 0;
        u16 len;
        int i, processed, rxdone = 0;
        bool eop;

        EM_RX_LOCK(rxr);

    ❶for (i = rxr->next_to_check, processed = 0; count != 0; ) {
            ❷if ((ifp->if_drv_flags & ❸IFF_DRV_RUNNING) == 0)
                    break;

        ❹bus_dmamap_sync(rxr->rxdma.dma_tag, ❺rxr->rxdma.dma_map,
                BUS_DMASYNC_POSTREAD);

            mp = sendmp = NULL;
            cur = ❻&rxr->rx_base[i];
            status = cur->status;
            if ((status & ❼E1000_RXD_STAT_DD) == 0)
                    break;
            len = le16toh(cur->length);
            eop = (status & ❽E1000_RXD_STAT_EOP) != 0;

            if ((cur->errors & ❾E1000_RXD_ERR_FRAME_ERR_MASK) ||
                (rxr->discard == TRUE)) {
                    ++ifp->if_ierrors;
                    ++rxr->rx_discarded;
                    if (!eop)
                            rxr->discard = TRUE;
```

```
                    else
                            rxr->discard = FALSE;
            ⑩em_rx_discard(rxr, i);
                    goto next_desc;
        }
```

...

This function's execution is contained primarily within a ❶ for loop. This
loop begins by ❷ verifying that the ❸ interface is up and running. Then it ❹
synchronizes the DMA buffer currently loaded in ❺ rxr->rxdma.dma_map, which
is ❻ rxr->rx_base.

The buffer ❻ rxr->rx_base[i] contains a descriptor that describes a
received packet. When a packet spans multiple mbufs, rxr->rx_base[i]
describes one mbuf in the chain.

If rxr->rx_base[i] lacks the ❼ E1000_RXD_STAT_DD flag, the for loop exits.
(The E1000_RXD_STAT_DD flag stands for *receive descriptor status: descriptor done.*
We'll see its effects shortly.)

If rxr->rx_base[i] describes the ❽ last mbuf in the chain, the Boolean variable eop, which stands for *end of packet*, is set to TRUE. (Needless to say, when a
packet requires only one mbuf, that mbuf is still the last mbuf in the chain.)

If the packet described by rxr->rx_base[i] contains any ❾ errors, it is
⑩ discarded. Note that I use the word *packet*, not *mbuf*, here, because every
mbuf in the packet is discarded.

Now let's look at the next part of em_rxeof:

...

```
            ❶mp = rxr->rx_buffers[i].m_head;
            mp->m_len = ❷len;
            rxr->rx_buffers[i].m_head = NULL;

            ❸if (rxr->fmp == NULL) {
                    mp->m_pkthdr.len = len;
                    ❹rxr->fmp = ❺rxr->lmp = mp;
            } else {
                    mp->m_flags &= ~M_PKTHDR;
                    ❻rxr->lmp->m_next = mp;
                    ❼rxr->lmp = mp;
                    rxr->fmp->m_pkthdr.len += len;
            }
```

...

Here, ❹ rxr->fmp and ❺ rxr->lmp point to the first and last mbuf in the
chain, ❶ mp is the mbuf described by rxr->rx_base[i], and ❷ len is mp's length.

So, this part simply ❸ identifies whether mp is the first mbuf in the chain.
If it is not, then mp is ❻ ❼ linked into the chain.

Here is the next part of em_rxeof:

...

```
            ❶if (eop) {
                    --count;
                    ❷sendmp = ❸rxr->fmp;
```

```
                        sendmp->m_pkthdr.rcvif = ifp;
                        ++ifp->if_ipackets;
                        ❹em_receive_checksum(cur, sendmp);
❺ #ifndef __NO_STRICT_ALIGNMENT
                        ❻if (adapter->max_frame_size >
                            (MCLBYTES - ETHER_ALIGN) &&
                          ❼em_fixup_rx(rxr) != 0)
                                goto skip;
       #endif
                        if (status & E1000_RXD_STAT_VP) {
                                sendmp->m_pkthdr.ether_vtag =
                                    le16toh(cur->special) &
                                    E1000_RXD_SPC_VLAN_MASK;
                                sendmp->m_flags |= M_VLANTAG;
                        }
       #ifndef __NO_STRICT_ALIGNMENT
       skip:
       #endif
                        ❽rxr->fmp = ❾rxr->lmp = ❿NULL;
                }
       ...
```

If mp is the ❶ last mbuf in the chain, ❷ sendmp is set to the ❸ first mbuf in the chain, and the header checksum is ❹ verified.

If our architecture requires ❺ strict alignment and ❻ jumbo frames are enabled, em_rxeof ❼ aligns the mbuf chain. (Jumbo frames are Ethernet packets with more than 1500 bytes of data.)

This part concludes by setting ❽ rxr->fmp and ❾ rxr->lmp to ❿ NULL. Here is the next part of em_rxeof:

```
       ...
       next_desc:
                cur->status = 0;
                ++rxdone;
                ++processed;

                if (❶++i == adapter->num_rx_desc)
                        i = 0;

                ❷if (sendmp != NULL) {
                        rxr->next_to_check = i;
                        EM_RX_UNLOCK(rxr);
                        ❸(*ifp->if_input)(ifp, ❹sendmp);
                        EM_RX_LOCK(rxr);
                        i = rxr->next_to_check;
                }

                if (processed == 8) {
                        ❺em_refresh_mbufs(rxr, i);
                        processed = 0;
                }
            }                                   /* The end of the for loop. */
       ...
```

Here, i is ❶ incremented so that em_rxeof can get to the next mbuf in the ring. Then, ❷ if sendmp points to an mbuf chain, em(4)'s input routine is ❸ executed to send that ❹ chain to the upper layers. Afterward, new mbufs are ❺ allocated for em(4).

NOTE   *When an mbuf chain is sent to the upper layers, drivers must not access those mbufs anymore. For all intents and purposes, those mbufs have been freed.*

To sum up, this for loop simply links together every mbuf in a received packet and then sends that to the upper layers. This continues until every packet in the ring has been processed or rx_process_limit is hit (rx_process_limit was described in "Packet Reception" on page 299).

Here is the final part of em_rxeof:

```
...
        if (e1000_rx_unrefreshed(rxr))
                em_refresh_mbufs(rxr, i);

        rxr->next_to_check = i;
        if (done != NULL)
                *done = rxdone;
        EM_RX_UNLOCK(rxr);

    ❶return ((status & E1000_RXD_STAT_DD) ? TRUE : FALSE);
}
```

If there are more packets to process, em_rxeof ❶ returns TRUE.

em_handle_rx Function

Recall that when em_rxeof returns TRUE, em_msix_rx queues a task structure (em_msix_rx was discussed in "Packet Reception" on page 299).

Here is that task structure's function:

```
static void
em_handle_rx(void *context, int pending)
{
        struct rx_ring *rxr = context;
        struct adapter *adapter = rxr->adapter;
        bool more;

        more = ❶em_rxeof(rxr, adapter->rx_process_limit, NULL);
        if (more)
                taskqueue_enqueue(rxr->tq, &rxr->rx_task);
        else
                E1000_WRITE_REG(&adapter->hw, E1000_IMS, rxr->ims);
}
```

This function is nearly identical to em_msix_rx. When there are more packets to process, ❶ em_rxeof just gets called again.

Packet Transmission

To transmit a packet, the network stack calls a driver's output routine. All output routines end by calling their interface's transmit or start routine. Here is em(4)'s start routine:

```
static void
em_start(struct ifnet *ifp)
{
        struct adapter *adapter = ifp->if_softc;
        struct tx_ring *txr = adapter->tx_rings;

        if (ifp->if_drv_flags & IFF_DRV_RUNNING) {
            ❶EM_TX_LOCK(txr);
            ❷em_start_locked(ifp, txr);
                EM_TX_UNLOCK(txr);
        }
}
```

This start routine ❶ acquires a lock and then calls ❷ em_start_locked.

em_start_locked Function

The em_start_locked function is defined as follows:

```
static void
em_start_locked(struct ifnet *ifp, struct tx_ring *txr)
{
        struct adapter *adapter = ifp->if_softc;
        struct mbuf *m_head;

        EM_TX_LOCK_ASSERT(txr);

        if ((ifp->if_drv_flags & (IFF_DRV_RUNNING | IFF_DRV_OACTIVE)) !=
            IFF_DRV_RUNNING)
                return;

        if (!adapter->link_active)
                return;

    ❶while (!IFQ_DRV_IS_EMPTY(&ifp->if_snd)) {
            ❷if (txr->tx_avail <= EM_TX_CLEANUP_THRESHOLD)
                ❸em_txeof(txr);

            ❹if (txr->tx_avail < EM_MAX_SCATTER) {
                    ❺ifp->if_drv_flags |= IFF_DRV_OACTIVE;
                    break;
            }

            ❻IFQ_DRV_DEQUEUE(❼&ifp->if_snd, ❽m_head);
            if (m_head == NULL)
                    break;
```

```
                if (❾em_xmit(txr, &m_head)) {
                        if (m_head == NULL)
                                break;
                        ifp->if_drv_flags |= IFF_DRV_OACTIVE;
                        IFQ_DRV_PREPEND(&ifp->if_snd, m_head);
                        break;
                }

                ETHER_BPF_MTAP(ifp, m_head);

                txr->watchdog_time = ticks;
                txr->queue_status = EM_QUEUE_WORKING;
        }
}
```

This function ❻ removes one ❽ mbuf from em(4)'s ❼ send queue and
❾ transmits it to the interface. This repeats until the send queue is ❶ empty.
(Send queues, as mentioned in Chapter 16, are populated by output routines.)

NOTE *The em_xmit function, which actually transmits the mbufs to the interface, is not
detailed in this book, because of its length. It is fairly straightforward, though, so you
shouldn't have any trouble with it.*

If the number of available transmit descriptors is ❷ less than or equal to
EM_TX_CLEANUP_THRESHOLD, ❸ em_txeof is called to reclaim the used descriptors.
(A transmit descriptor describes an outgoing packet. If a packet spans multiple
mbufs, a transmit descriptor describes one mbuf in the chain.)

If the number of available transmit descriptors is ❹ less than EM_MAX_SCATTER,
transfers are ❺ stopped.

em_txeof Function

The em_txeof function goes through the transmit descriptors and frees the
mbufs for packets that have been transmitted. Its function definition is listed
below, but because this function is fairly long and involved, I'll introduce it
in parts. Here is the first part:

```
static bool
em_txeof(struct tx_ring *txr)
{
        struct adapter *adapter = txr->adapter;
        struct ifnet *ifp = adapter->ifp;
        struct e1000_tx_desc *tx_desc, *eop_desc;
        struct em_buffer *tx_buffer;
        int processed, first, last, done;

        EM_TX_LOCK_ASSERT(txr);

        if (txr->tx_avail == adapter->num_tx_desc) {
                txr->queue_status = EM_QUEUE_IDLE;
                return (FALSE);
        }
```

```
          processed = 0;
    ❶first = txr->next_to_clean;
    ❷tx_desc = &txr->tx_base[first];
    ❸tx_buffer = &txr->tx_buffers[first];
    ❹last = tx_buffer->next_eop;
     eop_desc = &txr->tx_base[last];

     if (++last == adapter->num_tx_desc)
             last = 0;
    ❺done = last;
...
```

Here, ❶ first is the first mbuf in a chain that housed an outgoing packet,
❹ last is the last mbuf in that chain, and ❺ done is the mbuf after last.

NOTE   *Recall that transmit descriptors, and subsequently mbufs, are held in a ring buffer.*

The variables ❷ tx_desc and ❸ tx_buffer are temporary variables for a
transmit descriptor and its associated mbuf.

Now let's look at the next part of em_txeof:

```
...
        bus_dmamap_sync(txr->txdma.dma_tag, txr->txdma.dma_map,
            BUS_DMASYNC_POSTREAD);

    ❶while (eop_desc->upper.fields.status & E1000_TXD_STAT_DD) {
        ❷while (first != done) {
                ❸tx_desc->upper.data = 0;
                 tx_desc->lower.data = 0;
                 tx_desc->buffer_addr = 0;
                 ++txr->tx_avail;
                 ++processed;

                 if (tx_buffer->m_head) {
                         bus_dmamap_unload(txr->txtag,
                             tx_buffer->map);
                        ❹m_freem(tx_buffer->m_head);
                         tx_buffer->m_head = NULL;
                 }

                 tx_buffer->next_eop = -1;
                 txr->watchdog_time = ticks;

                 if (++first == adapter->num_tx_desc)
                         first = 0;
                 tx_buffer = &txr->tx_buffers[first];
                 tx_desc = &txr->tx_base[first];
        }

        ++ifp->if_opackets;

        last = tx_buffer->next_eop;
        ❺if (last != -1) {
```

```
                    eop_desc = &txr->tx_base[last];
                    if (++last == adapter->num_tx_desc)
                            last = 0;
                    done = last;
            } else
                    break;
    }

    bus_dmamap_sync(txr->txdma.dma_tag, txr->txdma.dma_map,
        BUS_DMASYNC_PREWRITE);
...
```

This ❷ while loop iterates through first to last, ❹ freeing their mbufs and ❸ zeroing their transmit descriptors. (em(4) has a finite number of transmit descriptors. Zeroing a descriptor makes it available again.)

This ❶ while loop ❺ determines whether another mbuf chain can be freed by this ❷ while loop.

Here is the final part of em_txeof:

```
...
    txr->next_to_clean = first;

    if (!processed && ((ticks - txr->watchdog_time) > EM_WATCHDOG))
            txr->queue_status = EM_QUEUE_HUNG;

❶if (txr->tx_avail > EM_MAX_SCATTER)
        ❷ifp->if_drv_flags &= ~IFF_DRV_OACTIVE;

    if (txr->tx_avail == adapter->num_tx_desc) {
            txr->queue_status = EM_QUEUE_IDLE;
        ❸return (FALSE);
    }

    ❹return (TRUE);
}
```

If there are more transmit descriptors to reclaim, em_txeof returns ❹ TRUE; otherwise, it returns ❸ FALSE.

If the number of available transmit descriptors is ❶ greater than EM_MAX_SCATTER, packets ❷ can be transmitted.

Post Packet Transmission

Whenever an interface transmits a packet, it sends an interrupt. Naturally, this causes its interrupt handler to execute. Here is what executes in em(4):

```
static void
em_msix_tx(void *arg)
{
        struct tx_ring *txr = arg;
        struct adapter *adapter = txr->adapter;
```

```
        bool more;

        ++txr->tx_irq;

        EM_TX_LOCK(txr);
        more = ❶em_txeof(txr);
        EM_TX_UNLOCK(txr);
        if (more)
                ❷taskqueue_enqueue(txr->tq, &txr->tx_task);
        else
                E1000_WRITE_REG(&adapter->hw, E1000_IMS, txr->ims);
}
```

NOTE   *Because of MSI, em(4) can use a different interrupt handler for post packet transmission and packet reception.*

This function simply ❶ reclaims the used transmit descriptors. If there are more descriptors to reclaim, a task structure is ❷ queued. Here is that task structure's function:

```
static void
em_handle_tx(void *context, int pending)
{
        struct tx_ring *txr = context;
        struct adapter *adapter = txr->adapter;
        struct ifnet *ifp = adapter->ifp;

        EM_TX_LOCK(txr);

        ❶em_txeof(txr);
        ❷em_start_locked(ifp, txr);
        E1000_WRITE_REG(&adapter->hw, E1000_IMS, txr->ims);

        EM_TX_UNLOCK(txr);
}
```

This function first ❶ reclaims any used transmit descriptors, after which any packets that may have been halted due to a lack of descriptors are ❷ transmitted.

Conclusion

This chapter and Chapter 16 gave a primer on network devices and drivers. If you're serious about writing network drivers, you should review em(4) in its entirety. I recommend beginning with its device_attach implementation: em_attach.

REFERENCES

Baldwin, John H. "Locking in the Multithreaded FreeBSD Kernel." *Proceedings of the BSDCon 2002 Conference*, February 2002.

Corbet, Jonathan, Alessandro Rubini, and Greg Kroah-Hartman. *Linux Device Drivers*. 3rd ed. Sebastopol, CA: O'Reilly Media, 2005.

Kernighan, Brian W. and Dennis M. Ritchie. *The C Programming Language*. 2nd ed. Englewood Cliffs, NJ: Prentice Hall PTR, 1988.

Kong, Joseph. *Designing BSD Rootkits*. San Francisco, CA: No Starch Press, 2007.

McKusick, Marshall Kirk and George V. Neville-Neil. *The Design and Implementation of the FreeBSD Operating System*. Boston, MA: Addison-Wesley Professional, 2005.

Neville-Neil, George V. "Networking from the Bottom Up: Device Drivers." Tutorial given at AsiaBSDCon, January 2010.

Oney, Walter. *Programming the Microsoft Windows Driver Model*. 2nd ed. Redmond, Washington: Microsoft Press, 2003.

Orwick, Penny and Guy Smith. *Developing Drivers with the Windows Driver Foundation*. Redmond, Washington: Microsoft Press, 2007.

Stevens, W. Richard. *Advanced Programming in the UNIX Environment*. Reading, MA: Addison-Wesley Professional, 1992.

van der Linden, Peter. *Expert C Programming*. Englewood Cliffs, NJ: Prentice Hall, 1994.

INDEX

cv_wait_sig function, 81
cv_wait_unlock function, 81
cv_wmesg function, 81

D

d (descriptor) argument, 38
dadone function, 227
dastart function, 227
dastrategy function, 226
data argument, 4
Data Carrier Detect (DCD), 107
data transfers for USB drivers, 262–264
d_close field, 209
d_close function, 57
d_drv1 field, 210
debug.sleep.test sysctl, 90–92
DECLARE_MODULE macro
  data argument, 4
  name argument, 4
  order argument, 4–5
  sub argument, 4
delaying execution
  callouts, 94–96
  event handlers for, 92–94
  load function, 89–90
  sleeping, 83–85
  sleep_modevent function, 88–89
  sleep_thread function, 90–91
  sysctl_debug_sleep_test function, 91
  taskqueues
    global, 97
    management routines for, 97–98
    overview, 96–97
  unload function, 91–92
  voluntary context switching, 83–85
descr argument, 46
descriptive fields for disk structures, 208–209
descriptor (d argument), 38
destroy_dev function, 9, 72
destroying tags for DMA, 198–199
devclass argument, 116
dev_clone event handler, 92, 103
DEV_MODULE macro, 15
device_attach function, 114
device_detach function, 114, 115
device_foo functions, 114–115
device_identify function, 114
device method table, 115
device_probe function, 114
device_resume function, 114
devices
  configuration of, 259
  defined, 1
  driver types, 1–2

device_shutdown function, 114
device_suspend function, 114
d_flags field, 209
d_foo function, 7–8, 72, 121
d_fwheads field, 209
d_fwsectors field, 209
d_ident field, 209
d_ioctl field, 209
d_ioctl function, 28, 58
direction field, 260
Direct Memory Access (DMA). *See* DMA
DISKFLAG_CANDELETE constant, 208
DISKFLAG_CANFLUSHCACHE constant, 208
DISKFLAG_NEEDSGIANT constant, 208
disk structures
  descriptive fields, 208–209
  driver private data, 210
  management routines for, 210
  mandatory media properties, 209
  optional media properties, 209
  storage device methods, 209
dismantling transfers using DMA, 196
DMA (Direct Memory Access)
  buffers
    bus_dmamap_load_mbuf_sg function, 201–202
    bus_dmamap_load_mbuf function, 201
    bus_dmamap_load_uio function, 202
    bus_dmamap_load function, 200–201
    bus_dmamap_unload function, 202
    bus_dma_segment structures, 199–200
    synchronizing, 205
  example using, 203–205
  maps, 199, 202–203
  overview, 193
  tags for
    creating, 197–198
    destroying, 198–199
  transfers using
    dismantling, 196
    initiating, 196
dmat argument, 198, 200, 205
d_maxsize field, 209
d_mediasize field, 209
dontcare_mask argument, 289
d_open field, 209
d_open function, 57
driver argument, 116
DRIVER_MODULE macro
  arg argument, 116
  busname argument, 116
  devclass argument, 116
  driver argument, 116
  evh argument, 116
  name argument, 116

I

IPMI driver, *continued*
  ipmi_pci_match function, 186
  ipmi_pci_probe function, 185–186
ipmi2_pci_attach function, 189–191
ipmi2_pci_probe function, 189
ipmi_attached variable, 186
ipmi_identifiers array, 186
ipmi_pci_attach function, 187–189
ipmi_pci_match function, 186
ipmi_pci_probe function, 185–186
IRQs (interrupt-request lines), 122
isochronous endpoints, 258
ithread argument, 126
ithread routine, 127

K

Keyboard Controller Style (KCS)
    mode, 188
KLDs (loadable kernel modules)
  block drivers, 15–16
  character drivers
    character device switch table, 8
    destroy_dev function, 9
    DEV_MODULE macro, 15
    d_foo function, 7–8
    echo_modevent function, 14
    echo_read function, 13–14
    echo_write function, 12–13
    loading, 15
    make_dev function, 9
  compiling and loading, 6–7
  DECLARE_MODULE macro
    data argument, 4
    name argument, 4
    order argument, 4–5
    sub argument, 4
  Hello, world! example, 5–6
  module event handlers, 2–3
kldunload -f command, 61

L

LED driver
  led_attach function, 178
  led_close function, 180
  led_detach function, 178–179
  led_identify function, 177
  led_open function, 179
  led_probe function, 177–178
  led_read function, 180–181
  led_write function, 181–182
len argument, 46
loadable kernel modules (KLDs). *See* KLDs

load function, 89–90
loading
  character drivers, 15
  KLDs, 6–7
lockfuncarg argument, 198
lockfunc argument, 198
locks, 65
longdesc argument, 19
lowaddr argument, 197
LP_BUSY flag, 157
LP_BYPASS flag, 156
lpt_attach function, 148–150
lpt_close function, 159–160
lptcontrol(8) utility, 162
lpt_detach function, 150
lpt_detect function, 147–148
lpt_identify function, 146
lpt_intr function, 156–157
lpt_ioctl function, 160–162
lpt_open function, 151–153
lpt_port_test function, 147, 148
lpt_probe function, 146
lpt_push_bytes function, 158–159
lpt_read function, 153–154
lpt_release_ppbus function, 162–163
lpt_request_ppbus function, 162
lpt_timeout function, 158
lpt_write function, 154–156

M

make_dev function, 9
Makefiles, 6
MALLOC_DECLARE macro, 20
MALLOC_DEFINE macro, 19
malloc function, 18
malloc_type structures
  MALLOC_DECLARE macro, 20
  MALLOC_DEFINE macro, 19
management routines
  for condition variables, 80–81
  for disk structures, 210
  for DMA maps, 199, 202–203
  for MSI (Message Signaled
    Interrupts), 297
  for mutex locks, 66–68
  for network interface media structures,
    289–291
  for network interface structures,
    286–288
  for rw (reader/writer) locks, 78–79
  for sx (shared/exclusive) locks, 73–75
  for taskqueues, 97–98

mandatory fields for USB drivers, 260
mandatory media properties for disk struc-
    tures, 209
manual_status flag, 262
maps, DMA, 199, 202–203
masks, for ignoring bits, 291
max_dev_transactions argument, 242, 243
MAX_EVENT constant, 88
maxsegsz argument, 198
maxsize argument, 198
max_tagged_dev_transactions argument, 243
mbuf argument, 201
mbuf chain, 293
mbuf structures, 293–294
M_ECHO structure, 22
media properties for disk structures
    mandatory, 209
    optional, 209
memory allocation
    contiguous physical memory, 22–25
    malloc_type structures
        MALLOC_DECLARE macro, 20
        MALLOC_DEFINE macro, 19
    overview, 17–19
memory barriers, 172
memory-mapped I/O (MMIO). *See* MMIO
Message Signaled Interrupts (MSI), 294
    implementing, 294–296
    management routines for, 297
methods structure for USB drivers, 265
mfi(4) code base, 241
mfi_intr function, 240
mfip_action function, 236–238
mfip_attach function, 234–235
mfip_detach function, 235–236
mfip_done function, 240–241
mfip_poll function, 238
mfip_start function, 238–240
mfi_startio function, 239, 252
MMIO (memory-mapped I/O). *See also*
    I/O operations; PMIO
    and memory barriers, 172
    reading from, 166–167
    stream operations, 169–172
    writing to, 167–169
M_NOWAIT constant, 19, 23
modem drivers. *See* virtual null modem
modeventtype_t argument, 3
MOD_QUIESCE constant, 61
module event handlers, 2–3
MSI (Message Signaled Interrupts), 294
    implementing, 294–296
    management routines for, 297
MSI message, 294

MSI-X (Extended Message Signaled
    Interrupts), 294
MSI-X message, 294
msleep_spin function, 85
MTX_DEF constant, 67
mtx_destroy function, 68
MTX_DUPOK constant, 67
mtx_init function, 67
MTX_NOPROFILE constant, 67
MTX_NOWITNESS constant, 67
MTX_QUIET constant, 67
MTX_RECURSE constant, 67
MTX_SPIN constant, 67
mtx_trylock function, 68
mtx_unlock_spin function, 68
mutex locks
    management routines for, 66–68
    race_modevent function, 71–72
    sleep mutexes, 66
    spin mutexes, 65–66
M_WAITOK constant, 19, 23
mword value, 290–291
M_ZERO constant, 19, 23

N

name argument
    for DECLARE_MODULE macro, 4
    description of, 46
    for DRIVER_MODULE macro, 116
n argument, 30
network devices, 2
network drivers
    example of, 291–293
    mbuf structures, 293–294
    MSI (Message Signaled Interrupts), 294
        implementing, 294–296
        management routines for, 297
    network interface media structures,
        289–291
    network interface structures
        ether_ifattach function, 287–288
        ether_ifdetach function, 288
        management routines for, 286–288
    packets.
        post transmitting, 307–308
        receiving, 299–303
        transmitting, 304–307
network interface media structures,
    289–291
network interface structures
    ether_ifattach function, 287–288
    ether_ifdetach function, 288
    management routines for, 286–288

Newbus drivers
  device_foo functions, 114–115
  device method table, 115
  DRIVER_MODULE macro
    arg argument, 116
    busname argument, 116
    devclass argument, 116
    driver argument, 116
    evh argument, 116
    name argument, 116
  example of
    d_foo functions, 121
    foo_pci_attach function, 120–121
    foo_pci_detach function, 121–122
    foo_pci_probe function, 120
    loading, 122
  hardware resource management with,
    122–124
  overview, 113–114
nibble mode, 154
nmdm(4) driver, 99–100, 102
nmdm_alloc function, 105–106
nmdm_clone function, 104
nmdm_count variable, 103
nmdm_inwakeup function, 108
nmdm_modem function, 108–109
nmdm_modevent function, 103
nmdm_outwakeup function, 106
nmdm_param function, 109–110
nmdm_task_tty function, 106–107
nmdm_timeout function, 110, 111
no_pipe_ok flag, 262
np_rate variable, 110
nsegments argument, 198
ns_part variables, 106
number argument, 46

O

optional fields for USB drivers, 260–261
optional media properties for disk
    structures, 209
order argument, 4–5
output routines, 285–286

P

packets
  post transmitting, 307–308
  receiving
    em_handle_rx function, 303
    em_rxeof function, 300–303
  transmitting
    em_start_locked function, 304–305
    em_txeof function, 305–307

parallel port
  interrupt handlers on, 138–139
  printer driver example
    lpt_attach function, 148–150
    lpt_close function, 159–160
    lpt_detach function, 150
    lpt_detect function, 147–148
    lpt_identify function, 146
    lpt_intr function, 156–157
    lpt_ioctl function, 160–162
    lpt_open function, 151–153
    lpt_port_test function, 148
    lpt_probe function, 146
    lpt_push_bytes function, 158–159
    lpt_read function, 153–154
    lpt_release_ppbus function, 162–163
    lpt_request_ppbus function, 162
    lpt_timeout function, 158
    lpt_write function, 154–156
parent argument, 46, 197
pause function, 85
pci_alloc_msi function, 297
pci_alloc_msix function, 297
pci_msi_count function, 297
pci_msix_count function, 297
PCIR_BAR(x) macro, 189
pci_release_msi function, 297
_pcsid structures, 120
physical memory, contiguous, 22–25
pint_attach function, 133–134
pint_close function, 135–136
pint_detach function, 134
pint_identify function, 132
pint_intr function, 137–138
pint_open function, 134–135
pint_probe function, 132–133
pint_read function, 136–137
pint_write function, 136
pipe, defined, 257
pipe_bof flag, 262
PMIO (port-mapped I/O). *See also* I/O
    operations; MMIO
  i-Opener LEDs driver example
    led_attach function, 178
    led_close function, 180
    led_detach function, 178–179
    led_identify function, 177
    led_open function, 179
    led_probe function, 177–178
    led_read function, 180–181
    led_write function, 181–182
  and memory barriers, 172
  reading from, 166–167
  stream operations, 169–172
  writing to, 167–169

sleeping, 66, 83–85, 98

sleep_modevent function, 88–89

sleep mutexes, 66

sleep_thread function, 90–91

SMBIOS (System Management BIOS), 188

SMIC (Server Management Interface Chip) mode, 188

software interface modules (SIMs), 225

SPI (SCSI Parallel Interface), 226

spi_command structure, 220, 223

spin, defined, 65

spin mutexes, 65–66

stall_pipe flag, 262

start argument, 123

start routines, 286

static node, 47

status_callback argument, 290

storage device methods for disk structures, 209

storage drivers
  block I/O queues, 212–213
  block I/O structures, 210–211
  disk structures
    descriptive fields, 208–209
    driver private data, 210
    management routines for, 210
    mandatory media properties, 209
    optional media properties, 209
    storage device methods, 209
  flash memory driver example
    at45d_attach function, 217–218
    at45d_delayed_attach function, 218–219
    at45d_get_info function, 219–220
    at45d_get_status function, 220–221
    at45d_strategy function, 221
    at45d_task function, 221–223

strategy routines, 209

stream operations, 169–172

struct usb_xfer * argument, 262–264

sub argument, 4

sx (shared/exclusive) locks
  avoid holding exclusive locks for long periods of time, 82
  avoid recursing on exclusive locks, 81
  example of, 75–78
  management routines for, 73–75

sx_destroy function, 75

SX_DUPOK constant, 74

sx_init_flags function, 74

sx_init function, 74

SX_NOADAPTIVE constant, 74

SX_NOPROFILE constant, 74

SX_NOWITNESS constant, 74

SX_QUIET constant, 74

SX_RECURSE constant, 74

sx_slock_sig function, 74

sx_unlock function, 75

sx_xlock_sig function, 74

sx_xunlock function, 74

synchronization primitives, 65

synchronizing DMA buffers, 205

SYSCTL_ADD_* macros, 44, 46–47

SYSCTL_ADD_INT macro, 43

SYSCTL_ADD_LONG macro, 42

SYSCTL_ADD_NODE macro, 42, 43, 47

SYSCTL_ADD_OID macro, 46

SYSCTL_ADD_PROC macro, 43

SYSCTL_ADD_STRING macro, 43

SYSCTL_CHILDREN macro, 47

sysctl contexts, 42

sysctl_ctx_init function, 44

sysctl_debug_sleep_test function, 90, 91

SYSCTL_HANDLER_ARGS constant, 51

sysctl interface
  contexts for, 44
  dynamic sysctl, 44–47
  overview, 40–44
  SYSCTL_CHILDREN macro, 47
  sysctl_set_buffer_size function, 50–52
  SYSCTL_STATIC_CHILDREN macro, 47

sysctl_set_buffer_size function, 50–52

SYSCTL_STATIC_CHILDREN macro, 47

sysinit_elem_order enumeration, 4

<sys/malloc.h> header, 20

<sys/module.h> header, 4

SYS_RES_IOPORT constant, 123

SYS_RES_IRQ constant, 123

SYS_RES_MEMORY constant, 123

System Management BIOS (SMBIOS), 188

T

tags for DMA
  creating, 197–198
  destroying, 198–199

t argument, 30

TASK_INIT macro, 98

taskqueue_drain function, 98

taskqueue_enqueue function, 98

taskqueue_run function, 98

taskqueues
  global, 97
  management routines for, 97–98
  overview, 96–97

The Electronic Frontier Foundation (EFF) is the leading organization defending civil liberties in the digital world. We defend free speech on the Internet, fight illegal surveillance, promote the rights of innovators to develop new digital technologies, and work to ensure that the rights and freedoms we enjoy are enhanced — rather than eroded — as our use of technology grows.

PRIVACY   EFF has sued telecom giant AT&T for giving the NSA unfettered access to the private communications of millions of their customers. eff.org/nsa

FREE SPEECH   EFF's Coders' Rights Project is defending the rights of programmers and security researchers to publish their findings without fear of legal challenges. eff.org/freespeech

INNOVATION   EFF's Patent Busting Project challenges overbroad patents that threaten technological innovation. eff.org/patent

FAIR USE   EFF is fighting prohibitive standards that would take away your right to receive and use over-the-air television broadcasts any way you choose. eff.org/IP/fairuse

TRANSPARENCY   EFF has developed the Switzerland Network Testing Tool to give individuals the tools to test for covert traffic filtering. eff.org/transparency

INTERNATIONAL   EFF is working to ensure that international treaties do not restrict our free speech, privacy or digital consumer rights. eff.org/global

EFF.ORG

ELECTRONIC FRONTIER FOUNDATION

Protecting Rights and Promoting Freedom on the Electronic Frontier

EFF is a member-supported organization. Join Now! www.eff.org/support

FreeBSD Device Drivers is set in New Baskerville, TheSansMono Condensed, Futura, and Dogma.

This book was printed and bound at United Graphics in Mattoon, Illinois. The paper is 60# Husky Offset, which is certified by the Forest Stewardship Council (FSC). The book uses a layflat binding, which allows it to lie flat when open.

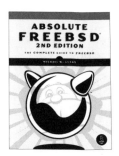

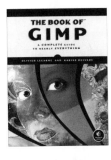